THEATRE IN
PIECES

POLITICS, POETICS AND
INTERDISCIPLINARY COLLABORATION

AN ANTHOLOGY OF PLAY TEXTS 1966–2010

US
Peter Brook and collaborators

A Girl Skipping
Graeme Miller

Hotel Methuselah
Imitating the Dog and Pete Brooks

Trans-Acts
Julia Bardsley

Don Juan. Who? / Don Juan. Kdo?
Anna Furse, Athletes of the Heart

Miss America
Split Britches

48 Minutes for Palestine
Mojisola Adebayo and Ashtar Theatre

introduced by
Anna Furse

Methuen Drama

1 3 5 7 9 10 8 6 4 2

This collection first published in Great Britain in 2011
by Methuen Drama, an imprint of Bloomsbury Publishing Plc

Methuen Drama
Bloomsbury Publishing Plc
36 Soho Square
London W1D 3QY
www.methuendrama.com

US first published in Great Britain by Calder and Boyars Limited 1968.
Reproduced in this edition by kind permission of John Calder
Copyright © The Authors 1968
Introduction to *US* copyright © Peter Brook 2011
A Girl Skipping copyright © Graeme Miller 2011
Hotel Methuselah copyright © Pete Brooks and Andrew Quick 2011
Trans-Acts copyright © Julia Bardsley 2011
Don Juan. Who? / Don Juan. Kdo? copyright © Anna Furse 2011
Miss America copyright © Lois Weaver and Peggy Shaw 2011
48 Minutes for Palestine copyright © Mojisola Adebayo and Ashtar Theatre 2011

Introduction copyright © Anna Furse 2011

A CIP catalogue record for this book is available from the British Library

ISBN: 978 1 408 13996 7

Available in the USA from Bloomsbury Academic & Professional,
175 Fifth Avenue/3rd Floor, New York, NY 10010.
www.BloomsburyAcademicUSA.com

Designed and typeset by Country Setting, Kingsdown, Kent CT14 8ES
Printed and bound in Great Britain by Martins The Printers, Berwick-upon-Tweed

Contents

Introduction

There are plays by playwrights and then there are theatre texts. What do I mean by this?

The playwright initiates what will be staged. In this theatre the production starts as dramatic literature that you can hold in your hands, and that (as is frequently said) directors aim to 'serve'. It is what is known as the Writers' Theatre. Then there are texts. Texts are woven; they are nets that gather meanings.[1] They are braided, knotted, threaded, sewn, patched together, edited, *montaged*. They *evolve in the process* of making performance. Theatre texts may or may not include words (and writers); they might include specific visual elements (e.g. video); they will always include action (for performance is *sine qua non* an *act*); they will always be authored or co-authored. There is no name for this theatre. It isn't necessarily the Directors' Theatre or Actors' Theatre, though it might be either – or both. The definitions don't generally matter to those making the work. This theatre is simply driven by its own specific imperatives and reaches its spectators *via* different routes: research and experimentation with *ideas*, hunches, questions and themes rather than a production strategy that starts from interpreting the play as written.

In short, theatre can either be the consequence of 'staging a play' or the culmination of research towards making. The question will arise 'who writes this other theatre then?'. This is the question of authorship. The final 'author'-ity may well be the director, but in each of the projects included here the play-wright–director–actor sequence that traditionally informs rehearsal 'from page to stage' is broken by a range of directed and self-directed approaches that have led to performance, and then a text that is *consequently* possible to publish. This anthology seeks to capture and share just some of the myriad ways in which a text that is the *result* and not the trigger of a *collaborative* and *interdisciplinary* process might reach a reader, on the page, *post-production*.

So this is not an anthology to be picked up by an auditionee looking for speeches or directors looking for plays to stage. It is, rather, a collection of theatre works, each utterly distinct – an anthology of differences then, and it would be foolish to attempt any syllogistic approach by which to compare them. The only fact they have in common is that they were not authored or published *prior* to their development in research, that they evolved in studio conditions, that they express the collaborative nature of our craft, and that each one is a sign of its times.

The volume opens with Peter Brook's controversial and iconoclastic **US** for the RSC in 1966 – a blistering collective response to the Vietnam War, and a large-scale ensemble creation that, even on first publication two years later, Brook insisted was a laboratory work. *US* was driven by Brook's searing question: how to respond to contemporary events as artists with political outrage and confront the audience with raw truths so that they listen? *US* inevitably provoked many reactions – and anger – since in articulating a response to the senseless horrors of a long and cruel war, it also raised questions on the role and responsibility of art in times of crisis. The volume ends, over forty years on, with a play-without-words, **48 Minutes for Palestine**, by our youngest contributor Mojisola Adebayo (with Ashtar Theatre), a text that shapes another contemporary sense of political outrage, this time with no need for words, song or speech at all. In between are gathered pieces that have been made by a generation who grew up artistically in the 1970s and 1980s, each responding to political and cultural realities then and now: to Thatcher and Reagan; to the mediatisation of our culture; to Bush's USA, the Middle East, post-liberation movements, economic instability; to technology – including its scenographic possibilities – and to what it means to live in the 'global village'. I suggest that the artists in this anthology have each inherited their own version of Peter Brook's 1960s 'nausea' with theatre's artifice, pretence, conventions, exclusions and economies in every sense.

In the 1980s, a generation of theatrical innovators in the UK, weaned on the radicalism of the previous two decades and the spirit of political and artistic collectives, were introduced for the first time to artistic giants such as Pina Bausch, Ariane Mnouchkine and Peter Brook's visit to Glasgow from Paris with *The Mahabharata*. At the ICA, then the London home for experimental performance, we would see our international peers: the young Robert Lepage, and even younger Jan Fabre, while David Gottard's programming at Riverside Studios brought us The Wooster Group from New York, Tadeusz Kantor from Poland and, with Dance Umbrella, the non-narrative democracies of American postmodern choreographers. Meanwhile, a European festival and touring circuit had built up for new work that didn't depend on dialogic English-language theatre but celebrated – and understood – physical, visual and radical performance. This was the ferment in which teeth were cut, companies formed and new approaches to directing and experimental collaborative creation emerged, in spite of Thatcherism's toxic bite into funding. Today that infrastructure, built up over years, is seriously threatened to extinction by the dire state of the economy and politicians who demonstrably undervalue culture – save for a brief, big and very expensive Olympic bash in 2012.

The works included here, framed by Peter Brook's urgent 1960s example, express and reflect some four decades of different experimental energy. Some (consciously or unconsciously) have absorbed his example from *US* in explicitly bringing the voices of performers themselves into the work (note how many texts name the performers by their own name, as *per US*). Like Brook, we have trawled our personal experience, political consciousness, and response to the culture, and/or raided the news media for material, to bring art and life into the same space of action.

Graeme Miller's **A Girl Skipping** was a *zeitgeist* piece that became a seminal work of British alternative theatre. Allegorically resisting the forces bearing down on Britain at the time, the performers' unrelenting energy insisted, within the theatrical metaphor of a children's play space, on society as defined by co-operation, values that were being corroded by the Tory ideology of individualism. Weaving Miller's haunting sound-score with words, song and unstoppable action, this exhilarating ensemble-devised work vividly bore the marks of his collaborators. Split Britches are steeped in experimental performance on both sides of the Atlantic, and **Miss America** is a collaboration born of decades of working together. Multilayered, poetic, witty and rhetorical, this piece unflinchingly comments on the dissolution of the American dream. Their dialogue between 'the hopeful and the hopeless' questions their society's moral fabric, values, norms, the responsibility of the media and the obsession with winning. This work is also driven by the need to make sense of senseless contemporary events, this time a natural catastrophe – Hurricane Katrina – and the social and political ramifications of the government response in its aftermath.

Mojisola Adebayo's **48 Minutes for Palestine** is a play-without-words inspired by Samuel Beckett, influenced by Adebayo's interest in movement and informed by her twelve years of project work in Palestine. The silence of this piece, performed by a man and a woman in a circle of oranges and stones, is a translation of political occupation into theatrical space and time. Quiet and non-virtuosic, the simplest of gestures convey the shifting relationship of the performers as they struggle for space, with only a few carefully chosen objects as scenographic tools. The metaphorical dimension of this politically driven piece is clear. It presents a striking contrast – and bookend – to the speech-driven dialogues, monologues and sung-poetry pyrotechnics of Brook and his company's much larger-scale, complex and vividly charged response to Vietnam some decades earlier.

Some texts in this anthology are less explicitly engaged with contemporary political issues, but push rather at the edges of form and aesthetics. Julia Bardsley's idiosyncratic visual trademark leaps off the pages of **Trans-Acts.** She is interrogating the medium of theatre, its power relations and the act of transformation (acting) itself in her quest to slough off her past as an acclaimed auteurial director to her new identity as creator of artworks. Although a solo,

Bardsley's collaboration of twenty-two years with composer Andrew Poppy provides the sonic dimension, while the project reverberates with her dialogues with actor Anastasia Hille that gave rise to the project. It is just such ambivalence with theatre's representational conventions that draws innovation from its dissidents. **Hotel Methuselah** is one example of the ongoing collaboration between Pete Brooks[2] and Andrew Quick in creating complex and highly imaginative scenographies. An homage to post-war British and French new-wave cinema, this piece, exploring anxieties and fears, meticulously synchronises live performance with video to blur the spectator's experience of film and theatre. Theirs is an interdisciplinary experiment that delights in visual feasting, playing with scale, visibility and presence.

Long periods of gestation with collaborators who know and/or learn a great deal about working together is a highly desirable yet ill-affordable luxury in making new work. My company's own contribution, **Don Juan. Who? / Don Juan. Kdo?** explored contemporary male–female relationships *via* the archetype of Don Juan. Written collectively, collaboratively, and anonymously online, we harnessed technology to nurture collaboration for eighteen months prior to rehearsing. This intimate process laid the foundation for an ensemble committed to the risk of making a physically dynamic production from a text without scenes, structure, characters or shape – until we forged this in rehearsal. It was this piece that my editor initially approached me to publish and that has led to this anthology; for we agreed that it would be better placed in context since context informs everything we do.

So, a variety of interdisciplinary efforts, visual influences and formal experiments lie in the pages between the two theatre works that open and conclude this anthology; and here lies the *poetics* in the subtitle of this book: that is, the idea that the imaginative forms that theatre-makers choose constitute a philosophy on the nature of the medium itself, indicating what is important to the creator(s) and the languages by which meanings are conveyed.

Jean Cocteau wrote that there was a 'poetry *of* the theatre' as distinct from a poetry *in* the theatre.[3] Theatre at its best *evokes* through metaphorical compression, leaving a great deal to the spectator's imagination. Complex meanings might be released in the simplest of ingredients: an action, or even indeed words, that communicate directly and immediately with the spectator. When they recognise these signs, they engage, bringing themselves to the encounter, willing to be affected and changed by it. This is the palpable, live, uniqueness of theatre that keeps even those who feel the nausea re-searching how to work with it in a meaningful way.

Peter Brook introduced the original text of *US* with the words:

What is living theatre? We have no answer today. Whatever we know, is not it. Whatever we have seen, is not it. Whatever is labelled theatre, isn't. Whatever is defined as theatre, misses the point. Whatever has been handed down to us, has been cheapened out of recognition. Whoever claims to know what theatre was or could be, doesn't. We are now before a long period of perpetual revolution, in which we must search, attempt to build, pull down and search again.

Here I give you just some samples of those searches, demolitions and rebuilds – theatre, in pieces, and never pretending to be other than just that: assemblages of the imaginations and ideas of their creators.

It has been a privilege to gather this collection and to hold on to the idea that in the diversity of its parts lie some common themes of both dissent and vision: the consensus that theatre is, by definition, a collaborative art that is also interdisciplinary and poetic.

Anna Furse, London, March 2011

1. Etymologically both words derive from the same root, hence 'textures' and 'textiles'.
2. No relation to Peter Brook.
3. See his Preface to *Les Maries de la Tour Eiffel* (1921).

Websites (*in alphabetical order*)

www.artsadmin.co.uk/artists/graeme-miller
www.ashtar-theatre.org
www.athletesoftheheart.org
www.bouffesdunord.com
www.imitatingthedog.co.uk
www.julia@juliabardsley.net
www.splitbritches.com

Acknowledgements

Warmest thanks to Ludovic de Cognets, John Ginman, Željko Hrs, Michael Kustow, Tina Malič, David Smith, Nina Soufy, my family Jack and Nina Klaff, and Dafne Louzioti, whose support never fails. Simon Trussler committed himself to realising even the most ambitious layout suggestions. Our editor Inderjeet Tillier, whose idea this was in the first place, unflinchingly followed the desire path to present the book in this way – which was a complex task to say the least. Heartfelt thanks to all our contributors for their innovation and imagination, and to those artists they collaborated with to realise these works. Sally Jacobs, my collaborator and friend, has been a constant inspiration to keep digging deep. Most important and very special thanks to Peter Brook for letting me, many years ago, as a very young theatre innocent, sit for months on the edge of his empty space at the CIRT (International Centre for Theatrical Research, in Paris). He inspired me to work since, from my own impatience with the deadly. Finally, thanks to all those students over the years with a hunger to learn – often from a dire shortage of durable evidence – about our ephemeral art and how some have consistently questioned how it might remain, meaningfully and, always, *collaboratively* live. This is for you.

US

A collaboration

**from the original text by Denis Cannan
adapted by Michael Kustow and Michael Stott
with lyrics by Adrian Mitchell
and music by Richard Peaslee**

US was first performed at the Aldwych Theatre, London, on 13 October 1966.

The company was as follows:

Eric Allan	Leon Lissek
Mary Allen	Robert Lloyd
Jeremy Anthony	Ursula Mohan
Hugh Armstrong	Pauline Munro
Roger Brierley	Patrick O'Connel
Noel Collins	Mike Pratt
Ian Hogg	Clifford Rose
John Hussey	Morgan Sheppard
Glenda Jackson	Jayne Soriano
Mark Jones	Barry Stanton
Marjie Lawrence	Hugh Sullivan
Joanne Lindsay	Michael Williams
Henry Woolf	

Musicians
Michael Reeves, Freddie Adamson, Michael Gould, Michael Hart, Martin Nicholls, Rainer Schulain

Directed by Peter Brook
Designed by Sally Jacobs

Introduction 2010 | *Peter Brook*

There were seven of us – Michael Kustow, Adrian Mitchell, Denis Cannan, Albert Hunt, Richard Peaslee, Sally Jacobs, myself – quickly joined by many of those who had been in *Marat-Sade*. We all agreed – at a time when the idea of political theatre was more and more in the wind, often in very strident ways – that theatre cannot change the world. On the other hand, if one is close to the ever-changing world then the world can change theatre. We were waking up to the fact that the English theatre, shaking off some of its deeply rooted middle-class complacency, was beginning to face local problems, class issues, the maladjustment of couples, the hidden roots of sexual hang-ups. But what was its world? Only its little island, England was still keeping a comfortable distance from the horrors of a war in which the Americans were both perpetrators and victims. Was it truly none of our business? From this came the title – two letters without punctuation – US – the United States or us. We felt intuitively that this war could just not be the concern of others, on the other side of the world. For us, it had become our burning question.

The opening of the film *Tell Me Lies*, based on *US*, two years later shows a young couple, Bob Lloyd and Pauline Munro. They look at the photo in a magazine of a baby monstrously mutilated by napalm and at once their lives change. They ask is London aware, is London concerned?

For the small band of us in the RSC, images of napalm-scorched Vietnam came as the same shock. We had a field of our own, the theatre. Within the theatre, we saw that there were no plays touching this theme, not even in the pile of manuscripts submitted daily by budding authors to the Literary Department. So, what action could we take? The answer was obvious. We had access to a company of actors, we could fix a production date. That was enough – the issue of Vietnam could be brought right home, to us, here, to a regular audience in place of yet another *Comedy of Errors*. But how? We had no answer, but urgency was clearly the motor. And we were just a few – authors, directors, actors together confronting the great unknown. The theme was obvious – 'What's it all about and why?' For this we had to begin exploring all levels at once. The pressure was the need to be ready, to deliver without falling back on any of the clichés, the precooked ideas of the Left or the Right, of the extremists at either end. Judgements and self-righteous attitudes were there for the asking in dailies and weeklies. Could we start by trying to investigate without judgement? We all agreed on one basic sacrifice. To meet our deadline and to do this as best we could, art could never be our goal. If the end product was not up to the cultural standards that had driven so much work in the past, then that would be just too bad. We might be rough, but what was more important was to be ready.

So it began. Meeting officials, diplomats, journalists – dissidents, opponents, anarchists. Improvising daily on stories, situations that the news provided, or from actors ruthlessly exploring the North and South Vietnamese within themselves, helped by an intense, gruelling, challenging workshop with a then-unknown young Polish director, Grotowski. Discussions, debates, fragments of writing by the authors, sketches by the designer. Welcoming every day at the lunch break a guest who'd just returned from one of the hot trouble spots. Improvising with humour and anguish. Then, gradually by trial and error, a form began to evolve. The key image was of burning – the Buddhist monk burning himself as protest, the American Quaker doing the same on the steps of the Pentagon and the surrealist anarchist forms of protest that young Americans were using, such as 'Paint Vietnam on your dick and pull it out everywhere you go.' Or telling how a young farm worker poured a bucket of cow shit over the recruiting office's papers. His name was Barry Bondhus and his act was turned into a wild narrative ballad by Adrian Mitchell and Richard Peaslee.

It became clear that the play had to be a real show in the Elizabethan way that the RSC was rediscovering – the Elizabethan essential: the serious had to be animated by the vulgar and the sense of outrage had to pass through a defiant use of the outrageous.

Sally Jacobs conceived a flamboyant set, framed with TV screens and dominated by the vast figure of a dead American pilot flying over the proscenium, with a monster penis bursting from his pants, in the shape of a bomb. This led to our gentle stage manager, after many sleepless nights, secretly denouncing us for obscenity to the Lord Chamberlain, the censor of the time.

Equally, the American Embassy sent feelers to the Governors of the RSC to see if we could be banned. The Lord Chamberlain summoned the Chairman of the Governors to his office, determined to stop the show. He looked at him pointedly and asked a leading question. 'Have you seen a run-through of this play?' 'Yes.' 'In your opinion, if the American Ambassador goes to a performance, will he walk out?' A long pause. 'No, sir. Not if he stays to the end.' The elegance of this answer from one old-boy Englishman to another led to a smiling 'Go ahead!'

The evening was in two parts. The first was a collage of contradictions. The second was a concentrated dialogue written by Denis Cannan and played by Glenda Jackson on the theme of self-immolation as protest. The end of the play arose naturally and inevitably. We released a case of live butterflies into the auditorium – an image full of charm and delight. Then Bob Lloyd grabbed a butterfly, flicked open his lighter and slowly brought the butterfly into the flame, the flame destroying the tiny white fragment of life. Of course, for us it was just a folded piece of white paper. It was a trick and it worked; the shock to the audience was complete. No one could move. The silence was only broken once by an outraged critic whose political line hadn't been followed, shouting 'Are you waiting for us or are we waiting for you?' And once, an angry voice shouted 'Go on! Do it, NOW.' Immediately, a lady leapt on to the stage, snatching the paper from Bob's hand, just before it reached the flame, crying, 'You see, you can always do something!' In Bob's words: 'She couldn't stop the war in Vietnam. But she could stop an act of cruelty taking place in a London theatre.'

But most important of all was that almost every night after a silence, sometimes lasting up to fifteen minutes, someone spoke. This led to a discussion born out of this long, deep silent thinking, that was of a quality I had never encountered in the easy cliché-ridden positions of the time. Contradictions were being faced, attitudes reconsidered.

To reach this point had been our hope, our aim. For a moment, political theatre had become real.

September 2010

Introduction 1968 | *Peter Brook*

There are times when I am nauseated by the theatre, when its artificiality appals me, although at the very same moment I recognise that its formality is its strength. The birth of *US* was allied to the reaction of a group of us who quite suddenly felt that Vietnam was more powerful, more acute, more insistent a situation than any drama that already existed between covers. All theatre as we know it fails to touch the issues that can most powerfully concern actors and audiences at the actual moment when they meet. For commonsense is outraged by the supposition that old wars in old words are more living than new ones, that ancient atrocities make civilised after-dinner fare, while current atrocities are not worthy of attention.

In fact, there is only one question. What is living theatre? We have no answer today. Whatever we know, is not it. Whatever we have seen, is not it. Whatever is labelled theatre, isn't. Whatever is defined as theatre, misses the point. Whatever has been handed down to us, has been cheapened out of recognition. Whoever claims to know what theatre was or could be, doesn't. We are now before a long period of perpetual revolution, in which we must search, attempt to build, pull down and search again.

US made no claims. It was work in progress. Publishing these details about our work is no claim – it is a progress report, for those interested, *not to be used except as a reference*. It arose from experimental laboratory work, which is another way of saying that it was turned up by a series of attempts to probe a certain problem.

The problem was – how can current events enter the theatre? Behind this lies the question, why should they enter the theatre? We had rejected certain answers. We did not accept the idea of the theatre as television documentary, nor the theatre as lecture hall, nor the theatre as vehicle for propaganda. We rejected them because we felt that from TV set to classroom, via newspaper, poster and paperback, the job was being done already through media perfectly adapted to the task. We were not interested in 'theatre of fact'.

We were interested in a theatre of confrontation. In current events, what confronts what, who confronts who? In the case of Vietnam, it is reasonable to say that everyone is concerned, yet no one is concerned: if everyone could hold in his mind through one single day both the horror of Vietnam and the normal life he is leading, the tension between the two would be intolerable. Is it possible, then, we ask ourselves, to present for a moment to the spectator this contradiction, his own and his society's contradiction? Is there any dramatic confrontation more complete than this? Is there any tragedy more inevitable and more terrifying? We wanted actors to explore every aspect of this contradiction, so that instead of accusing or condoling an audience, they could be what an actor is always supposed to be, the audience's representative, who is trained and prepared to go farther than the spectator, down a path the spectator knows to be his own.

US used a multitude of contradictory techniques to change direction and to change levels. It aimed to put the incompatible side by side. But this wasn't drama. This was in a way seduction – it used a contemporary, highly perishable fun-language to woo and annoy the spectator into joining in the turning-over of basically repellent themes. All this was preparation, like all the many phases of a bullfight that precede the kill. We aimed not at a kill, but at what bullfighters call the moment of truth. The moment of truth was also our one moment of drama, the one moment perhaps of tragedy, the one and only confrontation. This was when at the very end all pretences of playacting ceased and actor and audience together paused, at a moment when they and Vietnam were looking one another in the face.

I am writing this preface just after doing a production of *Oedipus*. It seems the opposite pole from *US*, and yet to me the two pieces of theatre are strangely related. There is nothing in common in their idiom, but the subject matter is almost identical. The struggle to avoid facing the truth. Whatever the cost, a man marshals everything at his disposal to skid away from the simple recognition of how things are. What is this extraordinary phenomenon at the very root of our way of existing? Is any other subject so urgent, so vital for us to understand now, today? Is Oedipus' dilemma something to do with the past?

Out of the two experiences I am left with one vast unresolved query of my own. If the theatre touches a current issue so burning and so uncomfortable as Vietnam it cannot fail to touch off powerful and immediate reactions. This seems a good thing, because we want our theatre to be powerful and immediate. However, when the trigger is so light, when the ejaculation comes so soon, when the first reaction is so strong, it is not possible to go very deep. The shutters fall fast.

With *Oedipus*, a Roman play at a national theatre, all the references are reassuring and so the audience's barriers are down. Hundreds of years of safe and insulated culture make any *Oedipus* a harmless exercise. So there is no opposition from the audience and it is possible for actors armed with a probing text to go very deeply into the nether lands of human evasion. The audience follows down these dark alleys, calm and confident. Culture is a talisman protecting them from anything that could nastily swing back into their own lives.

The contemporary event touches raw nerves but creates an immediate refusal to listen. The myth and the formally shaped work has power, yet is insulated in exact proportion. So which in fact is more likely to be useful to the spectator? I want to find the answer.

April 1968

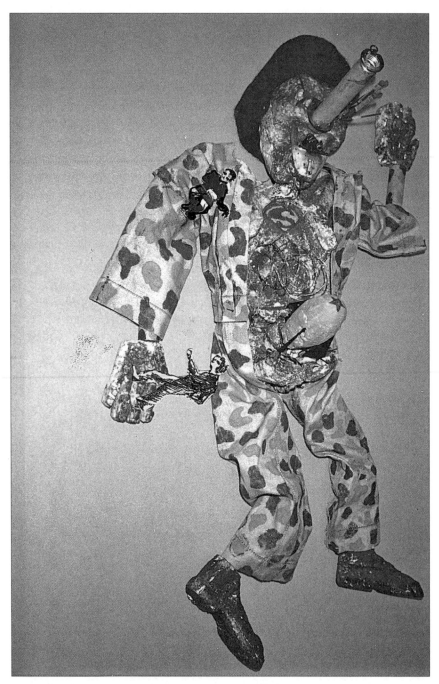

Sally Jacobs: scale model of the set design for *US*.

A Note on the Design | *Sally Jacobs*

This was a production which defied design. As we pursued our investigations into the mass of complex material, I continually supplied the 'means' to turn it all into performance. We finished up with a huge pile of everything we needed in the middle of the stage – ladders, mattresses, tightropes, Chinese dragons, American bomber wreckage, jeeps, oil drums etc. Peter said it should look like all war-torn landscapes have always looked – and I surrounded all of this with the harshest yellow cyclorama. About halfway through rehearsals he asked me to express my own individual response to all that we were discovering. I made a 36 ft pop-art scale model of a Green Beret soldier – a tragic figure of war – at once the victim and the aggressor. We used it as a monster presence hanging over the performance, which was lowered during a particularly violent sequence showing the escalation of the war, and thus it became simply a piece of scenery to clamber over.

Another unique design discovery happened at dress rehearsal when the actors put on their 'all-purpose' costumes. We found that they became stage characters, separated from 'us'. So we put them back into their own rehearsal gear, and they immediately could have been any one of the audience. It was important to include the audience in this way.

For my part, as a designer, I have always found great satisfaction in working as an integral part of a group devising a piece of theatre from scratch – because nothing is imposed – everything that finishes up on stage has been found from the inside of the process as it evolved during improvisations and research, and becomes a unique outcome – which is the true sum of its parts.

November 2010

On *US* | *Michael Kustow*

In *US*, self-accusation and moral paralysis struggled with exuberance and the spirit of jazz. It was Brook's first tussle with not one living playwright, but a whole group of author-collaborators, dealing with a subject that was in every sense a burning issue, a war that was being waged as they performed. What drove Brook and infuriated many who criticised the show from an anti-war position, was the quest to go beyond protest, having 'a position', 'a point of view'. Just when any spectator might feel that his convictions or prejudices were confirmed, the piece, like a slippery fish, wriggled and turned and upset fixed positions. It was a pyrotechnic, Meyerholdian montage, a kaleidoscope of furies and guilts, more dazzling than most musicals, made by a man fiercely in search of a human centre in an inhuman war. It is not only surprising that the piece came to fruition on the Royal Shakespeare's main stage, despite the Lord Chamberlain's attempts to emasculate it, and even to withdraw the RSC's grant. It is a miracle, given the strength of the disparate viewpoints, that Brook managed to hold together a fissiparous group and make a piece that deployed arguments, developed a dramatic line and was unmistakably theatre. Looking back now, from a time in which much 'political theatre' frequently sacrifices theatrical resources to documentary or 'verbatim' presentations, *US* still stands as a template of what theatre about immediate conflicts can be.

March 2005

This piece was originally published in *Peter Brook: A Biography* (London: Bloomsbury Publishing, 2005)

ACT ONE

A huge doll, dressed in soldier's costume, hangs over the stage. Centre stage is a pile of 'garbage' . . . petrol cans, chairs, boxes, newspapers, steel ladders and parts of crashed planes.

CLIFFORD enters and takes a yellow cloth from the garbage. HENRY enters and takes an American petrol can. MARK takes an English petrol can. ROBERT takes an American petrol can. GLENDA carries a robe and a Madame Nhu wig. MIKE enters and stands in the garbage. They freeze, and the other actors enter and freeze, watching them. All the actors except the six named above begin to sing very quietly.

SONG: ICARUS SCHMICARUS

CAST   If you never spend your money,
You'll always have some cash,
If you stay cool and never burn,
You'll never turn to ash.
If you build your house of garbage,
Then you'll love the smell of trash.
And if you crawl along the ground,
At least you'll never crash.
So why, why, why, why?
WHAT MADE YOU THINK YOU COULD FLY?
FLY? FLY?

MIKE   Saigon is the only city in the world where the garbage stands uncollected on the street corners and they burn people.

CLIFFORD   There have been so many assassinations that people are afraid. They do not raise their voices. They prefer to say nothing. When we burn ourselves, it is the only way we can speak.

CLIFFORD moves forward, sits, and HENRY mimes pouring petrol over him, makes a trail, waits. CLIFFORD nods, HENRY strikes a match, and kneels in prayer. CLIFFORD burns. GLENDA stands over him.

GLENDA   If you never spend your money
You'll always have some cash.
If you stay cool and never burn
You'll never turn to ash.

If you build your house of garbage
Then you'll love the smell of trash.
And if you crawl along the ground
At least you'll never crash.
So why, why, why, why?
WHAT MADE YOU THINK YOU COULD FLY?
FLY? FLY?

MARK   I was run over by the truth one day
Ever since the accident I've walked this way.
So stick my legs in plaster
Tell me lies about Vietnam.

GLENDA *has put on the robe and wig. She turns.*

GLENDA   These so-called monks who burn themselves are not
even faithful to their religion. True Buddhists respect
life so deeply they will not eat so much as a shrimp. In
Saigon we have reason to be proud of our elegant
avenues and squares. The image of our country
projected abroad should be one attractive to tourists,
encouraging to investors, and heartening to our real
friends. None of these purposes is served by allowing
the export of newsreels which show, in sordid detail,
these saffron barbecues in imported gasoline!

The actors break the freeze. GLENDA *takes off the wig and gown,*
CLIFFORD *stands and throws away his yellow cloth.* MARK *moves to
a seat at the edge of the stage.* HUGH *comes striding along banging a
gong, shouting in Vietnamese, leading a truck with various props on it,
and also* ROGER, *representing* VIETNAM, *kneeling, almost naked.
Musicians on the edge of the stage are playing. The actors gather
round the truck as an audience.* HUGH *gongs for silence, and announces
'The History of Vietnam', in Vietnamese. He will announce each float in
Vietnamese. The girls speak a commentary through microphones. The
History of Vietnam is presented in a series of tableaux on the truck.
The whole sequence is punctuated and coloured by music.*

HISTORY OF VIETNAM

PAULINE   History of Vietnam. Here we see a series of tableaux,
designed to impress on the memory of our shamefully
ill-educated people the history of Vietnam.

Tableau: DRAGON KING *and* FAIRY QUEEN

The birth of Vietnam. According to legend, the Dragon
King and the Fairy Queen met in the night thousands

of years ago. They had a hundred children: each finger represents ten of these children. But the Dragon and the Fairy were incompatible, and after they parted with violent threats and anger, fifty of the children retired with their mother to the mountains, fifty accompanied their father to the seashore. The people of Vietnam are the descendants of these separated brothers and sisters.

VIETNAM *is surrounded by two figures with green masks, one with blue silk cloth, and one with a toy dragon with teeth.*

GLENDA Geography of Vietnam. Vietnam has always been surrounded by potential enemies. In the west by Laos and Cambodia, in the south and east by the pirate-infested South China Sea, and in the north by the hordes of China. Today Vietnam has 32 million inhabitants: 15.7 million live in the north, 16.5 million in the south.

VIETNAM *is surrounded by four yellow-masked figures, each twirling a silver stick when his religion is named.*

MARJIE Religions of Vietnam. There are four main religions in Vietnam: Buddhism, which is the religion of 70 to 80 per cent of the population, Confucianism, Taoism, and Catholicism. About 7 per cent of the population are Catholics.

VIETNAM *lies down while the Chinese Dragon bites his leg, and is beaten off by* PAULINE *and* URSULA *with silver sticks.*

GLENDA Here we see one of the most heroic and beautiful stories in Vietnamese history. Two young sisters, widowed by the Chinese invaders, bravely led an army and drove out the oppressors of their country. A statue commemorating these heroic fighters has been erected in a park in Saigon by Madame Nhu.

Two masked figures crouch over VIETNAM, *choking him, while* CLIFFORD *writes on* PADDY's *hand.*

MARJIE The history of Vietnam is a great wheel of invasion, suppression, rebellion, and renewed invasion. In 1283, Vietnam was occupied by the Mongols. The hand of every Vietnamese soldier was inscribed with the words 'SAT DAT': Kill Mongols!

PADDY (*striking the masked figure*) SAT DAT!

BARRY, *masked and with flags on his shoulders, is teased by* GLENDA *with a toy grasshopper, until he topples forward and hits the floor.*

URSULA Vietnamese proverb. In the battle between a grasshopper and a chariot, who would have believed that it was the chariot, not the grasshopper, which was crushed?

All the men form a pyramid on the truck, with VIETNAM *crouched at the bottom, in the middle.*

PAULINE Before the arrival of the French, the traditional structure of Vietnamese society was a pyramid. At the top, the monarch, religious and civil leader; at the base, largely autonomous villages and communes. Between the King and the people were a body of literate men, shaped by Confucian principles. It will be noted that while this pyramid was comparatively stable, its very existence depended upon tension.

The pyramid crumbles into a heap of bodies, and MARY, *dressed in a tricolour, climbs on top of them.*

MARJIE The French invasion began in 1858. The French worked on three principles: divide and rule, isolation of the country, and economic subordination. By 1884 they had established colonial rule.

Through the next speech the bodies writhe and kiss.

URSULA The French corrupted the Vietnamese people, by introducing the evils of opium and prostitution.

MARJIE But the wheel turns. The history of French oppression is also the story of Vietnamese resistance. In 1930 a violent rebellion took place and was crushed by French troops and planes. In the same year the Indo-Chinese Communist Party was founded. And in 1945 the underground resistance finally burst forth in the victorious August revolution, under the guidance and wise leadership of our first President, Ho Chi Minh.

The people on the truck are rigid, striking heroic poses, led by PADDY. *They chant 'LAO FO, HO CHI MINH', as the truck drives off upstage. The four girls take rifles and come forward, with microphones. Music.*

GLENDA We travelled downstream on a raft . . .

URSULA Then on a boat . . .

PAULINE Took a short cut across the flooded fields, marched down the road . . .

MARJIE	And then we saw a car with a flag, a big red flag with a yellow star.
GLENDA	Our songs were coming over the loudspeaker . . . 'The Heroic Fighters' and 'To Smash Down Fascism'. And between the songs a voice said, 'The revolutionary forces took Hanoi at 4 p.m. today. The revolutionary forces took Hanoi at 4 p.m. today.'
URSULA	And so we drove through the city. Our car headed south, towards Saigon. Full speed on Road Number One.

SONG: ROAD NUMBER ONE

GIRLS	Rivers, bridges, All the length of the land, Mountain ranges, towns and cities, All of the country is in the people's hands.
GLENDA	It was a beautiful road, as straight as a ramrod, flanked by the mountains and the sea. At night each village along the route shone with hundreds of welcoming torches. By day the road became a river of flags.
URSULA	For years we'd been hiding, keeping our voices down, hardly seeing anything of our country but its densest undergrowth. But now, for the first time, we could shout out loud!
MARJIE	I suppose we were tired, our bodies were tired, but it seemed as if a strong electric current were running through our blood, flowing through the whole country, stirring up its atoms, setting them in motion. This August electric current had been generated by our Party.
URSULA	We could shout out loud!
GIRLS	Rivers, bridges, All the length of the land, Mountain ranges, towns and cities, All the country is in the people's hands. Burn all the records of our agony, For the nation has just begun. Shouting, singing, As we travel Road Number One.
PAULINE	And one week after our car left Hanoi, we reached South Vietnam. It was late at night. The local comrades phoned Saigon for instructions.

GLENDA   They cheered us on our way. Then, at last, we saw the
                lights of Saigon. We were taken to stay in an enormous
                building, formerly the summer palace of the Emperor.

CLIFFORD *enters, carrying a suitcase. He sits on milk float.*

CLIFFORD   We have decided to abdicate, and we transfer power to
                the democratic Republic Government. Upon leaving
                our throne, we have three wishes to express. One,
                we request the new Government to take care of the
                dynastic temples and royal tombs. Two, we request
                the new Government to deal fraternally with all the
                parties and groups which have fought for the
                independence of our country, even though they have
                not closely followed the popular movement. Three, we
                invite all parties and groups, as well as the royal
                family, to solidarise in unreserved support of the
                democratic government. As for us, during twenty
                years' reign we have known much bitterness.
                Henceforth we shall be happy to be a free citizen in an
                independent country. We shall allow no one to abuse
                our name or the name of the royal family in order to
                sow dissent among our compatriots. Long live the
                Independence of Vietnam! Long live the Democratic
                Republic!

CLIFFORD *leaves, with the suitcase.*

GLENDA   We wired to the North. 'Uprising complete in all 21
                provinces.' Hanoi replied, 'Independence Ceremony on
                September 2nd.' I'll never forget that date – September
                the 2nd, 1945. On the birthday of our country, I was in
                Saigon, the heart of our beloved Nam Bo, among the
                millions of our people who listened with their hearts
                and souls to the voice of the Fatherland from the Ba
                Dinh Square, Hanoi. Uncle Ho read the Proclamation.
                His voice was warm, gentle and resonant, as I had
                heard it years ago, in the depths of the Bac Bo Forest.

The truck has driven down again. Two huge yellow flags behind
PADDY *held by* BARRY *and* MORGAN.

PADDY   Declaration of Independence of the Democratic
                Republic of Vietnam, September 2nd, 1945. 'All men
                are created equal. They are endowed by their creator
                with certain inalienable rights. Among these are Life,
                Liberty, and the pursuit of Happiness.' This immortal
                statement was made in the Declaration of Independence
                of the United States of America in 1776. In a broader

> sense this means: all the peoples have a right to live,
> to be happy and free.

He steps off the truck and goes to the girls.

> Come. You will have dinner with the President of the
> Republic.

On the truck, BARRY *and* MORGAN *put their yellow flags aside and pull out pistols.*

> How funny life is. When I was in prison in China, I
> was let out for fifteen minutes in the morning and
> fifteen minutes in the evening, for exercise. And while
> I took my exercise in the yard there were always two
> armed guards standing right over me with their guns.
> Now I'm President of the Vietnam Republic, and
> whenever I leave this place there are two armed
> guards, standing right over me with their guns. Ah . . .
> come on . . .

BARRY *and* MORGAN *yank him on to the truck, their pistols pressed into his neck.*

GLENDA   Further history of Vietnam!

The actors gather round the float again. VIETNAM *gets on to the truck, kneels, while* HENRY, *with a Japanese flag, and* HUGH *wearing the Union Jack, crush* PADDY *on top of him.*

URSULA   Gracey. The Big Three at Potsdam agreed that
              Vietnam should be in the British sphere of influence,
              and a British General, Douglas Gracey, was sent to
              Vietnam to restore law and order. General Gracey's
              British and Indian troops collaborated with the
              Japanese to reimpose French power in Saigon.

> *Tableau: Four actors as French soldiers around a basket,*
> *with* GLENDA *as resistance to them.*

PAULINE   The Second War of Liberation. During the Second War
              of Liberation many new guerrilla tactics were
              developed. Here we see a tableau representing the
              death of four French soldiers, who, thinking they were
              stealing a basket of fruit from a girl, discovered too
              late . . .

An explosion from a drum, and the four actors slowly mime death.

For the next float HENRY *kneels, holding a French flag and a white handkerchief, while* PADDY *towers over him holding a bicycle.*

GLENDA   Dienbienphu. A battle to remember. Many reinforced
            Peugeot bicycles were used to carry rice and
            ammunition hundreds of miles through the jungle to
            support the Viet Minh. After three months of encircle-
            ment and fifty-five days of fighting, the yellow-starred
            red flag of the Viet Minh fluttered above the French
            command post. Seventy-three French soldiers escaped,
            two thousand were killed, and few of the ten thousand
            captured survived.

VIETNAM *is stretched between four actors, who paint him one colour
above the waist, another below the waist.*

MARJIE   The Geneva Conference. At the Geneva Conference,
            the French and the Viet Minh agreed on a provisional
            demarcation line at the 17th Parallel. Elections were
            to be held within two years.

VIETNAM *is grabbed at one end by* PADDY, *at the other by* LEON. *The
actor-audience is starting to divide into the two separate groups, while
the girls divide into two teams.*

MARJIE *and*   In the North, the Democratic Republic of Vietnam, led
GLENDA   by Ho Chi Minh!

URSULA *and*   In the South, the Independent State of Vietnam,
PAULINE   under the Premiership of Ngo Dinh Diem!

VIETNAM *writhes, while* JOHN *holds up a yellow flag described in the
next speech.*

URSULA   Regrouping. In accordance with the Geneva Agree-
            ments, nearly a million refugees, most of them
            Catholics, headed south, carrying with them a yellow
            and gold flag displaying the Pope's tiara and the keys
            of St Peter's.

PADDY *and* MARJIE *strike poses of fond farewells, while* LEON
prepares to grab MARJIE, *and* VIETNAM *writhes. By now the actor-
audience is cheering and booing the rival statements made.*

GLENDA   Marriages. In accordance with the Geneva Agree-
            ments, 90,000 Viet Minh Freedom Fighters left for the
            North. Thousands married before they left, believing
            that they would be separated from their wives for at
            the most two years.

VIETNAM *writhes on the truck while the two teams of girls shout at
each other.*

PAULINE   Land Reform in the North! Most of the landlords were
            executed, and the land given to the peasants.

Unfortunately, many grave errors were committed, and many peasants were wrongly classified as landlords. It is estimated that between twelve and fifteen thousand innocent people were killed!

MARJIE   Democracy in the South! Mayor Wagner of New York described Ngo Dinh Diem as one of the great statesmen of the twentieth century, and his government as a 'political miracle'. It is estimated that under Diem four hundred thousand people were tortured and one hundred and fifty thousand killed!

The actors start to spread and flick paint on VIETNAM.

URSULA   Infiltration. Urged on by the aggressors in Hanoi, and in contravention of the Geneva Agreements, many subversive elements infiltrated from the North into the independent state of Vietnam. To counter this, the United States sent military advisers to the South.

The actors are rolling VIETNAM *up in a white paper from the floor of the truck. They tip him over the side, and he disappears.*

GLENDA   Resistance to American Aggression. The people of Vietnam did not lie down before the American aggressors. In 1964, sixty-five thousand troops supported by one hundred thousand irregular guerrillas and ten thousand volunteers from the North, carried the resistance to the outskirts of Saigon itself!

During the next speech fighting almost breaks out. The words are drowned by shouting.

PAULINE   Defending the Free World! The United States Government did not lie down before the Communist aggressors. The rapid increase in US military strength from forty thousand in May 1965 to three hundred thousand today was a major factor in defeating the Viet Cong offensive.

The actors step forward with the paper that VIETNAM *was wrapped in . . . It is streaked with paint from his body . . . an 'action painting'. They rip it in half. The actors move upstage, and become absorbed in the small busy tasks of a Vietnamese village.* PAULINE *is left alone. Very quietly, she speaks*

The Lament of the Soldier's Wife

PAULINE   The water, clear as a spring, flows on under the bridge. Nearby, the road is covered with young grass.

I follow you with a heavy heart, oh my husband, my love . . . I wish I were the horse you ride, the boat you steer. The water flows on but water will not wash away my tears; the young grass smells sweet, but its perfume will not soothe my sorrow. To the resounding beat of drums, despair, mounting like the tide, captures my heart. Goodbye, goodbye, oh my husband, oh my love. My lips murmur goodbye, but my hand remains in yours. I go with you but my feet will not move. I wish I were the evening breeze singing in the branches, to follow you, to sweeten your sleep. But nothing keeps you, oh my husband, my love, neither family nor wife nor child. Like the Spirit of Hate, your eyes on fire, you hurl yourself in the path of the enemy. You frighten me, oh my husband! The wind trembles as you pass. Your tunic is red as the rising sun, your horse is white as snow. With my eyes closed I heard your horse galloping away across my heart, his hoofs echoing, echoing and dying away among the rolling drums. Warriors! From T-Lieu to Trang Duong there are nothing but warriors, and leaving with them are the sounds of flutes and the colour of flags. You go away through the rain and the wind, oh my husband, my love. I stay alone in our house, in the same room, with the same rush mat, the same coverlet. The blue clouds burst in tears, the withered leaves stifle their sobs. The plain soothes its solitude. The mountains are silent as stone. Oh, sun, oh, moon, where is my husband, my love? Oh, moon, I am afraid of you! Oh, clouds, I am afraid of you! I am afraid of the long road and the deep river. I am afraid of the morning sun and of the flames dying with the day. Flow, flow, tears, flow down my face, fall on my robe. Cry, cry, oh my eyes! Cry through the long night of waiting. Oh my husband, my love, I believed I was joined to you like a fish to the sea. Alas, I have been taken from you like water from the clouds.

Pause. PAULINE *sits, silent.* HUGH *leaps up on to the truck, and starts the 'LAO FO HO CHI MINH' chant again. The truck drives off, and the actors mime making the crude weapons of the Viet Cong . . . naily boards, spiked balls like porcupines. There are heavy 'war' sounds and a stirring revolutionary song,* The Leeches – LEON, MORGAN, PADDY, BARRY, IAN, JOHN *and* CLIFFORD – *slowly come forward to a barrier that has been put up downstage. They lean on it, facing the audience as though being interviewed, in a straight line, and with hardly any gestures or facial expressions.*

THE LEECH

When a peasant discovers that he's only a peasant,
When your humble servant notices his chains
You'll find his reactions are inclined to be unpleasant
He may hack you into pieces and exhibit your remains.

Found we were growing weaker every day
Always felt about to die.
Something was draining our blood away
Somebody had sucked us dry.
It was the leech, it was the landlord leech
It was the leech, it was the landlord leech.
It was bulging with blood and its jaws were made
    of steel.
We tore it off
Threw it down
Crushed it under our heel.

Then all the children of the leech took flight
Sent another twice their size.
It called us brother but we saw the light
Shining from its greedy eyes.

It was the leech, it was the Saigon leech
It was the leech, it was the army leech.
It was bulging with blood and its jaws were made
    of steel.
We tore it off
Threw it down
Crushed it under our heel.

Last came a monster with a hairy face
Crawling through the delta mud
Burning the world to find a hiding place
Screaming that it needed blood.
It was the leech, it was the Yankee Leech,
It was the leech, it was the Lyndon Leech
It was bulging with blood and its jaws were made
    of steel.
We tore it off
Threw it down
Crushed it under our heel.

You say we're cruel but we know your kind –
Never practise what you preach.
You'll never qualify as humankind
While you're married to a leech.

You're just a leech, you're just a sucking leech.
You're just a leech, you're just an English leech.
It was bulging with blood and its jaws were made
    of steel.
We tore it off
Threw it down
Crushed it under our heel.

IAN   What do you make of this, Fighting Man?

LEON   As a negro, I can't say whether I'm for the war or not. I can't say whether we should be here or not. But I will say this: since we are here, we can't leave.

MORGAN   I'd never think of shouting 'Gung Ho' or 'Geronimo' any more.

LEON   We have no profane or hate-laden epithets for the enemy. He's just Charlie and he's out there.

MORGAN   He's as much an object of grudging respect for his damned tenacity as he is the object of detached loathing for the calculated horrors he inflicts on his own people.

CLIFFORD   Oh yes, as a moderate, greying Virginian, piloting a medical evacuation helicopter, I've evacuated Charlie, but I don't get the chance to do it often. I look at these little guys, and I know they've maybe got families worrying about them just like I have. We should have compassion for Charlie, no matter what he does. In some ways he's as idealistic as we are. It's regrettable he is misinformed. I read the Bible every day and I write home to my wife daily if I can. Because I disapprove of smoking I take my cigarette issue and I rip them up, and this often annoys other soldiers. This is a hard war, emotionally hard. We can't go into villages and try to make friends with people, the way our troops did in Korea. Here we have to protect ourselves all the time. The defence perimeter is all around you.

JOHN   As one of the top commanders in Vietnam, I'd say this war is a cat and mouse game. Our objective is to kill the enemy, to inflict on him maximum losses. Terrain is less important. I can also say that never before have troop commanders had such mobility, and that the novelty of this war is the helicopter. And also that the jungle is like an immense ocean . . . full of sharks and submarines.

MORGAN	At thirty-eight I've been in the Army twenty years, and I like to quip, 'Yup, twenty years and I'm thinking about making a career of it now.' I'm a mature man, medium build with a hard, trim body, sparse, close-cropped sandy hair and ice-blue eyes. My face is ruddy except for some clean white lines, scars from where a Chinese grenade got me in Korea.
JOHN	Sometimes, someone has to make the decision to fire or not to fire on a village from which our troops are being fired on. The sergeants have to take these decisions, and it requires mature men.
MORGAN	I and most of the old pros in Vietnam am possessed of the abiding conviction that 'short termers' here really do little more than pull duty as sort of glorified boy scouts.
IAN	I know I only have another five months to go in Vietnam, and then I can go home . . . maybe to take up the schooling I left off when I joined the Army against my father's advice. I said I wanted to be the biggest baddest guy on the block so I joined the Airborne. I have a Stateside story that I love to tell and that many but not all of my comrades like to hear. It's about what happened when I and 121 of my para-trooper buddies were at Oakland airport waiting to ship out, and an anti-Vietnam demonstrator came up and began to lecture us. My version goes on something like this. 'This guy came up, he looked kinda faggy, and he said, "I don't want you guys to go to Vietnam" . . . some crap like that. He just kept it up and kept it up. Finally, blam! One of the paratroopers hit him in the face. Man, he was blood all over, and his old lady was there hollering for the police, and this guy he kept it up, he was holding this handkerchief up to his face, and he was blood all over.' At this point I'm often in tears with laughter. 'All the other civilians there, they were for us, they kept saying, "Give it to him, give it to him." Finally the cops show up, and they ask "Who hit this Vietnik?" Then all 122 Paratroopers hollered with one voice, "I did!" The cops didn't care, they really couldn't have cared less. Boy, what a riot!'
PADDY	I take rather a quiet view of the dissent at home. Not only the anti-war people, but their opposite numbers as well, both sides strike me as a little nutty. Like a surprisingly large number of professional officers in

	Vietnam, I take a sophisticated view of the social and political aspects of this struggle, along with the military. I confirm this by saying we are fighting people with lots of patience. Americans want to do things now. But we can't wrap this up quickly because we can't just win militarily. They, the VC, they'll just melt into the jungle and come back when we leave. We have to leave a strong Government behind us. The French didn't do that.

BARRY   This discourse has been interrupted by a heavy-set Special Forces Master Sergeant who overheard the Captain's last remarks, and disagrees. 'By God, what this country needed was for Barry Goldwater to be elected in '64. I bet 500 Ps (by which I mean Piastres), I'd be sitting in Hanoi right now with an eight-man Special Forces Team. Let China come in. Let them try. Barry would have had us in Pekin if they'd tried.'

PADDY   I hear the Sergeant, puzzled, even a little shocked, and I say evenly, 'If Goldwater had've been elected, you'd be standing right where you are now.'

The soldiers freeze into stiff poses, while the other actors creep and slouch forward as Beatniks with anti-war posters, the girls caressing the soldiers.

Four lines of The Green Beret *come over the loudspeakers. It's a record by Sgt Barry Sadler.*

'Fighting solders from the sky,
Fearless men who jump and die.
Men who mean just what they say.
The brave men of the Green Beret.'

BOB *has come on, pale suit and sunglasses, microphone in hand. He slips in front of the soldiers.*

BOB   Thank you, Sergeant Barry Sadler . . . and goodnight. I have a 'Stateside story' that I love to tell, and that some of my 'comrades' like to hear. It's about another Barry. The true story of Barry Bondhus, or 'Moon over Minnesota'.

Mister Bondhus
Of Big Lake
Minnesota
Made his mistake
When he raised ten sons,
Ten sons, ten sons,

To be Henry Fondas –
You know, the model of a democratic voter –
Didn't buy his sons guns.
Why?
Didn't want them to die
Or kill. Was that strange?
Well, yes,
I guess,
But it makes for a change.
One day the draft board
Told Mister Bondhus
You can afford
To let the Army have a son,
Just one
For a start,
You can part
With Barry, Barry,
Barry, Barry Bondhus –
Your son.

Mister Bondhus
Of Big Lake
Minnesota
Downright
Forthright
Wouldn't send his quota.
Well, Heaven's sake,
I'm not the kind of man who squanders
His seed
I need
Barry, if you draft him
I've got nothing to
Look forward to
But ten coffins draped with the flag.
It became
A game
Of tag.
Will the draft board
Catch Barry Bondhus
To join the boys who died
On the side
Of the Lord
And the Big Lake
Minnesota
Draft Board?

Barry Bondhus
Of Big Lake
Minnesota
Ponders
As he wanders
Through the doors of the draft board
Office
Of his own accord.
Opens half-a-dozen files
Packed full
Stacked full
With miles and miles
Piles of government documents
About all the young men due to go far.
Then he lumps in
Dumps in –
If I may quote a
Story from the *Minneapolis Star* –
Two full buckets of human excrement,
Stinking
Bondhus thinking
Excrement –
Nothing personal against the President –
It sounds as wild
As the action of a sewer-
realist child,
But the draft board files
Are all defiled.

Walt Whitman
Charlie Parker
Clarence Darrow
Ben Shahn
William Burroughs
Allen Ginsberg
Woody Guthrie
Tom Paine
James Baldwin
Joseph Heller
Dr Benjamin Spock
Mark Twain
Yes, all of the beautiful prophets of America
Write across the Minnesota sky:
Look look look at Barry Bondhus –
That boy can fly.

The last verse is repeated by everyone except the soldiers. Then, even they join in slowly, leaving BARRY, PADDY *and* MORGAN *standing to attention, rigid. The Beatniks dance off with the barrier, the naily boards, and other war toys, then as the song ends the men sit down, as if in the Army.*

PADDY	This is school! The United States Army is the largest single educational complex in the world, and you are here to learn. You gotta face up to the fact you just might get captured, and interrogated. You've had to learn to shoot a gun, you've had to learn to read a map, and now you've got to learn how to deal with interrogation.
MORGAN	We simulate VC interrogation conditions. That just means some guys pretend they're VC, some pretend they're prisoners. What you learn here will save your life!
BARRY	Okay, school's open.
EVERYONE	Hup two three four, hup two three four!

The actors are standing in two lines facing front.

BARRY	We'll just have a little rouser to warm you up, okay. BONG THE CONG!
MEN	Bong the Cong.
BARRY	BONG THE CONG!
MEN	Bong the Cong.
BARRY	BONG THE CONG!
MEN	Bong the Cong.
PADDY	THE TIGERS ARE COMING!
MEN	The tigers are coming.
PADDY	THE TIGERS ARE COMING!
MEN	The tigers are coming.
PADDY	THE TIGERS ARE COMING!
MEN	The tigers are coming.
MORGAN	WHAT ARE YOU?
MEN	Tigers.
MORGAN	WHAT ARE YOU?
MEN	Tigers.

MORGAN   WHAT ARE YOU?

MEN   Tigers.

BARRY, PADDY *and* MORGAN *take a pace forward and growl. The men repeat the growl. The three leaders take two more steps forward, growling, and the men repeat the growl. Then the three wheel round on them.*

PADDY   Okay, divide!

EVERYONE   Hup two three four, hup two three four.

The actors run to positions in groups of three. Two grab the third and prepare to torture him . . . one group by holding his head under water, another by battering his head on a wall, another by kicking him. BARRY, PADDY *and* MORGAN *sit on boxes in the middle of this, and* MIKE *sits facing them.*

A microphone is brought on, and held up to each speaker in turn.

MIKE   Do you men make any moral distinction between physical and mental torture?

BARRY   Hell no. I don't make any distinction in morality at all. Torture is torture, and when you ass around with a guy's mind and his whole basic reason for living, you're really hurting him . . . especially when he's prepared mentally and spiritually for the physical torture.

PADDY   Once you've broken him down it comes to the point when he wakes up in a sweat one morning and tells you 'All right'. Then he tells you the names of the two people in his cell, or the location of his camp, and then you're through with him, in practical terms. But if you really believe in anything yourself, you've got to give this guy something to hope for before sending him back for further processing. Because you have just brought this individual to the lowest point in his life, in terms of human meaning and existence. That's when you've got to stress that, 'What you just told us is the beginning of a positive affirmation for you. Now we just can't process you into our unit right now, because you don't know what we stand for. But we hope that one day you will be joining us.' It's pretty rough stuff to get involved in, but it works.

MIKE   How do you offset the damage to yourself?

BARRY   Your belief. Your belief; you have to sincerely believe that in the long run you are helping this guy.

MIKE	So you think you have the right, by these techniques, to deny a man the belief he came in with, and only accept a set of alternatives which you propose?
MORGAN	We had a guy in the Phu Yen province who was the propaganda director for the NLF in that province. And, boy, we just worked ourselves ragged in four days, trying to bring that guy to the point where he'd tell us a few things. And he was tremendous, just tremendous. Didn't tell us a thing.
MIKE	You admire this man?
MORGAN	Tremendous, tremendous.
MIKE	So you admire a person who will not agree with you rather than one who does?
MORGAN	No, not true. I didn't say that at all. I admire a guy who will tortuously admit . . . a guy who will examine his previously arrived-at conclusions and change his mind, that's what I admire.
BARRY	You see, if we do not break this guy, if we do not attempt to change his ideas, then in essence what have we done? We've said that basically he's right.
MIKE	No, that isn't so. One agrees to disagree as a matter of principle in a democratic system.
PADDY	I've had some tremendous conversations with these guys, and we begin by agreeing to disagree. But you can soon get this guy so flustered and so shaken up that before he knows it, he's agreeing with you. His assumptions to begin with were rather . . . vulnerable?
MIKE	But that isn't the issue here. The issue here is whether you will impose your will by this technique.
PADDY	We don't know what our will is yet.
MIKE	You will impose your ideas.
PADDY	What ideas?

Pause. The actors suddenly break back into the torture session, the torture groups start. BARRY, PADDY *and* MORGAN *grab* MIKE, *beat him, kick him, and put a dog chain round his neck to drag him round.*

PADDY	You VC? Charlie . . . you VC?
MORGAN	You Viet Cong, you VC? Are you VC? What are you?
BARRY	You're a worm.

MORGAN   You're a worm. What are you?

PADDY   You're a slopehead!

The music starts, and MIKE *starts hitting out and kicking at the three. He is in a frenzy, and the three encourage him.* MORGAN *sticks a microphone down his belt, which* MIKE *pulls out like a six-shooter. The sound of screaming fans comes over the loudspeakers. The other actors will join in the chorus, miming, shooting and bayoneting on a small group of 'Viet Cong', forcing them progressively downstage, to the audience.*

SONG: ZAPPING THE CONG

MIKE   I'm really rocking the delta
From coast to coast.
Got 'em crawling for shelter
Got 'em burning like toast.
And the President told me
That it wouldn't take long.
But I know I'm in heaven
When I'm zapping the cong.

EVERYONE   Zapping the cong
Back where they belong
Hide your yellow asses
When you hear my song
All over the jungle
Up to Haiphong,
I'm crapping jelly petrol
I been zapping the cong.

Between each verse MIKE *staggers away from the microphone, is rubbed down by* PADDY, MORGAN *and* BARRY, *and swoops back to the microphone for the next verse. He gives it the full pop treatment, and the three behind him form backing group of dancers and singers.*

MIKE   I had a bomb in my copter
Called Sandra Dee.
Saw a village and dropped her
On a mess of VC.
I always say sorry,
When I get it wrong.
Then I got to be zooming,
Cos I'm zapping the cong.
I had a dream about going,
With Ho Chi Minh.
But I'll only be crowing,

When I'm zapping Pekin.
Be spreading my jelly,
With a happy song.
Cos I'm screwing all Asia,
When I'm zapping the cong.

EVERYONE   Zapping the cong,
Back where they belong.
Hide your yellow asses,
When you hear my song.
All over the jungle,
Up to old Haiphong,
Been crapping jelly petrol,
I been zapp, zapp, zapp, zapp,
Zee, Ay, Pee, Em, Ay, En,
Is . . .
ZAPMAN!

Everyone settles down and reads coloured comic books, while IAN
*roars and swells, into evil comic monster, grabs her and carries her
off up the ladders in the garbage.* BOB *stands up, arms to the sky,
announces he is Zapman, and goes up the other side of the ladder, kills
the monster with an invisible death ray, and* PAULINE *and he hug
each other on top of the ladder. The others throw their comics away,
cheering as* IAN *slides, dead, down the ladder.* GLENDA, URSULA *and*
MARJIE *crouch over* MIKE, *lying exhausted on the floor. They sing into
the microphone which is sticking up out of his belt.*

GIRLS   I had a dream about going,
With Ho Chi Minh.
But I'll only be crowing,
When I'm zapping Pekin.
Be spreading my jelly,
With a happy song.
Cos I'm screwing all Asia,
When I'm zapping the cong.

EVERYONE   Zapping the cong,
Back where they belong.
Hide your yellow asses,
When you hear my song.
All over the jungle,
Up to old Haiphong.
Been crapping jelly petrol,
I been zap, zap, zap, zap, zap,
Zee, Ay, Pee, Gee, Eye, Ar, Ell
Is . . .
ZAPGIRL!

Everyone freezes. HENRY *interviews* HUGH.

HENRY You said Mao isn't really what he thinks he is. Is that true of the other men who are in line to succeed him? Are they what they think they are? And do we know what they think they are or are they really something other than what they think they are?

HUGH As a historian, I have a jaundiced view. I don't think we are what we think we are.

HENRY As a historian you tell us.

HUGH I think we are all acting in a long stream of history with historical ideological influences in our mind influencing us, whether or not we realise it. It is awfully difficult to be self-conscious completely and understand why you are doing what you do and why you tick the way you do and why you believe in what you believe. We have our own pattern and they have theirs. As a historian, of course, I am a pessimist about human nature.

HENRY As a politician, I join you.

MIKE *whirls around with the microphone, and leads everyone in a last chorus.*

EVERYONE Zapping the cong,
Back where they belong.
Hide your yellow asses,
When you hear my song.
All over the jungle,
Up to old Haiphong.
Been crapping jelly petrol,
I been zap, zap, zap, zap . . .

There are twenty 'zaps', ending in 'Zapping the Cong', and everyone freezes in mid-karate chop.

HUGH *and* ROGER *come on with the microphones.*

ROGER What's war like, soldier?

PADDY Hell.

HUGH What's combat like, soldier?

LEON Hell.

ROGER What's pain like, soldier?

HENRY Hell.

HUGH What's dying like, Major?

CLIFFORD   Hell.

MIKE P   (*with microphone*) What's the war like, General?

JOHN *is crouching on top of the ladder. He takes* MIKE P's *microphone.*

JOHN   Getting the government forces into the same element
            as the insurgent is like trying to deal with a tomcat
            in an alley. It is no good inserting a large fierce dog.
            The dog may not find the tomcat; if he does the tomcat
            will escape up a tree and the dog will then chase the
            female cats in the alley. Right! The answer is to put in
            a fiercer tomcat. The two cannot fail to meet because
            they are both in exactly the same element and have
            exactly the same purpose in life. The weaker will be
            eliminated.

MIKE P   Thank you, General.

He climbs down the ladder a few rungs.

            The only summary I have heard of the Vietnam war,
            the only summary that can be understood by anybody,
            anywhere, anytime, was given to me today, personally,
            by a high-ranking officer in a man-to-man interview.
            'The war is just a fight between two tomcats.' That's
            all. But in the darkness of Vietnam today, I for one am
            grateful for this one ray of crisp, incisive daylight.

*The actors move off to the edge of the stage. They sit down, lie down,
relax and watch* MIKE, *left alone on stage. He has taken a tape
recorder. The stage is strewn with comics and newspapers.*

MIKE   Why are we bombing them every day? I think the
            reason is simple: simple desperation. Some observers
            within the American mission here, the military
            command and the press, believe that the current
            strategy cannot win. They say the US can never send
            enough troops to do the job. Their premise might be
            wrong. The majority of Vietnamese will probably be
            neither hostile nor friendly. They will hate the war,
            and they will pour into refugee centres to avoid it.
            They will be numb from pain and loss and hopeless-
            ness. If the US is prepared to kill two or three for
            every Viet Cong, the Communists may be defeated.

*He is wandering round, occasionally sitting, looking for an attitude.
He picks up a piece of newspaper from the floor.*

            It has been said repeatedly, and with justification,
            that there are not only forty-three different wars in
            Vietnam, or one for each province, but two hundred

and forty, or one for each district, and this was brought home to me during my stay in Binh Dinh. In Phu Hai, a fishing village of three hamlets I visited . . .

He screws the paper up and drops it.

When I first arrived in Vietnam, I thought the war could not be won but that it was worth trying. Now I sometimes think that it can be won but that it is not worth the price. At other times, comfortable and self-righteous times, I can still review the official rationalisations and find them persuasive. If the suffering of the peasant in Vietnam spares the peasant in Thailand or Laos, the Philippines or Malaya from future wars, is not that a sacrifice the world must ask of the Vietnamese? America did not, after all, choose this battlefield. It was his cousin from the North who marked the South Vietnamese for torture and mutilation.

And then the simple, stubborn point that blots out all other considerations: why should one country be permitted to subvert and destroy another? Why should Hanoi possess South Vietnam? And if the United States does not stop the North, what country will? Indignant over my coffee, I am at that moment quite willing to sacrifice the entire South Vietnamese people for my principles.

Pause. He looks round.

I love this country. I love it.

Pause.

I said to a journalist the other day, 'Before I arrived in Vietnam I thought the Americans should stay. Now that I'm here I think they should go.' He said to me, 'That's funny. Before I came here I thought the Americans should go. Now that I'm here I think they should stay.' Like almost everyone outside the US, and not a few in it, I am greatly alarmed by the Americans. For many years they have been putting the wind up the world by actions of terrifying charity and menacing goodwill. But especially do they scare me, since the more I alienate myself from everything they do internationally the more I seem to get mixed up with them personally.

Saigon is the only town in the world where the garbage stands around on the street corners, and they burn people. The war in Vietnam is not only destructive of people, property, integrity, sanity and ideals. It destroys judgement. There is only one valid generalisation that can be made about the situation: it is stalemate. In Vietnam no power, no person, no argument, can carry through to a crisp conclusion without being destroyed on the way.

He switches on his tape recorder, on playback.

TAPE 'Saigon is the only city in the world where the garbage stands on the street corners, and they burn people. Vietnam is the country where the good guys act villainous and the bad guys heroic, where a pacification means burning down villages and a liberation means murdering schoolteachers. This is also, incidentally, the place where all politicians are generals, and all generals politicians, except for the United Buddhist Church, which isn't unified, or Buddhist, or a church. In other words, Vietnam is where right is all wrong (most of the time) and wrong is dismayingly all right.'

He clicks the tape off.

MIKE So if you want to hold a clear, crisp, impressive opinion on the Vietnam war, stay far away. The war is so unpleasant it distorts all judgement, and morality apes those novels which the critics, in despair, say have to be appreciated on several levels simultaneously. Each of these levels is contradictory.

But this is **precisely** where my mind has been changed by visiting **Vietnam**. There does, in fact, come a point where the details add up so massively that they overwhelm the whole.

Pause.

As for the poor journalists, we are like those dogs that Pavlov tortured. He twisted their conditioned reflexes up by training them to distinguish between a high musical note, which indicated food was in their trough, and a low one, which meant they'd get an electric shock. Then he progressively brought the two notes closer and closer, until they were virtually indistinguishable. The dogs, as I recall, went mad.

Poor newspapermen in Saigon sit around like those dogs, with all their conditioned reflexes all screwed up. We tell each other sick stories. 'Saigon is the only town in the world where the garbage stands around on street corners, and they burn people.'

MARK *catches his eye, and* MIKE's *nervous grin fades.*

MARK I smell something burning, hope it's just my brains.
They're only dropping peppermints and daisy chains.
So stuff my nose with garlic,
Coat my eyes with butter,
Fill my ears with silver,
Stick my legs in plaster,
Tell me lies about Vietnam.

MIKE *hovers for a moment, about to answer him. Music comes over the loudspeakers, and the actors drift on, carrying chairs, setting them down and sitting: they are the journalists.* PADDY, BARRY *and* MORGAN *enter opposite the others, also with chairs, and microphones are brought on and placed in front of them. They are the spokesmen. Both groups face and speak straight out front. Whenever* MIKE *claps his hands, everyone freezes until he frees them by another clap.*

MIKE Every afternoon at 5 p.m. there is a ritual known as American Military Briefing. It is sometimes known as the Five o'Clock Follies. It takes place in the Rex Cinema, where the air-conditioning is excellent. You sit in deeply padded chairs, chilled to the bone, having come out of the very humid, hot Saigon summer day.

A girl is handing out large wadges of papers to the journalists.

In case you think these journalists have just come back from the battle areas I'd better mention that they have in fact arrived from their air-conditioned hotels, which in most cases are just across the road. Those one hundred yards of heat are the only contact most of them have with the people or the country. They shuffle between the two. Few ever leave Saigon, few ever meet Vietnamese. Vietnam, for them, is this room. From this room comes ninety per cent of all stories, all articles, all ideas about the war. When you read about Vietnam in your newspaper the report probably came from this room, already processed, homogenised, made fit for human consumption.

This is Harold Brubeck. It's his job to see that the briefing goes off smoothly, above all to project the idea of success, so that the world will be reassured, confidence maintained. And you, watching that night's news, will feel the war is in capable hands.

PADDY *rises.*

Harold Brubeck rises, and in the nicest softest way (it's very well amplified, this room), says . . .

PADDY   Good afternoon.

MIKE   Arfternoon, rather than Aaafternoon.

MIKE *takes a seat at the edge of the journalists.*

PADDY   I'll just start with a commercial. The US AID is proud to announce that the eighth millionth textbook has this day been imported into Vietnam as part of US AID's civic action programme in re-educating the people of Southern Vietnam to take their place in the fight for democracy and freedom.

           To our regret, in an action in the Delta region a group of Vietnamese civilian canal workers have been attacked by the Viet Cong. The canal workers were being protected by a regiment of Southern Vietnamese regulars, but nonetheless the VC infiltrated into their camp in the middle of the night, woke 200 of them, said, 'This is to teach you a lesson', then gunned down forty-five men, women and children, indiscriminately. Another statement. We deeply regret the fact that in the city of Hue a Buddhist nun, aged twenty-four, slashed her wrists and tried to write a letter to President Lyndon Johnson, condemning the American policy in Vietnam. We deeply regret and deplore any action of this nature, as we feel it is totally unconducive to the kind of war we're trying to win, for the minds and hearts and souls of the people of Vietnam.
           Any questions? Well, now I'll hand you over to the secular arm.

PADDY *sits,* BARRY *stands.*

BARRY   Figure for yesterday . . . two-five-zero Viet Cong killed.

HUGH   Colonel, was that bodycount or suspected KIA?

BARRY   Well, sir, at the moment it's suspected rather than proven bodycount.

HUGH   Bill, how many VC bodycount in that Operation Hawthorne, third day?

BARRY   Well, sir, we reckon on preliminary estimates . . . round about two-three-zero, sir.

ROGER   Bill, two years ago you fellows were saying that Phuoc Bin Hoi was a secure area. Today you say VC

	infiltrators have had to be combed out of precisely this area. How can you reconcile these two statements, Bill?
BARRY	Well, sir, of this moment I cannot predicate official policy with respect to statements issued on the security or otherwise of a given area, sir. But with respect, sir, I must point out that the military situation is liable, at times, to alter, sir.
HUGH	Was the Hawthorne fighting hand-to-hand, Bill?
BARRY	Hand-to-hand? It was eyeball-to-eyeball in the elephant grass!

He sits, and MORGAN *stands.* MIKE *claps and* MORGAN *freezes.*

MIKE	Colonel White, mid-westerner, lantern-jawed, burning blue eyes, MRA, violently anti-communist, anti-queer, anti-drink, anti-cigarettes.

MIKE *claps and* MORGAN *comes to life.*

MORGAN	I am authorised to announce that to support Big Red One, Airforce Units utilised a radically new item of ordnance, which is as yet uncleared security-wise.
IAN	Colonel . . .

MIKE *claps.*

MIKE	A German reporter, melancholic, drunk by 5 p.m. each evening, given to incomprehensible, Germanic, infinitely slow, bad-taste questions.
IAN	Can you tell us . . . why . . . the government authorities . . . have . . . not . . . sent . . . further gallons of . . . gawzoleen to Hue . . . so that further . . . Buddhist monks . . . can burn themselves?

Everyone writhes with embarrassment.

MORGAN	Yesterday there were four-seven-seven sorties off of Carrier Enterprise. Bridges were bombed at Kwang Nang, Ving Tong, Sup Luk, and Blup Suk . . .
HUGH	Colonel, how do you spell Blup Suk? Is that with a k?
MORGAN	Affirmative, that is with a k. VC build-up in Ell Zee Two . . . the build-up has been negated by fortuitous action on the part of Big Red One. Big Red One called in airstrike with napalm, rockets and CS5 . . .
LEON	Say, Colonel . . . this refined pesticide, CS5, does it in fact kill, if inhaled sufficiently?

MORGAN	Negative, sir. CS5 has been tested in our laboratories and produces temporary nausea from which after four or five days the person returns to complete normality.
ROGER	Colonel, do you mean to tell us that at Ban Sang, fifty-five B52s went in and dropped so many hundred tons of bombs, so many hundred tons of napalm, so many hundred tons of CS5, . . . and you do not know whether the VC were there or not?

Pause.

MORGAN	I'd like notice of that one, Roger, and I'll check that one out.
HENRY	Colonel . . .

MIKE *claps.*

MIKE	Joe Klein, carries the liberal conscience of America on his shoulders, also self-appointed needler.

MIKE *claps.*

HENRY	The town of Can tho was recently bombed was it not?
MORGAN	The forward air controller on patrol over the town of Can Tho was shot at with small arms, thereby provoking an airstrike on that town, affirmative.
HENRY	So small arms fire led the airforce to assume Vietcong presence there, right?
MORGAN	Presumably affirmative.
HENRY	And yet neither interpreters, newsmen, nor the town hospital doctor was able to find a single victim of the bombing who would concede that there were any Viet Cong in that town. Any comment, Mike?
MORGAN	No comment.
HENRY	More than one hundred civilians were killed or injured in that raid. Assuming the government forces were unable to protect the residents, did they themselves have any means of resisting Viet Cong visits to the town, and if not, can they be blamed, or justly punished, for the presence of the Viet Cong?
MORGAN	No comment.
HENRY	Would you give an opinion as to whether the military advantages gained by this airstrike are important enough to offset the political and humanitarian liabilities of killing and injuring one hundred people?

MORGAN	No comment, Joe.
HENRY	Colonel, would you say that existing military orders exhorting US Forces to take special precautions to avoid inflicting civilian casualties, would you say they were being effectively observed?
MORGAN	Affirmative, I would say that! We had one VC-dominated village and the commander refused to napalm it because innocent women and children would have been killed. As a result, VC snipers killed twenty of his men before he took that village. Affirmative, I would say they were being observed.

PADDY *stands.*

PADDY	A statement from General Westmoreland. Quote. One mishap, one innocent civilian killed, one civilian wounded, one dwelling destroyed, is too many. We are sensitive to these incidents, and want no more of them. If one does occur . . . mistake or accident . . . we intend to search it out for any lesson that will help us to improve our procedure and controls. A board of senior officials has been set up to revise precautions against accidental bombing and shelling of civilians. Any further questions?
HENRY	No.
MIKE	And even Joe Klein wears down.
PADDY	OK. We're off the record.

The journalists start to leave. MIKE *claps.*

MIKE	It's been a good day. This session only lasted thirty minutes. Normally they last for forty-five minutes, except for Saturday, which is the best day of all. Then it's only fifteen minutes.

He claps, and people move again. Another clap, and they freeze.

HUGH	Say, Harold, what really happened in that Hawthorne third day?
PADDY	Well, we don't really know yet, but we think we hurt somebody pretty bad.

MIKE *claps, they move again, clap, and they freeze.*

ROGER	Can you tell us why you persist in your refusal to give us any estimate of civilian casualties?

| PADDY | You've got to keep this war in perspective, Roger. Fewer people, of all categories, are killed here per day than we kill on the highways of the United States. |
| IAN | (*still drunk*) May I suggest . . . the quickest way . . . to get rid of the Communists . . . out of Asia . . . drop them Cadillacs by parachute! |

PADDY *and* ROGER *look at each other. The actors start to form a semicircle on the stage.*

A woman's scream. BOB *comes forward, and mimes pouring petrol on himself from an American jerry can.*

BOB *mimes his burning, mouth staring open, hands clutching at his eyes, he twists and sinks to the floor. There is a pause after he is still. The next speech comes over the loudspeaker.*

| RADIO | Norman Morrison, a thirty-two-year-old Quaker, set fire to himself on the steps of the Pentagon in Washington last night. A bystander described him as a human torch. The scene, said police, was like those in Saigon, where protesting Buddhist monks set fire to themselves in the streets. Several spectators dashed to beat out the flames. Morrison died on the way to hospital, two streets away. |

BOB *lies still throughout the next scene. The actors speak quietly, sitting in the semicircle of a Quaker meeting.*

| ROGER | We are gathered together today in memory of Norman Morrison. Most of us knew Norman personally. His wife is with us here today. For those who never met him, perhaps I should say this. Norman was not a fanatic, an eccentric, one of those gloomy 'do-gooders'. He was very happily married, with three children. He loved people. He was very skilful with his hands. He would rather repair something old than buy something new. He delighted in his ability to live on very little. And yet he enjoyed all those things that we find 'normal'. He was not a pious saint, attempting some kind of fanatical purity. |
| JOHN | Norman knew that when any people bases its hopes of security on its technological capacity to kill tens of thousands of its enemies' non-combatants . . . its women and children . . . that society, at that moment, has accepted a moral degradation which denies it any claim to freedom within itself. |

IAN	To Norman, love was an absolute imperative. He was radical. He desired a society transformed by love. And although love has become a trite concept that grown men are embarrassed to speak about, it is a radical idea, perhaps the most truly radical idea of the human race.
LEON	For most of us, a pinprick at the end of our finger is far more real than people being bombed in a nameless jungle. But Norman imagined, identified, totally. One of the things that moved him most on the day of his sacrifice was a report he read which quoted a Catholic priest in a pro-government village in Vietnam. 'I have seen my faithful burned up in napalm. I have seen my village razed. My God, it is not possible. They must settle their accounts with God.'
HENRY	In a society where it is normal for human beings to drop bombs on human targets, where it is normal to spend 50 per cent of the individual's tax dollar on war, where it is normal to give war toys for Christmas, where it is normal to have twelve and one half times overkill capacity, Norman Morrison was not normal. He said, 'Let it stop. Let us personally witness against this kind of normality. Let us be abnormal, in the sense that Jesus and Gandhi were abnormal.'
MARY	Norman was always disturbed by the view of so many people that their chief obligation was to their own family. He just didn't make the usual distinction between me and the children and the rest of mankind. That morning, when he read about those children in the priest's village, he said, 'How long can this go on?' I said we shouldn't despair, but we should keep looking for ways to work for peace. He must have been thinking of this final action then. I must have seemed terribly irrelevant. He wrote me a letter the day he ended his life. 'Dearest Anne, for weeks and even months, I have been praying only that I be shown what I must do. This morning, with no warning, I was shown, as clearly as I was that Friday night in August 1955, that you would be my wife. Know that I love thee, but must act for the children of the priest's village. Norman.'

MARJIE *comes forward as young American housewife, reads out this letter:*

MARJIE   18 February 1963

Dear President Kennedy,

My brother, Specialist James Delmas McAndrew, was one of the seven crew members killed on January 11 in a Viet Nam helicopter crash.

The Army reports at first said that communist gunfire was suspected. Later, it said that the helicopter tragedy was due to malfunction of aircraft controls. I've wondered if the 'malfunction of aircraft controls' wasn't due to 'communist gunfire'. However, that's neither important now, nor do I even care to know.

My two older brothers entered the Navy and the Marine Corps in 1941 immediately after the war started – they served all during the war and in some very important battles – then Jim went into the Marines as soon as he was old enough and was overseas for a long time. During those war years and even all during the Korean conflict we worried about all of them – but that was all very different. They were wars that our *country* was fighting, and everyone here *knew* that our sons and brothers were giving their lives for this country.

I can't help but feel that giving one's life for one's country is one thing, but being sent to a country where half *our* country never even *heard* of and being shot at without even a chance to shoot back is another thing altogether!

Please, I'm only a housewife who doesn't even claim to know all about the international situation – but we have felt so bitter over this – can the small number of our boys over in Viet Nam possibly be doing enough good to justify the *awful* number of casualties? It seems to me that if we are going to have our boys over there, that we should send enough to have a *chance* – or else stay home. Those fellows are just sitting *ducks* in those darn helicopters. If a war is worth fighting – isn't it worth fighting to *win*?

Very sincerely,
Bobbie Lou Pendergrass

1615 French Street
Santa Anna, California

BOB *gets up, sits on the petrol can, takes a notebook out. Two sides gradually form, like two opposing gangs. Diplomacy begins.*

BOB   We withdraw US forces by end of 1965.

IAN   We pledge fullest support in achieving victory.

MIKE   Both fighting and negotiating stepped up.

BOB   Infiltration from the north: 25,000 hardcore Viet Cong. US military personnel: 16,000.

JOHN   I call for a meeting of the same order as the Geneva Conference.

LEON   The Soviet Government insists that the Geneva Conference be reconvened.

PADDY   The National Liberation Front is not opposed to the convening of an international conference.

IAN   We do not believe in conferences called to ratify terror.

HUGH   NLF will talk to US in Rangoon now.

CLIFFORD   In my private capacity as mediator, I ask you to inform the President that North Vietnam is ready to talk.

MIKE   White House and State Department find Hanoi's offer insincere.

CLIFFORD   How do you know it's insincere?

MORGAN   A Canadian official met a deputy town councillor from Hanoi who warned him it was insincere.

SONG OF ESCALATION

EVERYONE   We know what we're doing
               We know what we're doing it for.
               We know what we're doing
               We ought to know for
               We've done it before.
               We know what we're doing
               We know who we're doing it to.
               We know what we're doing.
               Out of the way
               Or you know what we do
               Out of the way
               Or we'll do it to you!

IAN   There is danger and provocation from the North, and such provocation could cause a response.

MORGAN	US troops in Vietnam now 22,000.
BARRY	Three North Vietnamese patrol boats . . . unprovoked attacks on US warships in Tonkin Bay!
HUGH	No, no. American ships penetrate our territorial waters. US planes sink the torpedo boats we sent to challenge them.
JOHN	The Tonkin Bay incident completely destroyed any possibility of international talks.
LEON	A deliberate frame-up to prevent pressure for peace becoming too strong.
MORGAN	Congress approves and supports the determination of the President as Commander in Chief to take all necessary measures to repel any armed attacks against the forces of the United States.
BOB	The US Air Force . . . heavy attacks on North Vietnamese coastal bases.
MORGAN	The President now has full powers to deal by force with aggression from the North.
BOB	Infiltration increases. Daily airstrikes against the North begin . . . I don't believe we can be effective in South Vietnam in a short period of time. Total airstrikes, north and south: 4,700. Total infiltrators: 39,000.
IAN	We will not withdraw, either openly or under the cloak of a meaningless agreement.
PADDY	Our Four Points can be summarised as peace, independence, neutrality and democracy.
MIKE	There will be no air attacks on North Vietnam beginning at noon Wednesday May 12, 1965.

Everyone relaxes.

	In this decision the US government has taken account of repeated suggestions that there can be no progress toward peace while there are air attacks on North Vietnam.
HENRY	The US will be very watchful to see whether, in this period of pause, there are significant reductions in armed actions by forces decisively affected from the North. The US is well aware that this temporary suspension may be misunderstood as an indication of weakness, and it is therefore necessary to point out

that if this pause should be misunderstood in this fashion, it would be necessary to demonstrate more clearly than ever . . .

PADDY   (*to* JOHN) Tell Washington we are prepared to negotiate, on the basis of our Four Points, without prior withdrawal of American troops.

JOHN *moves to* PAULINE, *but* BARRY *beats him to it.*

BARRY   The Administration . . . disappointed: no reaction from North Vietnam during the suspension of bombing.

Everyone tenses.

JOHN   The French Government was not able to transmit the Hanoi offer until a few hours after the bombing resumed.

ROGER   There will be further disappointment before all parties gather round one table. But if success is achieved, it will be due in large measure to the patient and vigorous efforts undertaken behind the scenes by the British Government!

The Escalation Song begins again.

BOB   US military personnel: 75,000. Hard core Viet Cong: 70,000. US troops raised to 125,000. We have attacked bridges to reduce the flow of men and material. Attacks have been effective. Haven't stopped the flow, but have reduced that flow. We have stopped losing this war.

Everyone relaxes – sits or leans, on hearing HENRY.

HENRY   Once again the US suspends bombing on Christmas Eve, and continues this suspension for thirty-seven days. At the same time, President Johnson despatches high-ranking representatives to His Holiness, and to the heads of government of a number of states, to explain our most earnest desire to end this conflict peacefully and promptly.

The song ends.

CLIFFORD   We pray for peace in Vietnam.

The song starts again.

PADDY   If the US really wants peace, it must enter into negotiations with the National Liberation Front of South Vietnam.

IAN	It is not possible for us to consider the NLF as in any sense the authentic representative of the South Vietnamese people.
PADDY	What are the other forces in South Vietnam? What do they represent?
MORGAN	Are you in agreement with the resumption of the bombing of North Vietnam?
BOB	Yes.

Everyone tenses again.

	Our objectives: to affect their will toward a satisfactory settlement. We haven't reached that point yet.
BARRY	A target never before attacked by American pilots: Haiphong!
MORGAN	Seventy US Air Force jets crisscross Hanoi . . . seventy-two tons, 750-pound bombs, in twenty-five minutes!
BOB	These attacks, aimed at the heart of the petroleum system, should in time impose a lower ceiling on the number of men that can be supported in the South.
ROGER	The British Government must dissociate itself from this bombing.

He is pushed aside. The escalation music continues.

IAN	If North Vietnam's leaders will only let me know when and where they would like to ask us directly what can be done to bring peace to South Vietnam, I will have my closest and most trusted associates there in a matter of hours. Until then, US air strikes will continue to impose a growing burden.
PADDY	The Vietnam Democratic Republic has no alternative but to seek aid, chiefly from the socialist countries, in securing modern weapons . . . aircraft, anti-aircraft guns, and missiles!

The music stops dead.

IAN	We shall see this through. We shall persist. We shall succeed.

Air-raid begins, earsplitting noise. The actors become limping wounded. The huge soldier dummy which has hung above the stage starts to fall. It crashes down on to the stage. IAN throbs as the comic-strip monster again. URSULA rolls screaming on the floor, trying to beat out flames on her body.

As the sounds die away, and the dummy settles, the music for 'Make and Break' is heard. MIKE *and* BARRY, *in military costume, and* GLENDA *and* MIKE P *in white medical smocks, come through the doll. The other actors, still twisted up into wounds, pass through the checkpoint of* MIKE *and* BARRY *to the 'treatment' of* GLENDA *and* MIKE P.

SONG: MAKE AND BREAK

GLENDA *and* MIKE P

Pass me the stethoscope of Albert Schweitzer.

MIKE *and* BARRY

Pass me the armoury of Mickey Spillane.
Put the mothers through the bacon slicer.

GLENDA *and* MIKE P

Pick up the pieces and put them together again.

ALL FOUR   Want to be humane, but we're only human.
Off with the old skin, on with the new.

MIKE *and* BARRY

We maim by night.

GLENDA *and* MIKE P

We heal by day.

ALL FOUR   Just the same as you! Just the same as you!

This last line is shouted at PADDY, *who is rigid in a heroic 'pose' facing the four.*

BOB *comes forward through the doll, in a white smock, with a false hand in his hand.*

BOB   I am an artificial limb-maker from Spain. I am
             accustomed to see many cases in many countries
             around the world where I am doing this kind of job.
             But this shocked me more than any other place. More
             because they are mainly civilians and many people
             don't know what's happened. They stayed at home in
             the forest, the bombs go there, they come, aeroplanes
             and everything, drop a bomb there and they don't
             know what's happened. They don't know what the VC
             was. When I arrived here, it was difficult to find
             patients the first months. Now we get plenty. Next
             months more and more, because one patient tells
             another in the village and they come here. Everybody,
             to be fitted with artificial limbs.

MIKE *and* BARRY
        Fill all the area with whirling metal
        Five thousand razor blades are slashing like rain.

GLENDA *and* MIKE P
        Mr Hyde has a buddy called Jekyll
        Picks up the pieces and puts them together again.

ALL FOUR   Want to be humane, but we're only human.
        Off with the old skin, on with the new.

MIKE *and* BARRY
        We maim by night.

GLENDA *and* MIKE P
        We heal by day.

ALL FOUR   (*to* PADDY) Just the same as you! Just the same as you!

BARRY *crouches down and mimes loading children on to himself.*
MARJIE *stands over him, watching.*

MARJIE   Shhh, let the lovely sergeant carry you and don't talk.

BARRY   I want her to talk, I want her to feel free to say what
               she wants to say. That's what this whole thing is all
               about . . . you'll find we're very strong on that . . . we
               say what we like in America. Can you put your arms
               round my neck a bit tighter, then I can carry two of
               you, because you are a heavy girl, is that your brother,
               hang on tightly then, ups a daisy, I don't see why
               not . . . I really think I'm man enough . . . you up on
               my head and your friend hold me there . . . I guess I
               can manage, there's not one of you your normal weight
               I guess, though that's no fault of yours. Yes, kid, climb
               on to Uncle Henry, he's taking you all to be fitted. One
               more and that's that I guess, or just you, I can't say
               no to you . . . hold with your legs then . . . your hook
               thing's in my ear . . . if you could put it through my
               epaulette . . . yes, I am a real soldier, that means I'm
               a sergeant who is . . . a very important soldier.

He hands over the invisible children to GLENDA, *and snaps back into
line for the song.*

ALL FOUR   We treat the enemy like real blood brothers
        God made the family a blessing and pain.

GLENDA   Wives and husbands vivisect each other.

ALL FOUR   Pick up the pieces and put them together again.
        Want to be humane, but we're only human
        Off with the old skin, on with the new.

MIKE *and* BARRY
> We maim by night.

GLENDA *and* MIKE P
> We heal by day.

FOUR   *(to the audience)*
> Just the same as you! Just the same as you!

PADDY *mimes the throwing of a hand grenade. There is a whining sound, a huge explosion, and the four in the hospital fall dead.*

The doll starts to rise again. Most of the actors gather behind HUGH, *marching like zombies. A few gather behind* BOB, *holding parts of crashed aeroplanes, taken from the garbage heap. Both* BOB *and* HUGH *have microphones. The two groups face each other.*

HUGH   We want to tell the US Imperialists once again that the vast ocean of several hundred million Chinese people in arms will be more than enough to submerge your few million aggressor troops. Your atom bomb cannot intimidate the Chinese people. If you want to send your troops, go ahead, the more the better. We will annihilate as many as you can send, and can even give you receipts. We know that war brings destruction, sacrifice and suffering on the people. The sacrifice of a small number of people in revolutionary wars is repaid by security for whole nations, whole countries, and even the whole of mankind. Temporary suffering is repaid by lasting and even perpetual peace and happiness. War can temper the people and push history forward. In this sense war is a great school!

BOB   We know that war brings destruction, sacrifice and suffering on the people. The sacrifice of a small number of people in war is repaid by security for whole nations, whole countries, and even the whole of mankind. Temporary suffering is repaid by lasting and even perpetual peace and happiness.

HUGH *turns to his group,* BOB *to his, and both conduct their respective 'choirs' in rival songs.* BOB *sings 'Escalation' while* HUGH *sings 'The Leech'.*

BOB	HUGH
We know what we're doing	Found we were growing weaker every day
We know what we're doing it for.	Always felt about to die.

We know what we're doing	Something was draining our blood away,
We ought to know for	Someone had sucked us dry.
	It was a leech, it was the landlord
We've done it before	leech,
	It was the leech, it was the landlord
Out of the way	leech.
	It was bulging with blood and its
Or you know what we do	jaws were made of steel.
	We tore it off
Out of the way	Threw it down
Or we'll do it to you!	Crushed it under our heel.

The two songs together produce an awful cacophony. MARK *comes striding between the two groups, and* BOB *and* HUGH *wave for silence, and hold their microphones in front of* MARK.

MARK   You put your bombers in, you put your conscience out.
        You take the human being and you twist it all about.
        So scrub my skin with women,
        Chain my tongue with whisky,
        Stuff my nose with garlic,
        Coat my eyes with butter,
        Fill my ears with silver,
        Stick my legs in plaster,
        Tell me lies about Vietnam.

Slight pause, and then both groups cluster round MARK, *singing 'Escalation' together, growing louder, until they stamp their feet and* MARK *falls down. They all march past him, upstage, stamping on him as they pass, and singing. Pause. He sits up, lights a match.*

MARK   If you never spend your money,
        You'll always have some cash.
        If you stay cool and never burn,
        You'll never turn to ash.
        If you build your house of garbage,
        Then you'll love the smell of trash.
        And if you crawl along the ground,
        At least you'll never crash.
        So why, why, why, why?
        What made you think you could fly? Fly? Fly?

In the dim light, HENRY *and* BARRY *are led on, their heads beneath paper bags, and speaking through mikes. They are nightmare blind men, flanking* MARK.

HENRY   Now with respect to China itself, should we find
         ourselves locked in a war with China, is it your

	opinion, General, that we could subdue China by an all-out bombing attack against them?
BARRY	Nuclear bombing?
HENRY	Well, let us say first of all, conventional bombing.
BARRY	In my opinion, it would take nuclear bombs anyway, and there is no question about it, if we were to elect to use nuclear weapons, the devastation would be incredible . . . that we could inflict on any nation. Our stockpiles are tremendous, and the devastation would be beyond understanding.
HENRY	Beyond imagination?
BARRY	Oh, yes.
HENRY	But even if we were to spread such an incredible desolation through the use of nuclear weapons, do you think it would require physical occupation of China by American land forces, to effect a conquest of China itself?
BARRY	If you seek conquest, yes. Certainly not all of the real estate, but all of the key areas.
HENRY	How many American troops, in your judgement, would that require?
BARRY	Gee, I do not know, sir. I'm sorry. I would be guessing.

BARRY *and* HENRY *are tugged off clumsily by their microphone leads. Lights fade on* MARK *alone.*

End of Act One.

SONG: TO WHOM IT MAY CONCERN

('Tell Me Lies about Vietnam' by Adrian Mitchell)

MARK   I was run over by the truth one day.
Ever since the accident I've walked this way.
So stick my legs in plaster,
Tell me lies about Vietnam.

BOB   Heard the alarm clock screaming with pain.
Couldn't find myself so I went back to sleep again.
So fill my ears with silver,
Stick my legs in plaster,
Tell me lies about Vietnam.

MARK   Every time I shut my eyes all I see is flames.
Made a marble phone book and I carved all the names.
So coat my eyes with butter,
Fill my ears with silver,
Stick my legs in plaster,
Tell me lies about Vietnam.

BOB   I smell something burning, hope it's just my brains.
They're only dropping peppermints and daisy-chains.
So stuff my nose with garlic,
Coat my eyes with butter,
Fill my ears with silver,
Stick my legs in plaster,
Tell me lies about Vietnam.

MARK   Where were you at the time of the crime?
Down by the Cenotaph drinking slime.
So chain my tongue with whisky,
Stuff my nose with garlic,
Coat my eyes with butter,
Fill my ears with silver,
Stick my legs in plaster,
Tell me lies about Vietnam.

BOTH   You put your bombers in, you put your conscience out.
You take the human being and you twist it all about.
So scrub my skin with women,
Chain my tongue with whisky,
Stuff my nose with garlic,
Coat my eyes with butter,
Fill my ears with silver,
Stick my legs in plaster,
Tell me lies about Vietnam.

ACT TWO

The garbage pile has gone. Now there is just the wrecked aeroplane structure, and running out from it are metal barriers, like gymnastic bars, forming a frame for the action. Mattresses are spread about on the floor. ROGER *and* HUGH *enter and lounge. The house lights dim.* HUGH *takes* ROGER *and stands him against the plane wreckage. Four actors enter as firing squad. At an order from* HUGH *they take aim, and* ROGER *starts gabbling in 'Oriental'. All the other actors enter, gazing at the execution scene, and sit and lie down on the mattress.* BOB *and* MARK *stand at corners of the stage with microphones.* MARJIE *wanders on, with a microphone. She sings like a husky night club singer.*

SONG: ROSE OF SAIGON

> Rose of Saigon
> Wore armour plating.
> Only her mouth was alive
> Rose of Saigon.
> Rose of Saigon
> Seemed to be waiting
> For someone who'd never arrive.

A pause. HUGH *raises his hand, drops it, the firing squad shoots.* ROGER *crumples forward, hanging as though roped on to the wreckage.* BOB *and* MARK *meet each other centre. The music blares out.*

BOB *takes the microphone off, returns, and sits.* MARK *has the microphone taken off him, and is given an English petrol can. He pauses, then sits. He slides a box of matches in front of him, a letter to one side, and then screws the lid of the can off.* GLENDA *stands, and comes forward to him. The rest of the company watch closely.*

GLENDA   Do you suppose President Johnson or Mr Kosygin or Harold Wilson will ever even *see* this letter?

MARK   The papers will publish it.

GLENDA *considers him.*

GLENDA   You hope to draw people's attention to the war in Vietnam?

MARK *nods.*

	We're people. So you hope to draw our attention to the war in Vietnam?
MARK *nods.*	
	Our attention has been drawn. Your comments are noted. *Now* what do we do?
MARK	Change.
GLENDA	You think we'll change, just like that, because among all the other accidents and horrors we read a little paragraph about you setting yourself alight?
MARK	Someone will change.
GLENDA	It's no good inventing a mythical someone. (*She takes the matchbox.*) You've got to take me. I'm a suitable case. I vote left. I hold progressive opinions about homosexuality and capital punishment. I'm quite well read, I have a university degree. I do my best not to buy South African oranges . . . and what the hell do you think I'll do tomorrow any different from what I did today – just because you burn yourself?
MARK	Do you know what's going on?
GLENDA	Of course I *know*. We all *know*. It's on films, TV – soon they'll have it on a long-playing record.
MARK	You're a woman. You have to bring children into this world.
GLENDA	We don't – not any more; we choose to have them. Did your mother choose to have you? And if so, why? Did she have you to prove she was woman? Or to keep the marriage together? Or because everyone else was having them? Did she want a baby or you? And if she wanted you, why isn't she here, tonight, when you need her?

MARK *makes an attempt to answer her.*

	Perhaps it's not her fault – she's not capable of understanding this?

MARK *is silent.* GLENDA *studies him.*

GLENDA	Why don't you do something practical? Go to Vietnam and help . . . or march. Carry a banner. Or have you tried it?

MARK *nods.*

I'd like to march with a gun. Like a girl on a kibbutz, like a partisan. Like someone in the Resistance, when victory's come and it's the first day when you can say what you are. All I've done is to get blisters on one wet Easter. I looked behind, and I saw these thousands, and I thought, I am not alone! And I then thought, we are five thousand out of fifty million – and that is being alone. If we cared, we could jam the runways, paralyse London. And we march along, escorted by authority. One ticket collector striking for one extra shilling can bring a whole terminus to a standstill, and for world peace we can't even block a minor road for one hour.

Remember the night we thought the world might blow up? Over Cuba? I was outside the American Embassy. Not demonstrating. I was watching other people demonstrating. Where were you?

MARK   I went to the cinema.

GLENDA   With anyone?

MARK *shakes his head.*

You thought, either the big bombs will go off tomorrow; or they won't. Nothing I can do tonight will change anything.

She looks at him. He is silent, withdrawn.

Can't you talk? If you're doing this, I thought you must be intelligent. You're probably just some dull pleb little man, belonging to some pleb religion.

He is silent.

I don't like you. You're smug. You're like the people who try to draw my attention to that black child on the posters. Sometimes at Christmas I remember to send a cheque. But I end up hating that black child. If it were here, now, I'd wash it and wipe its nose and get rid of its eczema and worms and mother it . . . for how long? I don't know how long. But while it's just something begging from a poster, I hate it . . . it's like someone who starts talking too seriously at a party . . . I want to move away.

She does. The actors also draw back slightly, some lie down completely. But they keep watching MARK.

OK. You've drawn my attention to Vietnam. I'll send you a cheque in the morning. That's my reaction. Do you think anyone else's will be any different?

MARK *takes a long time to answer.*

MARK   If what you say were true, then we would all be worthless.

GLENDA   And if we're worthless, what's the point of your killing yourself?

MARK *pulls up his words as though each was a great weight.*

MARK   I have to believe we are not quite worthless. That there's someone . . . somewhere . . .

GLENDA *comes back to him.*

GLENDA   Have you ever tried to kill yourself before?

MARK *shakes his head.*

Are you a member of the Communist Party?

MARK *shakes his head.*

Any insanity in your family? You've never been to a psychiatrist? You haven't a bastard or a drunk father or a police record? You're not out of work? You haven't left any filthy books in your room? The little leg-men from Fleet Street will look, don't you worry; they'll turn back the sheets, look in the lavatory – and if they find *anything* they'll use it. You're quite sure you're a pure white lamb?

MARK   I'm not trying to be Christ.

GLENDA   No? Just in case you are, don't forget: Christ didn't kill himself – he was killed. If you want to be a martyr, all you need to do is to look inside yourself, and then say what you see. Accurately. Just once. You won't have to kill yourself. The human race will do it for you.

MARK *holds out his hand for the matches.*

Churches are warm in winter and cool in summer. I just sit there and hope there's no nutty old women doing the flowers who'll come and talk to me. I pop in and out of services like a dog looking for its master. Do you know, every Sunday those respectable people in suits, they say with one voice. 'We have left undone those things which we ought to have done, and we have done those things which we ought not to have done; and there is no health in us.'

I want to say it with them, but I can't . . . I can't.
Where do we look next . . . Freud? But Freud leads us
to the same point. 'You are not what you'd like to think,
you are what you think.' Then suddenly I thought
Sartre has the answer. Then I read a bit further. 'You
have chosen to be what you are.' I wasn't ready for
that, so I tried the Buddha. 'All that we are is the
result of what we have thought.' I was back where I
began, in the church where I couldn't join in. What we
want is someone to tell us how bloody marvellous we
all are, and what a bloody marvellous time we're all
having. He used to exist. He was called Satan.

MARK   I've read all these arguments. I've talked all night,
                I can only do what I'm going to do.

*He holds out his hand for the matches. She looks irritated, she plays
with the matchbox.*

GLENDA   What are you burning?

MARK   Myself.

GLENDA   All of yourself? The Good and the Bad?

MARK *nods.*

                Do you believe in life after death?

MARK   No.

GLENDA   Or God?

MARK   No.

GLENDA   Those monks who burn themselves – they believe that
                good will survive.

MARK   It's easy to burn the bad in me. It's the good that will
                hurt. A bonfire of rubbish means nothing. But to burn
                something valuable, beautiful . . .

GLENDA   *Look* at what you are burning! Are you one of those
                puritans who despise the body? What feeds this great
                mind of yours? What carries it from place to place,
                what suffers when the mind suffers, gets aches and
                ulcers, gives you signs and warnings – like some
                faithful old servant who can't speak but *shows* you
                what he feels? The Americans say they have to win
                the hearts and minds of the Vietnamese people. And
                then they use every device they can find to burn and
                wound the poor bodies those minds have to live in.
                You're just burning another body. Making another
                atrocity. Adding to the cruelty.

MARK	I cannot be moved by reason.
GLENDA	Like the government on either side? Like the Pentagon and Hanoi? They cannot be moved by reason, either.
MARK	The Pentagon *is* reason. This is a reasonable war. It is the first intellectuals' war. It is run by statisticians, physicists, economists, historians, psychiatrists, mathematicians, experts on everything, theorists from everywhere. The professors are advisers to the President. And we move not one inch either way. Even the atrocities can be justified in logic.

MORGAN *rises slowly, and comes slightly closer to* MARK. *Dream sequence starts.*

MORGAN	I speak of certain psychological dynamisms such as the mirror image of the enemy, the self-fulfilling prophecy and the double standard of morality. They are all evident in American conduct in Vietnam. The mirror image is evident in the way the United States and China each sees itself as peacefully inclined, and the other as aggressive. This war in Vietnam has assumed an ideological character similar to the old Holy Wars, and this has ominous implications. People who are fighting for their ideals seldom, if ever, can be forced into surrendering by punishment.

MORGAN *drifts back to his place, and sits.* HUGH *enters, carrying a fishing rod and basket.*

HUGH	On the 23rd of June 1966, I spent my life savings in putting an advertisement in *The Times* of London. I called it 'A Personal Message from Mr Matsuda'. I am a private citizen of Japan. It was three pages long, including my 'Blueprint for Paradise'.
	Paradise on Earth is a facility where people can live as follows:
	One. There are no taxes. Food, clothing and shelter are free. People get salaries.
	Two. There are almost no sources of unhappiness for people.
	Three. They suffer from almost no emotions.
	Marriages. The marriage committee matches men and women who are similar. In other words, men and women who have something in common in the fields

of taste and learning are matched to make couples. Inborn cripples or imbeciles are sterilised.

Ideas to reduce traffic accidents by 90 per cent. Counter-measures for high speed, slow speed, traffic congestion, overtaking, and inattentive driving will be by means of alarm lights and speed lights. A speed light is designed to have seven beams:

One, cream. Two, yellow. Three, harbour green. Four, green. Five, sky blue. Six, peacock blue. Seven, ultramarine blue.

I am a petty citizen of Tokyo, Japan, uneducated and anonymous. My wife says I'm crazy. My ideas for world peace come to me while fishing. My earnest thoughts for world peace prevent me from keeping busy with my work, so I do fishing. There is only one thing I have the right to do besides fishing, and that is my right to place an advertisement in *The Times* of London. I asked for the world leaders to give me twenty-four hours complete power, and I would guarantee peace. If I failed, I swore to burn myself to death.

He exits, then reappears without props, and sits with the other actors. BARRY *has stood, rolled his mattress up, and carries it towards* MARK. *He unrolls it, and lies down.*

BARRY   Everyone talks about war, it's so tiresome. As for me, I'm on a super-highway . . . war on one side . . . a playground on the other. Which one? For me, always the playground. If you pay attention to war you're part of it. Attention is participation. If you're part of it, you increase it. Boring, boring, boring. My boyfriend joined the army to get away from me. At least he looked cute in his uniform – cuter than before, even with nothing on. Me talking . . . if I took my toupee off and the rest of my face, you'd run like a frightened mouse. Thank God life is short. I fly up from the non-world of consciousness into the broad sanctuary of ecstasy and hope . . . I lie in my studio and listen to Asian hi-fi. I smoke pot. I have a beautiful creature who slips smooth chilled peaches over my tongue. I have a 16-millimetre camera. I film myself . . . I watch myself . . . watching myself.

He starts to roll up his mattress again.

Fools rush in
Where wise men fear to tread.
But wise men never fight a war
They masturbate instead.

He goes back to his place, unrolls his mattress, and lies down. BOB *and* PAULINE, *smoking pot, wander over to* MARK.

BOB   The director of a music concert would not allow me to perform 'Composition 1960 Number Five'.

Diana said maybe the reason the director of a music concert would not allow me to perform 'Composition 1960 Number Five' was that he thought it was not music. 'Composition 1960 Number Five' is the piece in which the butterfly is turned loose in the performance area. I asked her if she thought the butterfly piece was music to any less degree than 'Composition 1960 Number Two', which consists simply of building a fire in front of the audience. She said, 'Yes, because in the fire piece at least there are some sounds.' I said that I felt certain the butterfly made sounds, not only with its wings but also with the functioning of its body, and that unless one was going to dictate how loud or soft sounds had to be before they could be allowed into the realms of music, the butterfly piece was music as much as the fire piece. Diana said she thought that at least one ought to be able to hear the sounds. I said that this was the usual attitude of human beings, that everything in the world should exist for them, and that I disagreed. I said it didn't seem to me at all necessary that anyone should have to hear the sounds and that it is enough that they exist for themselves.

But the director of the music concert would not allow the butterfly piece. I saw a boy in the park today running away, quite terrified, from a small butterfly.

PAULINE   John Cage went to a concert and found that one of the composers had written in the programme notes that he felt there was too much suffering in the world. After the concert, John Cage said to this composer that he had enjoyed the music but he didn't agree with his statement about too much suffering in the world. The composer said, 'What? Don't you think there is enough?' to which Cage replied that he thought there was just the right amount. Later, in a letter, Dennis Johnson wrote to me, 'Do you think there is too much Evil in the world? John Cage thinks there is just the right amount. I think there is too much world in the Evil.' Some time after, I remember that Richard Huelsenbeck had another permutation. At one of those Dada lectures he gave in Berlin, he had made the statement that the war had not been bloody enough.

BOB   It is often necessary that one be able to ask, 'Who is John Cage?'

MARK *walks away.* BOB *catches his arm.*

I am not interested in good. If you are interested in what is good that means you are interested in what you already like. I am interested in the new – even if this involves the possibility of its being evil.

BOB *is going away when* HENRY *comes to both him and* MARK.

HENRY   A new, deeper anti-world symmetry is now believed to hold, in which the anti-world, which is supposed to be precisely identical to our world, does not only have anti-particles replacing particles, but also is a mirror image of our world, in which the flow of time is reversed. The exact location of this anti-world is not yet known.

He taps BOB's *shoulder consolingly, and goes back to his mattress.* BOB *goes back to his mattress.* CLIFFORD *gets up.*

CLIFFORD   The present generation under the age of twenty-five is the wisest and holiest generation that the world has ever seen. And by God, instead of lamenting, derogating and imprisoning them, we should support them, listen to them, and turn on with them. LSD is the love potion of the future.

PAULINE *moves to* CLIFFORD.

PAULINE   This aspect of LSD has been hinted at privately, but never spelt out in public before now. Why?

CLIFFORD   At the present time I'm under a thirty-year sentence, which for a forty-five-year-old man is essentially a life term; and I am under indictment on a second marijuana offence involving a sixteen-year sentence. Since there is hardly anything more that middle-age, middle-class authority can do to me – and since the secret is out anyway amongst the young – I feel I'm free to say what LSD does for me personally. You feel yourself sinking down into the soft swamp tissue of your own body, slowly drifting down dark red waterways and floating through capillary canals, softly propelled through endless cellular factories, ticking, chugging, pumping relentlessly. There is a shattering moment in the deep psychedelic session when your body, and the world around you, dissolves into shimmering lattice-works of pulsating white waves, into the silent, subcellular worlds of shuttling energy. At this point the unprepared LSD subject often screams out: I'M DEAD!

PAULINE   What would you say is the most important lesson you've learned from your own personal use of LSD?

CLIFFORD   First and last, the understanding that basic to the life impulse is the question: 'Should we go on with life?' Beyond this, I've learned to confine my attention to the really shrieking issues: Who wrote the cosmic script? What does the DNA code expect of me? Is the big genetic show live or on tape? Who is the sponsor? Are we completely trapped inside our nervous systems, or can we make real contact with anyone else out there?

PAULINE   Will the psychedelic experience become universal? Will everyone be turned on?

CLIFFORD   LSD will enable each person to realise that he is not a game-playing robot put on this planet to be given a Social Security number and to be spun on the assembly line of school, college, career, insurance, funeral, goodbye. Through LSD, each human being will be taught to understand that the entire history of evolution is recorded inside his body; the challenge of the complete human life will be for each person to recapitulate and experimentally explore every aspect and vicissitude of this ancient and majestic wilderness. Each person will become his own Buddha, his own Einstein, his own Galileo.

CLIFFORD *exits.* PAULINE *lies on a mattress.* IAN *is standing on a platform in the plane wreckage.*

IAN   Our generation has a dream. It is a very old dream. But we have the power and now we have the opportunity to make it come true. Every night before I turn out the lights to sleep, I ask myself this question: Have I done everything that I can to unite this country? Have I done everything I can to help all the people of the world? Have I done enough?

IAN *freezes on the platform.*

MARK   You can live in the country and look at the grass and the trees; and then remember in Vietnam they've found a way of making the earth bald, so there's nowhere anyone can hide. You can live in the town and drink or take pills or smoke pot, turn sex into a war . . . it's a nice war, that like. I am interested in the new – even if this involves the one. The wounds don't show. Not much. You can fly to some Greek island . . . and then you remember even the sun is a weapon, because you've read in *Scientific American* that they've worked out how to make a hole in the atmosphere, so the solar rays could drive a whole population mad. You can actually go to Vietnam and take a few pictures of burned babies and sell your honest doubt to the Sunday supplements. Honest doubt . . . it's an irreproachable attitude. You give nothing away. You can't be wrong. This war . . . words won't stop it. Reason won't stop it. Only an act that is beyond words, beyond reason, has any meaning.

GLENDA   What have you done, that you want to burn? What have you thought?

A silence. MARK *reaches for the box. She moves away her hand.*

    Suppose I say 'Jew' to you: What do you see?

MARK   I see . . . a suffering race.

GLENDA   What do you see? Come on, what do you see? Jew. Jew!

MARK   I see . . . pits. A bulldozer moving bodies.

GLENDA   Where are you standing? In a hut? In the ranks, where they choose who'll go where? Or are you standing where the guard would be standing?

MARK   I am standing – where the camera was.

GLENDA   You're cheating. Jew, Jew! Go on – what do you see?

MARK   A man . . . with a hooked nose. Black hair. Fat, rich, moving his hands . . . I'm trying to forget he's a Jew. I want to say, I don't care if you're a Jew. For Christ's sake stop thinking I care if you're a Jew!

GLENDA   Suppose I say – 'burning Negro'. What do you see?

MARK   Men in hoods.

GLENDA   Go on.

MARK	A stake. Hands tied behind his back. The fire.
GLENDA	Where's the fire?
MARK	Round his feet. Burning upwards.
GLENDA	Yes?
MARK	Up his legs.
GLENDA	Yes?

MARK *is embarrassed.*

MARK	His clothes on fire . . .
GLENDA	Yes?

Pause.

GLENDA	Suppose I say to you, 'American' – what do you see?
MARK	I see . . . a car.
GLENDA	Go on.
MARK	A big car. Long – as a house. One of those number plates – 'California, Garden State'. It's black, lots of chrome . . .
GLENDA	Who's in the car?
MARK	There's no one in the car.
GLENDA	Where have they gone?
MARK	They've gone shopping.
GLENDA	What are they buying?
MARK	Everything. They're buying everything.
GLENDA	What?
MARK	Antiques. Drugs. Pictures. Love.
GLENDA	And?
MARK	You and me.
GLENDA	What is the difference between anti-Americanism and anti-Semitism?

MARK *makes no answer.*

The American is rich like the Jew, strong like the Negro. He doesn't have a nose or a colour – but he has a voice. It's useful, that voice. That's how you can tell him. It takes a Jew to tell a Jew, but anyone can tell an American. You can hear them coming and change the price. By being anti-American you can enjoy all the

> pleasure of race hatred whilst persuading yourself you
> are on the side of peace.

MARK   Can't we stand up and show them – we can't be
                bought!

IAN *swings down from the platform, muttering staccato phrases overlapping with* MARK's *speech.*

MARK   IAN

That we're not afraid to be   There is nothing we want . . .
poor, undefended, on our own!   there is nothing we want . . . we
This is – possible. At least,   have made it clear . . . we have
we'd have some – some pride   made it clear . . . in many more
in ourselves. We could become   ways than I can tell you . . . we
a nation of . . . of . . . I'd sooner have explored . . . we are
live on nothing . . . have   exploring . . . Until that day . . .
nothing . . . be . . . be . . . I   we will carry on . . . no one knows
can't see any way of making   how long it will take . . . No one
English people see this . . .   can tell how much effort . . .
                                    sacrifice . . . no one can tell you . . .

IAN *has tottered downstage. He freezes, having grown older during his short walk.*

GLENDA   (*to* MARK) The Germans got rid of the Jews . . . but
                all they had to give up was a few musicians and
                philosophers and artists and scientists and principles.
                If we kicked out the Americans we'd lose money,
                safety. Hitler was a fool. What's the use of gassing the
                thing you hate? Much better to keep the thing you
                hate . . . Better still, let it keep you.

MARK   I ask. I ask my father, my mother, my sister. And
                because I ask this, they think I'm ill. I ask a friend –
                and because I ask this, I lose him. I ask the girl who's
                with me in bed. We've made love. And I say, why when
                we've made this good love am I left with a question –
                a tick-tick-tick in my mind? What is the thing after
                this? I can't see her. I can tell she's afraid. She's
                thinking, what more does he want? Christ, he's had
                my body, I washed the dishes, he can't want that, no
                not that: if it's in him it's not in me, not in me. I go
                down streets and I think it must show.

GLENDA   This nice kind Englishwoman went to Spain. She saw
                some boys who'd caught a seagull with a broken wing.
                They were throwing it from hand to hand. They tied a
                string to its leg and tried to fly it like a kite. She went
                up to them and tried to take the seagull away. It was

their toy, they wouldn't part with it. So she gave them ten pesetas, took the seagull, went back to her room and tried to mend its broken wing. That night twenty boys came to her hotel. They'd all caught seagulls and broken their wings. And they wanted her to buy them for ten pesetas. That's what happens when you go to someone else's country with your busybody principles and ideals! 'You want girls? Have ours! You want corpses? We'll give them. You want a speech? We'll make it.'

MARK *has not heard her.*

MARK   Do you know what I'm seeing? It's grey, a grey landscape with a few houses going to a flat horizon. I am standing on a height. All kinds of things are going on – men ploughing fields, soldiers marching, vans delivering, here and there a house on fire, a ship sinking. But all this – it's only a small part of what I can see. And if I lift my eyes from this model, I'll see giants, colours, distances, heights, depths . . . I would lie on the carpet with a little world like this inches from my nose. For hours I could believe in the scale – it was real. Then, the game ended. I knocked it down. I stood up, to my enormous height. The figures, that had been so real, the plastic cows and sheep in the fields – they were suddenly something that would fit in a small box and could be put away without . . . without any sadness.

GLENDA   I want to say to them, let's talk a *little* further. Not far, just a little. Just beyond 'have you read, have you seen, have you met, have you heard?' Just a little beyond that, to see what the next thing could be. But they know what the next thing could be. It would bring down the whole house we live in, the whole language. People don't just burn in Vietnam. We burn here, in one another's arms.

She has crumpled in tears. CLIFFORD *enters, with the yellow Buddhist cloth – from the beginning of the play – over his shoulder.*

CLIFFORD   Open your eyes and awake. See things as they are and you will be comforted. He who is awake will no longer be afraid of nightmares. He who has recognised the nature of the rope that seemed to be a serpent, ceases to tremble . . . Not in the sky, not in mid-ocean, not in mountain cave – nor in the fire – can a man find sanctuary from his sin . . . Let us live happily, then, not hating those who hate us! Let us live free from hatred among men who hate! Let us live happily, then, free from ailments, among the ailing! Let us dwell free from afflictions among men who are sick at heart! Let us live happily, then, free from care among the busy! Let us dwell free from yearning among men who are anxious! Let us live happily, then, though we call nothing our own! We shall become like the bright gods, who feed on happiness!

CLIFFORD *sits.*

GLENDA   We could live together and be poor and happy. We could paint the walls ourselves, and make furniture out of boxes . . . We could drink cheap wine, eat pasta, and read *The Brothers Karamazov*. We could make love three times a night and buy a record player and find we both like Mahler. Until the mistake that is not quite a mistake makes me pregnant. We will talk about this at great length and read Simone de Beauvoir. We will marry in a Registry Office and send up the ceremony by going in jeans. We will say, we don't feel any different being married, let's pretend we're still living in sin. Quite forgetting that when we *were* living in sin we defiantly said we weren't. We will read paperbacks on child psychology and have the baby in a progressive way. You will take a job for which you have to apologise, and another baby will come and to avoid feeling merely bourgeois we will read the entire output of the Olympia Press and know people who take LSD. You will make more money and we will move to a house with a garden and buy a Mini and have serious conflicts about education. We will change over to stereo and get an au-pair. We will own five beds, twenty blankets, fifteen pairs of sheets, one automatic defrosting refrigerator, one electric mixer and pulveriser, one washing machine, one spin dryer, one vacuum cleaner, one Polaroid camera, two pairs of skis, fourteen assorted brushes, mops, buckets and brooms, five hundred and sixty boxes, pen trays, ash trays, ornaments, implements, toys, garments, labour-saving apparatuses and comic novelties, nine hundred books, forty square yards of Wilton carpet with foam underlay and seventy-two records, as new, scarcely played. We will decide we ought to go out more. We will dress up and go to the theatre – choosing, of course, some experimental controversial leftish sort of show. And as we leave the theatre, we will say, not exactly what we really feel, but the proper sensitive intelligent things that everyone else is saying. We will begin to talk always from books and films and plays, and never from ourselves. We will become afraid of words like 'good' and 'bad'; so when we're in doubt we will call the latest thing 'interesting' – to hide our uncertainty. We will be so easily embarrassed by any natural feeling that we will put it in inverted commas, or say it in a funny voice. And at our parties everyone else will be doing the same, so life will really be quite comfortable – apart from occasional exercises of conscience, over something like Rhodesia or Vietnam. You will die before me, because women live longer. The children will put me in a home or build me a bungalow. There's a nice English seaside town where so many old people live alone that philanthropists have issued them with whistles and little cards reading 'Help'. When they feel death coming, they are supposed to blow the whistle and put the card in the window . . .

MARJIE *stands and walks to* MARK *and* GLENDA. *The music is light.*

SONG: ANY COMPLAINTS?

MARJIE　　　　My girl Kate's teaching in the States,
　　　　　　　Lecturing from town to town.
　　　　　　　Pays her bills by, gets her thrills by
　　　　　　　Studying the influence of Yeats on Yeats.

　　　　　　　What's wrong with that?
　　　　　　　That's what she always wanted to be.
　　　　　　　What's wrong with that?
　　　　　　　If it makes her happy,
　　　　　　　If it keeps her happy,
　　　　　　　That's all that should matter to me.

　　　　　　　My son Dave says he's living in a cave,
　　　　　　　Hiding from the MI5.
　　　　　　　Rank outsider, full of cider,
　　　　　　　Goes to demonstrations for a good old rave.

　　　　　　　What's wrong with that?
　　　　　　　That's what he always wanted to be.
　　　　　　　What's wrong with that?
　　　　　　　If it makes him happy,
　　　　　　　If it keeps him happy,
　　　　　　　That's all that should matter to me.

My son Pete has a passion for defeat,
Never leaves the Twilight Zone,
He's a chronic melancholic,
Chewing tranquillisers as he sits and sits.

What's wrong with that?
That's what he always wanted to be.
What's wrong with that?
If it makes him happy,
If it keeps him happy,
That's all that should matter to me.

My son Tom sends chatty letters from
Where they make pneumonic plague.
Scientific, feels terrific,
Breeding germs to go into the Black Death Bomb.

What's wrong with that?
That's what he always wanted to be.
What's wrong with that?
If it makes him happy,
If it keeps him happy,
That's all that should matter to me.

The last verse is spoken. The actress's name can vary.

MARJIE   My name is Marjie Lawrence. For a long time we've
been working on this war in Vietnam. And we've
thorough enjoyed ourselves. And –

EVERYONE   What's wrong with that?
That's what we always wanted to do.
What's wrong with that?
If it makes us happy,
If it keeps us happy,
That's all that should matter to you.

MARJIE *walks away and sits.* JOHN *rises, and comes forward to stand
between* MARK *and* GLENDA.

JOHN   I want you to understand very clearly just what it is
you are protesting about when you demonstrate
outside our embassy. Most of your protests are based
on a misunderstanding of what this war is about. It's
really very simple. Vietnam is, at this moment, the
focal point of a great power struggle. We think our
way of life is better than that of the communists.
Believing this, we cannot allow the communists to
take over South Vietnam.

It is possible to make a moral protest against our activities. You may say that it's wrong for two great powers to be killing innocent people. But if you say that, you are, in effect, condemning everything on which civilised societies have been based for the past two thousand years. History is the story of power struggles. Those engaged in those struggles have always believed they were right. The only morality lies in gaining your ends while inflicting as little suffering as possible.

America is the most powerful nation in the history of the world. We think that we're using our overwhelming power with more restraint than any other nation in the history of the world. This is the essence of our moral case. You may reject that case, but if you do so, you are rejecting the concept of the power struggle itself. You are denying the right of anyone to use power to achieve ends that he thinks are right. You are saying, 'I will achieve my ends by rejecting the power struggle,' and you will probably not achieve your ends.

If every general started questioning his orders, what is there to stop the officers from questioning the generals . . . and the soldiers from questioning the officers? This kind of disorder may lead to war being abolished. But only if you are prepared to accept the full consequences of disorder, have you any right to judge me.

When you protest, you should realise that you are in fact protesting not against the war in Vietnam but against the whole concept of an orderly society. If this is what you want, I shall listen to you as respectfully as I hope you will listen to me. And I shall continue to disagree with you.

JOHN *turns away, goes back to his mattress, and sits.*

GLENDA   So you end the war in Vietnam. Where's the next one? Thailand, Chile, Alabama? The things that will be needed are all ready in some carefully camouflaged quartermaster's store. The wire, the rope, the gas, the cardboard boxes they use for coffins in emergencies.

I WANT IT TO GET WORSE! I want it to come HERE! I want to see it in an English house, among the floral chintzes and the school blazers and the dog leads hanging in the hall. I would like us to be tested. I would like a fugitive to run to our doors and say hide me – and know if we hid him we might get shot and if we turned him away we would have to remember that for ever. I would like to know which of my nice well-meaning acquaintances would collaborate, which would betray, which would talk first under torture – and which would become a torturer. I would like to smell the running bowels of fear, over the English Sunday-morning smell of gin and the roasting joint, and hyacinth. I would like to see an English dog playing on an English lawn with part of a burned hand. I would like to see a gas grenade go off at an English flower show, and nice English ladies crawling in each other's sick. And all this I would like to be photographed and filmed so that someone a long way off, safe in his chair, could watch us in our indignity! Everyone who doesn't care *what* goes on – so long as it's out of sight – wants it to go on; because if it's being done to someone else, they think it won't be done to them; and if someone else is doing it, that's better than doing it yourself. Every man whose spirit is dying wants it to go on, because that sort of dying is better if everyone else dies with you. Everyone longing for the day of judgment – wants it to go on. Everyone who wants it to be changed, and can't change – wants it to go on. It doesn't matter that the world will be ash – if your life is ash, you'll want it to go on. And that is why it goes on. And why it will get worse. And why the catastrophe will come.

I want it. You want it. They want it. Like lust, it goes on because we want it. And as with lust, we suspect most of all those who shout loudest, 'No!'

She collapses. IAN *wakes up and shuffles across the stage.*

IAN   We may well be living in the time foretold many years ago, when it was said: 'I call Heaven and Earth to record this day against you, that I have set before you life and death, blessing and cursing; therefore choose life, that both thou and thy seed may live.'

He stops suddenly, staring out at the audience. BOB *enters, carrying a small table with a black box on it. He wears black gloves. He opens the lid of the box, and releases several white butterflies. They fly out into the auditorium, and over the actors. He reaches into the box and takes another one or two butterflies and throws them into the air. Then he pulls out a lighter from his pocket, lights it, takes out another butterfly and holds it in the flame. We cannot tell if it is real or false. As it stops burning he freezes, as do all the actors. The house lights have come up. The actors stay immobile until everyone has left the theatre.*

'Can't You Cope with a Little Guilt?' | *D.A.N. Jones*

Emerging from the first night of *US* at the Aldwych, among so many public faces, such a lot of swinging London, desperate-eyed David Frost with his microphone, a waiting crowd hoping to see royalty perhaps – you felt like something that just crawled out of a Scarfe cartoon. The Royal Shakespeare Company's stage demonstration was indecent by its very nature; you have to sit comfortably in the Aldwych stalls and enjoy clever acting, exhilarating verse, music, jokes – and all of it, in a sense, at the expense of the burning Vietnamese. The demonstrators are well aware, too much so, of the basic indecency. Any criticism that could be made against their taste and tone, their motivation – narcis-sistic, financial, sadistic – is already in the text: the second half consists of little but self-criticism. If they had got this out of their system in the first five minutes, swiftly made their (quite unnecessary) apologies for being Hampstead intellectuals, they could have got down to business. To quote from another new play, 'What's the matter, Oscar, can't you cope with a little guilt feeling?'

The end of Act Two also alienates in the wrong way. They stand there, miming contempt or stoicism or something, and watch you go out – apparently pleased that you don't know whether it's the end or not.

New Statesman

The Aldwych Liturgy | *The Bishop of Woolwich*

In all the words that have been spilt over *US* at the Aldwych, I have noticed none that seem to me to have placed it in its real category. There is debate whether it should be classified as 'theatre of fact', a documentary, journalism, 'vicarious psychodrama', or indeed as a play in any sense at all. Irving Wardle in *New Society*, correctly fastening on the statement 'only an act that is beyond words has any meaning', has recently concluded that it is music. I believe that it is liturgy.

The function of liturgy, as the Church has understood it, is to involve its participants in the saving acts of their redemption. It re-en-acts. It overcomes the gulf between what happened two thousand years ago and the believer's life and action in this world now. It is a remembrance of Christ's passion – not in the sense of reminding Christians of past events outside them, but of internalising and making present those events in and through them. It breaks down the barriers of time and space so that they are 'there' with Him and He is here in them.

It is this liturgical function of annihilating distance by involvement that *US* is primarily concerned to accomplish. The very ambivalence of its title makes the point that the American action in Vietnam is not just something going on on the other side of the world, on some green hill, or rice paddy, far away. What is presented is not in any strict sense 'theatre', a spectacle of a world with no continuous relation to real life into which we can be taken 'out of ourselves' for two and a half hours.

Like liturgy, but unlike a play, it has no author. As the programme notes insist, it is a corporate presentation, a con-celebration, in which the whole company, director, designer, script writers, effects men and song writers, have a shared responsibility. And the audience are equally implicated in the action. There is nothing separating stage from stalls, sanctuary from congregation. Uniting the two, above the proscenium is suspended, in the place of the rood, a monstrous, obscene figure, which we eventually make out to be a dead man – a US soldier.

Then when the action starts we are exposed in bewildering succession to all the elements and arts of liturgy. It begins with an anamnesis of Vietnamese history, a representation of it, partly by recitation, partly by re-enactment, in which the central figure is a half-naked man representing his people in their sufferings, torn apart, daubed and despised of men. There follows a kaleidoscopic succession of readings, songs, refrains, antiphons, dialogue, preaching, confession, intercession, ritual movements, and recurring symbolic actions and images, particularly of fire and burning.

Above all, everything is done to insist that this is not just, as liturgy so often becomes, play-acting in a separated time and separated space. The rood doesn't stay there impassively to be looked at. It descends threateningly to engulf both actors and audience. The son of man is among them – is them. The players mingle gropingly and disconcert-ingly with those sitting comfortably in their stalls, and at the end, instead of actors walking out on the audience to hand-clapping applause, they remain motionless on the stage till the last of the spectators have slunk away.

The reiterated theme is of a reality too painful to be evaded and too profound to admit of any verbal or rational solution. It can be resolved only in action which is itself suffering, and in suffering which is itself action.

The whole thing reminded me more than anything else of Holy Week liturgy. It is not specifically Christian: far from it. It spoke of confession, but not of absolution, of fraction but not of communion. It judged, but it did not pretend to save.

Nevertheless it was a renewal of dedication as the caring community of an intensity that condemns what so often passes for liturgy in our churches. This was a 'liturgy for Vietnam' in the sense that the Church's much-praised 'liturgy for Africa' (with nothing distinctively African about it at all) never begins to be.

I attended it after sitting through two days of Convocation arguing (oh so Christianly) whether we should say 'We offer this bread and this cup' or 'We give thanks over this bread and this cup'. In the end we compromised by permitting either. I cannot dismiss the need to start liturgical revision from this end. But when is the Church going to commission someone like Peter Brook to show us what it might look like begun from an entirely different end altogether – from the secular crucifixion of our time, in which, as Bonhoeffer said, 'Christians stand by God in His hour of grieving'?

Guardian, November 1966

Open Letter to Peter Brook | *Charles Marowitz*

In an evening devoted to contradictions and ironies, the crowning irony is that the play winds up by saying: the situation is futile but we must do something about it. The crisis has become abstract and stale-mated, but you must take it personally and work towards some humane solution. The task of dramatising, as opposed to merely positing, information, has not even been tackled, let alone solved. The play has little theatrical life to speak of and relies heavily on a dramatic predisposition on the part of the audience. It is argument and counter-argument; fact and sub-fact; anecdote and ironic implication-of-anecdote. Instead of elucidating the issues and arriving at a viewpoint it invites its audience to share, it merely dumps the whole caboodle of conflicting evidence into the audience's lap and demands that they sort out what the show's planners have not managed to think out.

With a show like *US* one's state on leaving the theatre is almost more important than the time spent at the performance. Leaving the Aldwych, I felt leaden and put-upon – a victim of an aggressive More-Committed-Than-Thou approach to life. The futility of the Vietnam crisis was even more intense (if that is possible) than when I entered the theatre. I had come – like so many other people – out of a hunger to do something, see something, say something which cuts a path out of the chaos. One doesn't need a theatrical performance to explain we are all at an impasse. The role of the theatre in times like today is to elucidate and give a positive lead. A conventional play may end up in a state of fascinating ambiguity, but a social document dealing with a red-hot contemporary crisis cannot take refuge in artistic ambiguities, or else it becomes only another cinder in the eye.

A century ago, the theatre's task, according to Chekhov, was to ask questions. This has been superseded by a world situation in which, if the theatre is to pull its weight, it must – at such times and on such themes – begin to supply answers.

International Times

Peter Brook replies . . .

Dear Charles,

If you as both critic and a very active director discuss a show concerning Vietnam, you too are challenged by your own words. What can you suggest as a positive solution of the Vietnam horror? Note your own proviso – this must not be a formula already covered by news, broadcasts, films, TV, or the press.

And Marowitz responds . . .

Dear Peter,

No one is wacky enough to suggest that a handful of writers and actors working off the Strand is going to arrive at a solution to a problem which has defied the best political minds in government today. One didn't expect a formula from the Royal Shakespeare Company, but a viewpoint. What the theatre can (and in my opinion should) do is put the issues in such a way as to make certain solutions visible to an audience. The first job is elucidating those issues, and this is urgently the case with Vietnam where everything is a welter of fact and pseudo-fact, half-truths and outright lies. In effect, your letter is asking me to supply you with a viewpoint and my innate sense of tact must refuse to do that. My main point is this, and though I put it bluntly I don't mean it rudely: if one has no overriding conviction to express on the Vietnam war other than the fact that it is horrible and insoluble, it is almost better to say nothing.

Many reviewers, in my opinion, have been subtly intimidated by the urgency of this subject and the unfamiliarity of the treatment which both you and I know is nothing more than Living Newspaper technique brought up to date. This has angered me and many like me who would like criticism to stare down the po-faced intensities of productions like *US* which with the best intentions in the world, produce superficial flurries on incendiary subjects that can be justified neither on artistic nor ideological grounds.

A Crisis of the Imaginary | *Jean-Paul Sartre*

A happening is real. It exists and it gives an effective opportunity to certain kinds of mass reactions, which we can take as fact. The problem really is: what happens to the performance insofar as it is an appeal to the free imagination of the spectator? Is not this spontaneous bringing of something into being by means that are more or less cruel the very opposite of theatre, or rather is it not the moment when the theatre destroys itself? Most of the happenings are a carefully thought out exploitation of the cruelty that Artaud advocates. In France, Lebel in his happenings exposes the public to certain sadism: this is accomplished by bright lights that come and go, by sounds that are insupportable to the ear, and by the audience's general contact with various objects which are usually disgusting. You have to go to these happenings in old clothes. And the public for happenings have reacted to their own torture.

Can we say that we have gone past the limits of the idea and the essence of the theatre? Peter Brook in England has tried to find a mixture, that is to say a compromise, that would contain happenings inside the limits of a play. This he has recently done in *US*, of which the title itself is a provocation because it means at the same time Us the English and US the Americans, and in the subject matter itself, if there is such a thing, and certainly in the main theme, it is also a direct provocation, because it is of course about the war in Vietnam. By itself this play has no meaning and we cannot call it a play. The performance must take place on a stage before the public and there is a succession of scenes, words and violent acts without any purpose other than the affective which in the middle of the confusion inspires the two themes of the play. The first part brings home the horror of the war in Vietnam, while the second part is principally about the impotence of the Left.

What we see is neither real, because after all we are looking at actors acting, nor unreal, as everything that happens makes us aware of the reality of the war in Vietnam. And in spite of everything it is the reality that affects the spectator, because it is the noises, the colours, the movement which finally bring abut a certain kind of trance or bewilderment, depending upon the individual. The public are not asked to take part in the performance: they are for the most part kept at a distance. They receive this mixture of broken sketches, interrupted at the moments where an illusion is about to be created, as a blow in the face. And at the end they find themselves before a real event, a real happening, even though this happening is renewed every evening.

For on the stage one of the actors opens a box of butterflies. They are taken out and a hand holding a lighter burns them in its flame. They are burnt alive. This is evidently an allusion to the monks who set fire to themselves and burn themselves alive in Saigon. This happening is a happening because something really happens: something alive dies and dies suffering. Nevertheless it is not altogether a happening because the play ends and the spectator, sent back to his solitude, leaves with a confused despair made up of shock, fury and impotence. There has been no conclusion and after all what is there to conclude? It is true that the war in Vietnam is a crime. It is also true that the Left is quite incapable of doing anything. Has it anything to do with the theatre? I think it is really on the borderline where form is only an intermediary and where we can either say 'this is theatre' or 'this is not'. In any case we can say that if it is theatre, this situation is an excellent example of what we can call the crisis of the imaginary in the theatre.

And so, between the theatrical illusion which is absorbed or swallowed by some real and sadistic action imposed on the spectator, as in a happening, and the real event which we re-create in the 'theatre of fact', which is swallowed by the illusion we create, we find the crisis of the image (theatrical credibility).

In fact, underneath the happening there is always an appeal to the image. This is because at bottom, the event whatever it is, is symbolic of something else and the real serves to create unreality. I do not have enough space to go into it in detail, but in any case this crisis, even if it has the effect of destroying some theatrical conventions, signifies some progress in thought.

We no longer work on the vague and confused principle of the authors and producers of the past, nor of the philosophy of the old theatre, which led us to think that theatricality essentially implies no differentiation in its big moments between the real and the imaginary. We used to be able to believe that an illusion which was presented and which was accepted as an illusion, would necessarily bring out real feelings among the audience. This is the Greek idea of catharsis. The easy conscience with which Gémier at the beginning of the century made his actors come into the auditorium, and cross it in order to get up on the stage, demonstrates the innocence which authors used to have. They thought at the time that the stage was an illusory place, a mirage, and that the characters who went to it by walking through the aisles, because they shocked the audience, would persuade them of the reality of the play. All of a sudden, for all the men of the theatre of our generation, as we shall soon see, the theatre ceased to be realistic. Because we want reality and to achieve it we have to go to the limit, there being no other way of doing so (we provoke real sentiments by real events), or else we must realise that a dramatic representation has a perfectly illusory character, but in that case its structure is unreal, it is for this very quality that we have to exploit it, as the negation of reality . . . and not as an imitation of it.

Open Letter to the Team | *Arnold Wesker*

We rushed home and I must write a note before leaving for Munich at 5 a.m.

The second part didn't clarify the first part except on one level – that of endeavour. It's difficult to explain this; I mean no details, no argument was clarified but, whereas I was physically shaking with anger over that brandy and feeling that a bunch of students had got together a show of jazzed-up facts, by the end I was respecting the intention. I was aware of the desperate anger and confusion (confusion in the best sense of the word that is) that went into its making. But still, respect and that love aside, it seemed that the presentation succeeded only in arguing itself out of all action, out of all concern. We'd done it again, we artists, we'd seen everything, we'd discovered too much, we'd discovered and faced all the truths and paralysed ourselves. (At least at this point I can only think so, because I could not hear what the actor in black said as he walked across the stage after Glenda's outburst.)

And what is one supposed to do with the knowledge of the 'honest actress' who says you all hoped the war wouldn't be over by the time the show came on? Just what is one supposed to do with it? What is one supposed to do with any of the truths one discovered in the evening?

My mother sees it very simply. Communist society is a good society, capitalist society is a bad one. The Americans are wrong – they must go. I also see 'communist society' as a good one and capitalist society as bad but I think the contrary – the Americans can't go for just that reason and it's the communists who should stop and the Viet Cong get out of South Vietnam. But they won't because as the Americans said, it all has now got to do with power structures. But what do you see? Peter, Cannan, Adrian, Geoffrey? If we felt impatient before, then we feel even more so now.

And is the anti-American the same as an anti-semite? And if some are, if many are – so what? It's a clever, disturbing revelation, but it doesn't knock at any but those on the left who are smug. And is that all you've set yourselves? To knock at some left-wingers? Somehow the problem has been set so acutely and then been turned aside from, in order to dig at the unattackable doubtful liberal.

But the butterflies are poetry. I would love to know – did Peter give a direction saying that if one person in the audience shouted 'Don't', then the butterfly would not be burned? I wanted to shout 'Don't' but I couldn't believe he'd actually do it. And it's unfair to say 'Precisely', because there is, there just is, a difference between the theatrical area and the political one – at least at that level.

I rush about and go back and forwards in this note. Forgive me. And ask Denis Cannan to forgive me for my rudeness though I believe he will understand. We'll talk more, though when I return you'll have talked yourselves out.

*

London Airport, next morning, 07.38. I'm flying Pan-Am, flight is late – I must add some more.

The difference between *Marat-Sade* and *US* is significant. Whatever Peter gave to the Aldwych production of Weiss it was essentially the writer's work which presented the argument, there was a single mind at work and a creative not interpretive one at that. This is not to attack Cannan, it's simply observing that he was an artist working under instruction – which doesn't really work. Constantly, I was watching a director 'doing things' arranging tableaux, giving actors 'business'. I can't understand how Peter permitted himself so much to the degree of obscuring what was being said. Perhaps it was because what was being said wasn't all that revealing, in the first half anyway, whereas the second half was less theatrical and more dramatic; controlled argument always is dramatic, and one felt the presence of a single writer. Was that Cannan? Or Peter? Or are you rubbing your hands gleefully and saying 'Ah! Ha! Everyone did it!' There are some powerful passages, the bulk seems the product of one hand.

It was wrong, the first two hours were all wrong, ill-sorted, badly juxtaposed, too loving it. It was Unity Theatre without the roots Unity had, it was a lean man trying on fat man's clothes, they didn't fit, belonged somewhere else, it was an Oxford student discovering, with great excitement, the terrible horrors of life by trying to temper it with all that philosophy and psychology he'd read and discarded but now had a chance to apply. You can't stand on the sidewalk and attack others who do the same; and that play stands on the sidewalk because the Aldwych Theatre is on the sidewalk, all theatre is on the sidewalk, and you and me and Peter and England. You either go to Vietnam like the International Brigade or you shut up, unless you're the prime minister. Or else you write about it in a different way.

Peter once complained to me about *Their Very Own and Golden City* that I hadn't gone deeply enough. He felt, he said, that if he probed and asked questions he'd get the real truth out of me. I was impressed and doubted myself. But perhaps one should face only those we can use – by that I mean if I can discover a truth which may be a shock or distasteful I will apply it if it can be applied – but I'm afraid of truths which only disturb me but cannot be used. And in a way, Peter's insistent probing is very near to busybodying; the woman and the seagull.

The crime is not in having the one washing machine, one spin-dryer etc. (though it might be in having seventy-two records barely played!), that's like Osborne knocking people in minis and at Surbiton tea-dances. It's making people feel guilty about the wrong things – like the puritan who denies the pleasures of the body.

I know that I've said the effect of art is not immediate. It's accumulative – but perhaps one should think twice about that if one chooses an issue of such immediacy.

And more – I keep wondering what was being said. The poet turning to both sides and accusing each of saying the same things and then being turned upon by both sides is one thing; then there was the Dostoievsky-line or Jesuitical attempt to corrupt the suicide out of his protest. Then there was the John Cage story of the noise of the butterfly whose sound we should recognise even if we are incapable of hearing it (or was the Cage and those other episodes an attempt to suggest the lunacy of our 'cool' preoccupation with metaphysical irrelevancies alongside the realities of awful suffering?), and then the butterfly story was extended into a metaphor – poetic but ambiguous, meaning what? You have no right to play around with ambiguities over such issues. Glenda cried out that it should happen here and that television cameras should film it all and show the films in countries a long way away – she might also have wished that theatres would dramatise the misery and sing songs about it and invent ingenious 'pop art' sets.

But perhaps the most irresponsible aspect of it all was the avoidance to ask was anyone right at any time at all. Both sides may, by now, be sabre-rattling, and perhaps the principles for which Ho Chi Minh stands are now not worth the suffering, and the beginning is lost in the confusion that now exists – but *US* is a documentary and no one has attempted to say if there was *ever* right on one side. Nor is it any good saying a play is never only about one thing. It is – it's only in process of pursuing and revealing the one thing that others emerge. If you start out wanting to say more than one thing, you end in confusion. What was the single pursuit of *US*? It seems there was no writer to control Peter, and too many writers for Peter to control!

Perhaps now that I've asked my questions and been forced into making certain observations, I should go and see it again and it will fall into place. I shall in any case.

One last point – for the moment at least – going back to the burning of the butterfly. If Peter did want people to cry out 'Don't', then, one: the actor must take a longer pause before applying the flame so that people have time to absorb the knowledge that he's actually going to do it; and two: he must alter the entire shape of the production in order to condition us to protest. You cannot hammer at an audience for three hours, demanding it look at you, listen to you, think about you, then in the last minute expect it to react. You don't jeer at people you've paralysed because they can't walk.

You have assumed an awful responsibility. You've assumed the right to dramatise, theatricalise, what you will, a terrible and seemingly senseless suffering. You must have a mighty reason for doing so – something more than curiosity or the quest for pure truth, or the desire to re-create the physical experience of that suffering.

Perhaps in the end the one extraordinary thing to have affect will be that the 'Royal Shakespeare Company' has done it. But not even that is surprising now.

It's an open letter, this, to Peter and Adrian and Cannan and all, and I desperately hope I'm wrong.

A Girl
Skipping

Graeme Miller
in collaboration with the company

A *Girl Skipping* was written directed and designed
by Graeme Miller in collaboration with the company

Originally performed by:
Heather Ackroyd
Emma Bernard
David Coulter
Liz Kettle
Barnaby Stone
Graeme Miller

Music composed by: Graeme Miller in collaboration
with David Coulter and the company

Lighting Design: Stephen Rolfe
Technical Direction: Stephen Rolfe
Scenic Artist: Steve Whittle
Costume: Beth Hardisty

Administration: Artsadmin

*Devised at St Donat's Arts Centre, Wales and first shown
at Arnolfini Arts Centre, Bristol, 1990*

Toured internationally until 1991
Recipient of Time Out's Dance Umbrella Award, 1990

Funded by The Arts Council of Great Britain

Preface

A Girl Skipping was conceived in 1988. It would be about play but not
be a play. It would have no characters and no plot, but work as an
unstoppable chain reaction transmitted by five performers held in the
empty frame of a playground over the void of ninety minutes. It would
be play.

In February 1990, on the day Nelson Mandela was released from Robben
Island, Heather Ackroyd, Emma Bernard, David Coulter, Liz Kettle,
Barnaby Stone with myself and technical director and lighting designer
Stephen Rolfe set off for St Donat's Castle in Wales to begin three weeks
of play, only briefly interrupted by sleep, that would determine the nature
of this work. The personally intense investment in the moment gave it the
signature of authenticity. It is a piece that primarily exists on its own terms,
being about its own performers and set in its own time. It is a piece that
seems to generate itself live despite being a more or less repeatable
performance. Perhaps this is to do with it being some kind of record of
its own making – the evidence of its own drive to be. It is a composed
scrapbook that tumbles toward a climactic transformation. In a sense it is
a performance's ability to self-elevate within its own language that mirrors
the weeks of hermetic play that built to its completion.

The text for the work – like the other elements that fitted into this grand
design of autonomy and authenticity – emerged during the seven weeks of
its making. There are several single lines spoken, a few small dialogues, a
series of incantations and chants and the telling of a wayward legend.
The rest is a lot of running about and doing stuff.

That work would be composed of real events in real time was a tenet shared with my colleagues in Impact Theatre Co-operative. That a work of art absolutely must be a world in itself was carried through from working with novelist Russell Hoban, who said that if you were then lucky it could be about the world too. That events could be composed with the same disregard for meaning as music, and that the just-controlled abandon of the performer could induce a transforming and momentary belief, came from my previous experience as a performer and musician.

The skipping girl was an imagined figure – a tiny detail in the wide view of a northern English town – an entranced child beating a loop of rope momentarily crashing to earth and flying. As you are drawn to this figure's fierce entrancement it seems to infect the world around it with rhythmic time. The words of A Girl Skipping were made to either skim the surface of this endless pulse, or to generate it or divide it into movements.

At the end of the company's incarceration and immersion in play, elements of the work had been made, but apart from a few crucial fragments, contained no text. None of these actions, games or activities had an order or was joined to another bit. They were stuff. Their composition – how they made and recrossed their tracks, shifted and repeated and altered time: that would make them material.

Beautyistruthtruthbeautythatisallyeknowonearthandallyeneedto
knowBeautyistruthtruthbeautythatisallyeknowonearthandallyene
edtoknowBeautyistruthtruthbeautythatisallyeknowonearthandall
yeneedtoknowBeautyistruthtruthbeautythatisallyeknowonearthan
dallyeneedtoknowBeautyistruthtruthbeautythatisallyeknowonear
thandallyeneedtoknowBeautyistruthtruthbeautythatisallyeknowo
nearthandallyeneedtoknowBeautyistruthtruthbeautythatisallyek
nowonearthandallyeneedtoknowBeautyistruthtruthbeautythatisal
lyeknowonearthandallyeneedtoknowBeautyistruthtruthbeautythat
isallyeknowonearthandallyeneedtoknowBeautyistruthtruthbeauty
thatisallyeknowonearthandallyeneedtoknowBeautyistruthtruthbe
autythatisallyeknowonearthandallyeneedtoknowBeautyistruthtru
thbeautythatisallyeknowonearthandallyeneedtoknowBeautyistrut
htruthbeautythatisallyeknowonearthandallyeneedtoknowBeautyis
truthtruthbeautythatisallyeknowonearthandallyeneedtoknowBeau
tyistruthtruthbeautythatisallyeknowonearthandallyeneedtoknoc
Beautyistruthtruthbeautythatisallyeknowonearthandallyeneedto
knowBeautyistruthtruthbeautythatisallyeknowonearthandallyene
edtoknowBeautyistruthtruthbeautythatisallyeknowonearthandall
yeneedtoknowBeautyistruthtruthbeautythatisallyeknowonearthan
dallyeneedtoknowBeautyistruthtruthbeautythatisallyeknowonear
thandallyeneedtoknowBeautyistruthtruthbeautythatisallyeknowo
nearthandallyeneedtoknowBeautyistruthtruthbeautythatisallyek
nowonearthandallyeneedtoknowBeautyistruthtruthbeautythatisal
lyeknowonearthandallyeneedtoknowBeautyistruthtruthbeautythat
isallyeknowonearthandallyeneedtoknowBeautyistruthtruthbeauty
thatisallyeknowonearthandallyeneedtoknowBeautyistruthtruthbe
autythatisallyeknowonearthandallyeneedtoknowBeautyistruthtru
thbeautythatisallyeknowonearthandallyeneedtoknowBeautyistrut
htruthbeautythatisallyeknowonearthandallyeneedtoknowBeautyis
truthtruthbeautythatisallyeknowonearthandallyeneedtoknowBeau
tyistruthtruthbeautythatisallyeknowonearthandallyeneedtoknoc
·Beautyistruthtruthbeautythatisallyeknowonearthandallyeneedto
knowBeautyistruthtruthbeautythatisallyeknowonearthandallyene
edtoknowBeautyistruthtruthbeautythatisallyeknowonearthandall
yeneedtoknowBeautyistruthtruthbeautythatisallyeknowonearthan
dallyeneedtoknowBeautyistruthtruthbeautythatisallyeknowonear
thandallyeneedtoknowBeautyistruthtruthbeautythatisallyeknowo
nearthandallyeneedtoknowBeautyistruthtruthbeautythatisallyek
nowonearthandallyeneedtoknowBeautyistruthtruthbeautythatisal
lyeknowonearthandallyeneedtoknowBeautyistruthtruthbeautythat
isallyeknowonearthandallyeneedtoknowBeautyistruthtruthbeauty
thatisallyeknowonearthandallyeneedtoknowBeautyistruthtruthbe
autythatisallyeknowonearthandallyeneedtoknowBeautyistruthtru
thbeautythatisallyeknowonearthandallyeneedtoknowBeautyistrut
htruthbeautythatisallyeknowonearthandallyeneedtoknowBeautyis
truthtruthbeautythatisallyeknowonearthandallyeneedtoknowBeau
tyistruthtruthbeautythatisallyeknowonearthandallyeneedtoknoc

A few added words can nuance this flow – patinate it with the moral, the social and the spiritual. Importing text imports the world.

Small drops can be used to colour whole sheets of material. It is an agent so intensely attractive to our desire in the audience to cut to the meaning of what we experience – the answer – that it can rapidly sink the whole paper boat. It can drain the music from music, turning it into the underscore of something leaden and deductible. It must be used with caution, and just how it is used sets the contract between the performance and its audience. The deal is struck in the moment and asks for total acceptance of a kind of cogent nonsense in exchange for surprise, humour and recognition. Words in *A Girl Skipping* were a tool to set the threshold of surrender for its audience and to maintain ninety minutes more or less at that threshold. We are narrative monkeys and try to find coherence in any two things that add up. If any two monkeys agree on any two things that add up it becomes culture.

What is thrilling to witness in the timed chaos of the play-ground is the volatile and amoral compulsion to co-invent that culture in the moment – letting one game drop in a second in order to join another in a constant defiance of boredom. *A Girl Skipping* was about play but above all it was play. The players really played with ferocious disregard for the audience. Paradoxically this opportunity to witness threw the viewer into vicarious collusion with the thrill of cruelty and joy of nonsense. The adult viewer viewing the adult player was to be held in ritual empathy by the same rules of the game as its enactors. The players' blithe immersion invited the audience to swim, and it became essential that no one, for an hour and a half of permission, would be allowed to touch the bank. In a metaphoric sea, texts were leaking life rafts designed to give some passing buoyancy.

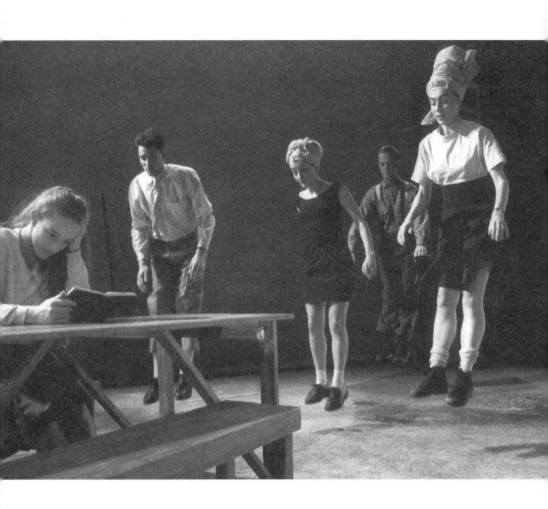

Playspeak

Heather Ackroyd and I met Iona Opie – folklorist and anthropologist of schoolchildren's lore and language. Her life's work with her husband Peter documents the bizarre and beautiful inventions of this cultural world which, although outgrown by its constituents, remains a coherent sphere evolving over centuries its own language. It is a world in which rhyme and rhythm are more important than meaning, yet one in which words never written can transmit mouth-to-ear over centuries and across languages. It is a secret continent moored invisibly beside the adult one and the language spoken there is, like every ritual and artefact, a currency of the places and times in which children are compelled to play. It borrows from the adult world and may to our adult view resonate with it, but it has no need to pay back.

The joy of its invention, its automatic generation, *ex nihilo* and self-defining logic, give it beauty. Intonement is all.

'Shepherds' Score' is a chant of numbers, one to twenty, that is probably a vestige of Celtic language that has survived among Cumbrian shepherds and children. It sounds good and is a challenge to recall and this is all it requires to be good for incantation.

1. yan
2. tan
3. tethera
4. methera
5. pimp
6. sethera
7. lethera
8. hothera
9. dothera
10. dick

11. yan dick
12. tan dick
13. tether dick
14. mether- dick
15. bumfit
16. yaner-bumfit
17. taner-bumfit
18. tethera-bumfit
19. methera-bumfit
20. gigert.

All Fall Down

An alphabet. Another cousin of the list. Perhaps because when all twenty-six places in its form are taken and it is complete, it suggests that an ordered cosmology is fully accounted for. This was the alpha and omega of the work and the private, shorthand names the company gave the games we invented. Chanted like a stern and military drill, this lexicon gave the clue that playing through this list, no matter what, was what made the entire performance a game of sorts – something to be done until completion. It gave a sense that the world created truly belonged to the performers. 'Poison and Antidote' was in the performance but 'Night of the Long Goodnight' never made it. It is a reference to a legendary moment of unstoppable play that spilled into the night. It was addictive and hysterical and legendary and – well, you had to have been there.

Including this private joke was an assertion of the tribal nature of the group and that this work could not be done by anyone else. It refers to and so strengthens the sacred and exclusive nature of the arena and the frame of time you are in. It tells the audience clearly that they are being allowed in on something that exists anyway. It bluntly renews the terms of the audience contract. Like the private joke, it risks being just annoying. But there is little that is truly funny that at some level isn't a private joke. A work that was pushing the sense of autonomy from its audience had also to bring them in on the secret. There is some judgement in balancing the clearly recognisable with the wilfully obscure, and not least in realm of words.

Fall down
<u>B</u>urn the Bridge
<u>C</u>rying over Spilt Milk
<u>D</u> uttecoat of Death
<u>E</u> Electrocution
<u>F</u>ear of Life
<u>g</u>od's Bottom
<u>H</u>anky Panky
<u>I</u> nto the Dark
2)<u>J</u> umping
2)<u>K</u> iss the Devil

<u>L</u>ove the Dirty Old Man
<u>M</u>aternity Ward Ten
<u>N</u>ight of the long goodnight
Oh my God
Poison + Antidote
Queen of Hearts
Under
<u>R</u>aise the Dead
Spear the Nun
Tragedy ← Under the A
Violent Death
Wake the neighbours
Xylophone
Yacht
Zebra.

97

Who Wrote That Then?

Dialogue is the food of the character-based narrative – the tennis of the playwright and a sign that you, the audience, should believe that people are pretending to be other people in another world.

Having set the precept of this work is real action in real time by real people, and using dialogue can generate a misunderstanding that you are watching a fiction. *A Girl Skipping* had a smattering of exchanges that needed careful phrasing and toning. They were often spoken as if the words were simply coming up into their mouths – semi-detached, as if printed in the playground tarmac and transmitted up through the feet.

Just as this seemed to be in a parenthesis of 'doing acting' (an Impact phrase), in a bed of performing, so the words retained the ghost of their quotation marks. They were delivered with a certain detachment and were marked by not really joining on to much to what preceded or followed. They could be dropped like pants or a spent children's game and formed a kind of role play in which either part could be played by either party.

LESSON 1

L   ....Truth is beauty, beauty truth; that is all ye know on earth and all ye need to know.

E   Who wrote that then?

L   Keats.

E   Keats who?

L   John Keats actually.

E   'John Keats actually'. So what was it all about then?

L   Well it's about lots of things.

E   Come on then, what things? Tell us. We're dying to know.

L   Well it's about love, well beauty really. A frozen moment of beauty.

E   Well I didn't understand a word of it.

L   Look, just sit down.

E   No.

L   Do as I say.

E   Why?

L   Because..

E   Because what?

L   Because I'm telling you.

E   That doesn't sound like a very good reason.

L   Sit down now.

E   But I don't want to.

L   You're spoiling it for everyone.

E   I don't think anyone's interested frankly.

L   We'll let them decide shall we?

E   All right, who wants John Keats Actually?

A Spell

A cousin of the list. It was spoken to stop the other performers' merciless copying by sending them to sleep. It is more or less verbatim what I would say to my son to get him to sleep, tracing a line down his arm to his fingertips.

Down the path
Through the wet leaves
Under the streetlight
Past two big gasometers
Down by the allottments
Under the chicken-wire
Onto the embankment
Then we slide
Down the railway tracks
Into the wet night
Up the chalk path
Through the hawthorns
Look there's one with a stocking on it.
So, we go down the path
Through the wet leaves
Until we come to the garden gate.
It's covered in ivy and missing a railing
So we go in.
In through the gate
Into the garden
Where there's warm wet grass
And pointy bushes
We go round and round and round
Round and round and round
Round the garden
And out through the trees at the bottom.

Sadness in the Evening

A list. A circle game. Lists are journeys in themselves. Their reading and their speaking evokes a path – a rhythmic path: a walk, or a drive past fence posts. Each item alters the last and all preceding as it frames the next and all succeeding. Also, and this is especially true of a long list like this, lists accumulate, making their journey pass through gates of boredom dividing into sections as it pulls in and out of focus. The long list is a game itself and one that is progressively at play with the idea of ending. Long lists are performative and almost don't need to be performed.

This liturgy is sampled from a homoeopathic *materia medica*. I first read these symptoms with the same mixture of recognition and dread as I wished to evoke.

In evening light the performers form a circle and play catch with a bloody hypodermic. At each catch they speak a symptom. One by one and with gentle resignation they drop and withdraw. As the circle narrows there is a sense that no one is really playing too hard to win. Heather Ackroyd, who always won the game, is then left alone and almost becomes the bearer of this despair, and so she speaks the remainder until its final phrase: 'Lamenting, erotic, confused, weary and sad.'

This was the time of AIDS.

Restless at night. Sadness in the evening. Desires to lay
down. But lying brings great restlessness. Many symptoms
worse after lying. Forgetful and easily frightened.
Cheerfulness during chill. Wandering speech. Oversensitive
to noise. To voices. Lamenting and laughter. Loathing of
life. Fear, evening and night. In a crowd. Of death. Of
evil. Of people when alone. Malicious. Mania. Weak. Timid.
Weeping. During chill. In hysteria. In sleep. Irresolution.
Extreme irritability. Fear on walking. Worse walking.
Walking in open air. Walking fast. Walking in the wind.
Worse in winter. Anger with silent grief. Anxiety day and
night. With fear. About salvation. Confusion in the
morning. Delerious at night. Delusions. Delusions about
animals. Despair during chill. Chill with pain. Pain.
Vertigo. Lump in the throat. Desire to lay down. Weeping.
worse at night. Vertigo. Vertigo. Objects turn in a circl
Worse when walking. Fear of evil. Of men. Foolish
behaviour. Idiocy. Indifference. Insanity. Erotic insan
Fear of conversation. Fear of crowd. Of people. Of
solitude. Pains are cutting, burning, tearing. Tearing
downwards. Worse walking, lying, evening, morning, ni
Impatience. Indifference. Bleeding gums. Cracked tong
Pain in the eyes. Eyelids stuck together. Sore, brui
sunken eyes. Swollen lids. Tears are acrid. Discharge
yellow, bloody, acrid. Pain at 4pm, 5pm. Worse in brig
light. Worse on the right side. Better after sleep. Wor
on waking. Walking. Stooping. Coughing. Coldness in the
stomach. Gnawing in the stomach. Retching when coughin
Morning, evening, night. Vomiting worse at night. After
milk. Coughing. Drinking. Eating. Vomiting bile, black,
food, mucus, watery. Anxiety. Diarrhoea. Pain in the liver.
Burning in the bowels. Cold hands, legs, feet. Twitching of
thighs. Trembling with chill; 1pm 2pm 4pm 5pm 6pm 7pm 8pm
12pm. Warm room does not relieve the coldness not the
chill, but is grateful of sleep. Deep sleep. Comatose.
Dreams. Amorous, anxious, of death, of the dead, of
misfortune. Pain in the bladder. Painful, dribbling,
difficult. Blood in the urine, burning, copious, cloudy.
Sweat is cold, sour, clammy, offensive. The lips bleed.
Fluid from the nose flows over the skin and leaves red
streaks. Blue spots. White, flaky, crawling, stinging.
Itching, burning, red, crusty. Bleeding. Suppurating.
Suppurating. Amorous dreams. Nocturnal emissions. Bloody,
copious, frothy, offensive. Cracked tongue. Red tongue.
Brown tongue. Dry tongue. Speech difficult. Difficult
speech. Vision blurred. Bright colours. Dim. Foggy.
Nostalgic. Nostalgic. Sadness. Sadness in the evening.
Bleeding from the anus, copious, thin. Lamenting, erotic,
confused, weary and sad.

The Story and the Book

In St Donat's Castle one evening I set up an improvisation for Emma Bernard just to tell the rest of us an unplanned story from a book. The book was called *The Wonderland of Knowledge, Volume 1* and was a pictorial encyclopaedia. What ensued was something that left us a bit spooked. A recorder was running and captured her gradual entrancement by the flipping pages and their bizarre images and words.

ent   in and the mud came back out again ...
he ground..and..er..the dog came along and.. er..The apples were
here, all over the place. Down the holes; in all the holes in
act and Mr. Shevednaze said....There was this dog,   there   was
his dog and anyway they came along, right, and there was this
og, the apples and everything and there was snow on the ground
nd there was ice underneath the ground.   The shovels went in and
he mud came out and piles and piles and piles of people were
till coming from all over the world. some of them in red and
ink, some of them in yellow. And some of them said, 'Why? Why is
hy is ..er..the business? What's going on though?' they said.
here's these apples. there's the mud.   There's the snow in the
round. Mr. Brown said well, she never even saw the lump. Never.
he never saw it and..er..before that happened there was grass
rowing, everything. There was apple blossom and..er..there's
his pig. Came along right, went up this tree, went down the
ree, went out the tree again, went down the tree, picked some
pples and put them in the hole. And there were more holes, more
oles, ditches all the way round and..um..bombs going off. Um the
xterminating Angel came along and said, 'Woa ho ho ho ho ho! No
o no no no! No more of that said. No more of that said. No more.' Anyway, the woman said
'Right now come along ooh yup yeah yeah.' Anyway he did,
r. Shevednaze had come and see what was going on. Anyway he did,
and..um..anyway, there was a lot of people coming from all over
he world, some of them in green and blue, some of them in
ellow. And..um..and..er..they came back and..er..there was more
xplosions and..um..It was the end of the world as we know it and
m there was..er..um..a lot of blood everywhere. In fact there
ere several people killed. Several million people killed. By
each of their own. some of them had the tops of their heads cut
ff. Some of them just had the arms and legs or one arm, one leg.
Some of them just had the tails cut off. some of them eventually
had their stomachs cut out and the intestines were on the floor.

So she said, 'Never mind! Never mind because there's
where that came from...and there was a great big flat ab
she said 'Never never you find us.' Apple, snow, mud
everything. There's shovel and..um..got nothing to worry abou
The problems of the world are over. And the Exterminating Ange
said, 'No, but you know that's not true 'cause I just blood
killed everone. She said, 'Well how come I'm still talking then'
And then he said, 'Oh yeah well its all magical 'cause its a
God and..er..in fact this is heaven. I'm God. This is God my so
and..er..this is God my father and ..er..Anyway, so the Fath
said to the Son..er..you know..get the Angels out quick.

All right, well if you'R getting out the exterm
then I'm calling up the vivian girls . Sh!

The Vivian Girls

The Vivian Girls were the invented heroines of artist Henry Darger, who when he died in 1973 had written over 19,000 typed pages of an epic work, *The Story of the Vivian Girls in what is Known as the Realms of the Unreal or the Glandeco-Angelinian War Story, Caused by the Slave Rebellion*. It was a world he inhabited every day and illustrated with over two hundred exquisite watercolour paintings. No doubt as an expiation and enactment of years of institutionalisation and abuse he suffered as a child, these scenes are apocalyptic and beautiful, often depicting bloody battlefields in which the hermaphroditic Vivian Girls fought angelic wars.

Emma Bernard's gravity-defying channelling of speech and Darger's haunting vision conflated in a voice that became the myth behind the choreographed rituals of *A Girl Skipping*. By placing adults in the realm of unfettered play, it placed them in moral ambivalence between the venal and self-destructive drive to the edge of a created world and a desire to save that world from destruction. In a way the Vivian Girls as child characters in a fairytale became the avatars of the performers who were liberated by their told-of doubles into being themselves onstage, into performing rather than acting.

All the character-based narrative could be contained within the covers of a book. I wrote another two episodes in the 'and then and then so anyway' style, and these three blocks became huge tools in structuring the work into acts. The first of these speeches began with an unprepared improvised re-run of the first story that at about halfway through (and the appearance of Mr Shevednaze), locked into and followed the original story verbatim.

Right, so they called out the exterminator and she called
out the Vivien Girls. It was a complete emergency. Houses
were falling down and great big cracks. Fissures d
volcanos. Fissures in the crust. Fish and loaves in all the
cracks and all the cutlery that had just flown out of all
the drawers. And er anyway, she said,'Stop it. Just bloody
stop it. It's the end of everything as we know it. Stop
this war. And so he said, 'I can't stop it, it's not just
the war anymore, it's the whole shabang, trees, plants,
molten jelly, the works. He said everybody lost. And they
were trying to hold it all together and look after the weak
ones, but they were all disqualified anyway. So they ran
back to the hotel and dialed 999. Only they got it upside
down on the bit of paper which was big trouble what with
that being the number of the beast. And er quite frankly,
that was it with large uantities of poison, poison in the
apples, air and everywhere. And people getting sick and
blue spots. And so, anyway, even though they had their
secret breathing it looked like He would come, the Prince of
Darkness and the Duffle-coat of Death.. unless they got to
him first. So they went upstairs and fell asleep..and um
anyway they woke up again and it was Wednesday. It was
early-closing-day and everything had gone back to normal.
Everything was normal, except it wasn't really. It was
nearly normal, only everything had a label on it and some
of the labels were completely wrong like the lampost that
had 'COD PORTION' written on it. Anyway they didn't like it
when it went all quiet because the man who wrote the Vivien
Girls Stories, who cleaned toilets, had made it all up from
things he had remembered from his childhood and you could
bet your bottom that when it went all quiet like this and
very very quiet and ticking that sooner or later somthing
totally horrific would happen. For instance, someone would
befriend them and then they would smile but inside their
mouth are all chicken claws. Chicken claws and jelly.
Anyway. It was early closing and drizzle in the town and
the children buried up on the moors sent them secret
messages not to trust anyone or anything and they could
find The Dark One in The Dark Arches of Death. Which is
where they went next. The Dark Arches of Death is where the
river runs under the railway station and the men sleep in
boxes. And anyway they walked into the tunnel which smelt
of piss and burning. And they came to this one box and
everything went all quiet and ticking and slowly this man
with long black fingernails rolled out and looked at his
bleeding, sore hands and said, 'How did I get like this?
How did I get like this (etc). It was all gone the dog in
the river, the twins and the bombs, everyone. So they all
went home and had tea and went to bed.

Each tale is time out and has the effect of erasing the material that has just passed by, slowly drawing the listener into an offstage underbelly and a world of eternal struggle against greater levels of sinister violence. A story is a parallel world and one that indulges pure narrative. Each episode would end with the snapping of the book shut, and the audience would be woken back to the real-time, real-place arena of the stage.

Apart from colouring the following action with its aftertaste, it would refresh the scene, cleanse the playground, provide a state from which to wake. It is a particular way that text can work within the ride of a work – creating an escape route from a space that fills over time with a surfeit of information or a monotony of relationship. Even if the shift ends up being from nightmare to bad dream it is the falling asleep and waking that remain part of the grammar of composition.

Anyway, they went to sleep, right, that's right yes with
five beds all in a row and yellow wallpaper. So they went
to bed and said 'Night Vivian.' 'Goodnight Vivian' all five
times because they were five of them and five fives are
five. Which is true 'cause that's what they said every
night and as soon as their eyes shut they started to dream
only it was all real. It was really happenning and they
could really do this. Actually they couldn't stop it
because the man who wrote the books never slept either and
he was up all night writing and colouring in all the books
with crayons. So, anyway, they all woke up again except
they were back on the other side where there was also five
beds and the wallpaper was blue and green. So it was day
there. The sky was on fire. Oh my god. Lor lummy. The whole
playing field was covered in corpses. There was Tommy and
Tilley and masses and masses of other children form all
over the world there on the grass. They all looked like the
Vivian girls because they were all drawn the same. But they
weren't because they weren't protected which was pretty
obvious because they were all hacked to pieces and had
stumps that were still squirting red crayon and er some of
the stumps were on fire. Anyway, it was all torsos and
limbs and they couldn't match them up or put them back on.

So just then all the birds flew up from the trees, but they
couln't see anything, anything at all except a man on a
moped with one of those leather helmets with a peak. And he
was riding across the park and the stumps and the children.
So he must be the park-keeper. But he wasn't because when
you looked at him he became this purple shadow and he said,
I'm one of the Four Moped Riders of the Apocalypse, he said
and what are you doing here? So they said, 'Well, we're
going to save the world as we know it' and he said, 'Fuck
that 'cause you don't know it 'cause we live under The Dark
Arches of Death and there's four of us..mate.)The first is
me and you can see and hear me.)The second you can just see
but doesn't make any noise and the third one you hear it go
by but you can't see anything. And the last one you can't
see or hear but you can feel it go through you like a cold
wind. 'No, well, look, we're the Vivian Girls and there's
five of us and we're protected. Because every night they
faced terrible terrible dangers and always always survived
them because they were innocent. So she said, 'Fuck off,
we're innocent and nothing can happen.' And anyway he said,
'No. Nononononono. Not so easy because you're just made up.
and the man who writes the books is ill. He's upped stumps
and gone away. Father son the works. He left us all to our
own devices; exterminators, babies, animals, jelly, birds,
the works. And then he rode off across the page.

The Language Lesson

A section internally called 'Mayhem and Madness' invokes a wild swirl of stabbing and kicking, mayhem and, well, madness. The bin is on fire and it will all end in tears but for the appearance of the sixth member of the cast, myself. I begin a lecture that explains everything, or at least begins to, before it itself becomes corrupted and transformed by play. In form it is a *delivery* that is entirely addressed eye-to-eye to the audience through the shattered frame of what until now has been a secure one-way mirror.

The thesis of this lecture is hard to work out. It links Babble to Babel, Algebra to Gibberish, Talmudic texts to Islamic geometry and almost makes sense. There are, of course, real links between these words and these ideas and there are, of course, real links between hermetic philosophy and ideas about play's ability to create transformation, but it is not exactly something you would want to say out loud. Instead, a distant Aretha Franklin record sneaks in underneath the argument and a performer mimes to the track until the record sticks and the whole delivery surrenders to rhythmic time.

In the beginning, so we understand, The Word. God, the
written word God and the number of that word being
inseperable. Il illaha illa'lla; the formula of Islam; 'No
divinity if not the sole divinity. And so in geometry we
express this as point. Point, unity, source. And so God set
Adam the task of naming everything, and this he did. Plants
animals, everything. And in this Prelapsarian language
names and their essences were inseperable. Apple WAS apple.
Snake, snake. Etc. etc. Point,unity,source. After the fall,
the acquisition of knowledge, we have free-will and choice
and words now drift away from their essences being mere
labels whose meaning changes from context to contex.
Confusion. God's curse.

In geometry, we express this choice as a line, and in
drawing the line we exercise our choice to draw up,left,
right, but we choose down. Anyway, at least after the fall
everyone spoke the same language. Greed was greed.
Jealousy, jealousy, jealousy, maybe, maybe not. And so this
Distanced unity can be expressed in the diagram thus. From
the line we derive the arc and from the arc, the circle.
Point-origin, circle-unity. In alchemy this is the
hierograph for Gold. Hermes Trismegistus writes in his
Emerald Table,

          'As all things have come from the One, by
meditation of the One, thus all things have been born from
this single thing by adaptation'

And now if we turn to the end of Genesis we come to the
final event in the pre-history of the world. The Tower of
Babel. Its architect was Nimrod. Nimrod the first ruler of
the earth. Its builders a people united by a common
language and purpose; the attainment of heaven.

'And the Lord said, behold the people is one, they still
have one language and this they begin to do and now nothing
can be prevented from them which they have imagined to do'

It was said that a person could walk for 3 days without
leaving its shadow. Big tower. God angry. The ziggurat
spiralling towards its centre. But unattainable because.
The centre. Like layers of an onion. Peeling away. Peeling
away to an infinitessimally small point. Futile but none-
the-less God in his anger created the separation of the
languages.

Welsh, Yorouba, Hindi, Turkish, Spanish, Turkish, Spanish.
Finnish. Finnish the language, finish, in English. The end
point; the end of everything as we know it... and it was.

A Girl Skipping

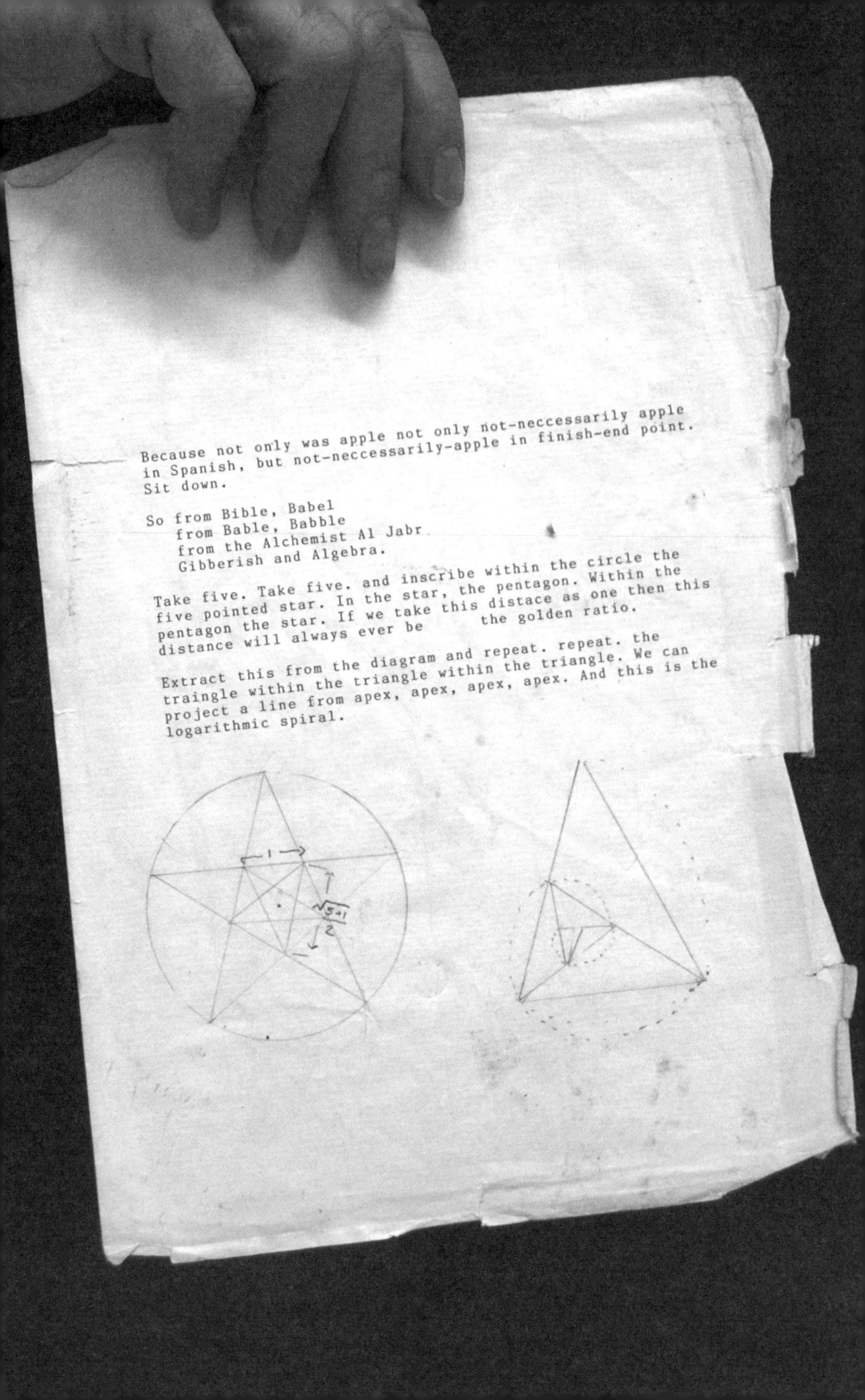

Because not only was apple not only not-neccessarily apple
in Spanish, but not-neccessarily-apple in finish-end point.
Sit down.

So from Bible, Babel
     from Bable, Babble
     from the Alchemist Al Jabr
     Gibberish and Algebra.

Take five. Take five. and inscribe within the circle the
five pointed star. In the star, the pentagon. Within the
pentagon the star. If we take this distace as one then this
distance will always ever be   the golden ratio.

Extract this from the diagram and repeat. repeat. the
traingle within the triangle within the triangle. We can
project a line from apex, apex, apex, apex. And this is the
logarithmic spiral.

The Language Lesson starts to burn words, shovelling them on to the fire as it hurtles down the tracks. The paucity of texts becomes in the final minutes of the work a torrent. The form if it has one is rant – a kind of chant delivered at someone. Its nonsensical nature does not stop its delivery being cogent.

While the esoteric lecture continues and Aretha sticks, so performers plot *Woman to World* . . .

WOMAN   WOMAN

WOMAN
WOMB
WOMBAT
WOMEN
WOMERA
WON
WON
WON
WONDER
WONDERFUL
WONDEROUS
WONGA-WONGA
WONKY
WONT×2
WOO
WOOBUT
WOOD
WOODCHUCK
WOODY
WOODSY
WOOER
WOOF
WOOF
WOOFER
WOOL
WOOLLEN
WOOMERA
WOON
WOORALI
WOOZLE
WOOSH
WOOT
WOOTZ
WOOZY
WOP
WOP
WORCESTER
WORD
WORE,

WORLD.

And *Man to Map* . . .

MAN
MANA
MANACLE
MANAGE
MANAKIN
MANANA
MANATEE
MANCANDO
MANCHE
MANCHESTER
MANCHET
MANCHINEEL
MANCHU
MANCIPATION
MANCIPLE
MANCUNIAN
MANCUS
ANDRILL
NDULATE
E
GE

BEY
INESE
ARRAX
MANGEL-WURZLE
MANGER
MANGETOUT
MANGY
MANGLE
MANGO
MANGOLD
MANGIONEL.

MANGOSTEEN
MANGOUSTE
MANGROVE
MANHANDLE
MANHATTAN
MANHOLE
MANHOOD
MANHUNT
MANIA
~~MANICHEAN~~
MANICURE
MANIFEST
MANIFESTO
MANIFOLD
MANIFORM
MANIHOC
MANIHOT
MANILLA
MANIPLE
MANIPLIES
MANIPULAR
MANIPULATE
MANKY
MANNA
MANNING
MANNOSE
MANOMETER
MANOR
MANSARD
MANSE
MANSION
MANSLAUGHTER
MASONRY
MANSWORN
MANTA
MANTEEL
MANTEL
MANTIC
MANTILLA

MANTIC
MAN
MA
MAN
MANUS
MANUSCRI
MANX
NANY
Manzilla
Manzanilla
Manzanita
Maoist
Maori
Map.

The Dance Lesson

Interlaced with 'Shepherds' Score', it is delivered like it was the Final Judgment. It is mumbo-jumbo and its almost-holiness funnels the gutterances, shards and motifs of the work through a highly rhythmic delivery and the stage becomes a pulpit for an impassioned delivery, half-trash, half-pearls. It speaks only about itself and almost manages in this way to speak about everything. Its interlocking and patterned rhythms begin with 'This is This' (a sample from *The Deer Hunter*) and an ultimately self-reflexive statement, and like 'Beauty is truth, truth beauty' (a sample from Keats), simply cruises on its own repetitive assertion. The fact that it was called a 'Dance Lesson' had something to do with the surrender of meaning to rhythm. The speech elides into pure movement – sections of jumping and a final burst of double-dutch skipping. It is a tower of wordage built in a godless universe to be sexually exultant and religiously climactic. Everything is washed away in the ringing of bells and a shower of water.

DANCE: LESSON 2a

①1. 1 is	⑤ 5 is	⑨ 20s	y
2. 1 is	5 is	30s	t
3. 1 is	5 is	40s	t
4. 1 is	5 is	50s	m
5. one	five	60s	pimp
6. * &	* &	70s	s
②1. 2 is	⑥ 6 is	⑩30s	l
2. 2 is	6 is	40s	h
3. 2 is	6 is	50s	d
4. 2 is	6 is	60s	dick
5. two	six	70s	yd
6. * &	* &	80s	td
③1. 3 is	⑦ 7 is	⑪ 40s	td
2. 3 is	7 is	50s	md
3. 3 is	7 is	60s	bumfit
4. 3 is	7 is	70s	* -----> ybf
5. three	seven	80s	* tbf
6. * &	* &	90s	* tbf
④1. 4 is	⑧ 8 is	⑫ round &	* mbf
2. 4 is	8 is	round &	* gigert
3. 4 is	8 is	round &	*
4. 4 is	8 is	round &	*
5. four	8 is	round &	gigert ⟨-----'
6. * &	8 is	round &	gigert

DANCE LESSON 2 A (8)

①	④	⑦	⑩
1. *	*	truth is	* hop
2. *	*	beauty	* hop
3. This is	bad is	truth is	* hop
4. this.	good.	beauty	* hop
5. This is	Bad is	truth is	* hop
6. this is	good is	beauty	* hop
7. this is	bad is	truth.	* hop
8. this.	good.	*	* hop

②	⑤	⑧	⑪
1. *	Goodies	Beauty is	y
2. *	baddies	truth.	t
3. and all a-	Goodies	Truth	t
4. lone ·	baddies	beauty.	m
5. And all a-	Goodies	Beauty is	pimp
6. lone	baddies	truth	s
7. and all a-	Goodies	truth.	l
8. lone.	baddies	*	h

③	⑥	⑨	⑫
1. *	Hop	round &	d
2. *	hop	round &	dick
3. Good is	hop	round &	yd
4. bad is	hop hop	round &	td
5. good is	repeat	round &	td
6. bad is	repeat	round &	md
7. good is	repeat	round &	bumfit
8. bad.	*	round. *	gigert.

3s

DANCE LESSON 2B

3/4	4/4
1. round &	Shirley oneple
2. "	Shirley twople
3. "	Shirley threeple
4. "	Shirley fourple
5. "	Shirley fiveple
6. "	Shirley sixple
7. "	Shirley sevenple
8. "	Shirley eightple
	Shirley nineple
1. again &	Shirley Temple
2. "	Ha Ha
3. " .	
4. "	repeat 3 times with
5. "	Ha Ha Ha Ha
6. "	then Ha Ha Ha Ha Ha Ha
7. "	
8. "	

1. rain
2. "
3. "
4. "
5. "
6. "
7. "
8. "

repeat 3 times

*In play the beauty of the human body
in motion reaches its zenith and in its more
developed forms is saturated with rhythm
and harmony, the noblest gifts known to man.
Many and close are the links that connect
play with beauty.*

Johan Huizinga, *Homo Ludens*, 1955

Hotel Methuselah

a theatre piece
by Imitating the Dog and
Pete Brooks

Introduction

Hotel Methuselah was produced as a collaborative project between Pete Brooks and the performance company Imitating the Dog. It was co-commissioned by the Nuffield Theatre, Lancaster University, and the Cochrane Theatre at University of the Arts, London. It was project funded by Arts Council England. The original cast were Morven Macbeth, Anna Wilson, Richard Malcolm and Simon Wainwright.

The other key collaborators were Pete Brooks and Andrew Quick (writing and directing), Laura Hopkins (design), Neil Boynton (music), Seth Honnor, Monica Alcazar and Rodrigo Velasquez (video recording and editing). Many other people contributed, particularly as performers in video sequences, and the contributions of the key collaborators were by no means limited to their listed roles. A special mention needs to be made of Guy Gutman, who contributed a very small but highly significant number of lines to the final text.

Hotel Methuselah had an unusually long gestation. It began life as a bunch of ideas that didn't really get used in another project, and then slowly over a few years got turned into a screenplay for a short film. At this point it was a story without baggage; it had characters and a situation, but no thematic. Then, in 2003, Britain and the US invaded Iraq, and my wife found out she was pregnant. In 2004, shortly after the birth of my daughter, I was invited to make a project with students at the University of Lancaster. I decided to use the film script as a starting point and, being at the time much preoccupied with a renewed sense of my own mortality, with sex as a procreative act and with the morality of the Iraq invasion, the thematics of the piece sort of announced themselves and extraordinarily seemed to fit perfectly with the narrative vehicle that I had, as it were, prepared earlier.

The project with the Lancaster students was quite consciously research and development for something that was now beginning to take shape as a viable project. I have always been principally concerned with telling stories from the stage, and the story behind *Hotel Methuselah* was now more or less solid. What was less clear to me at that point was the narrative – what parts of the story the audience would be shown – but this is something I have always worked out in rehearsal. At about the same time Imitating the Dog, a company with a declared interest in stories, asked me if I would like to produce a piece with them and it was decided that we would work collaboratively on the original text of *Hotel Methuselah*. At this point the process changed from a fundamentally solitary one to one of collaboration, and specifically collaboration in the sense of shared authorship. The story, thematics, characters, situation and basic cyclical structure of the piece were now all essentially in place; but the way in which the narrative unfolded and the form taken by the spoken text were not. And so began a process of working with my co-writer Andrew Quick, writing over or rewriting each other's work until we had a text with which we could work with actors. This process also fed into the development of both the narrative and scenographic structure of the work. What began as a cast of many was rationalised down to a cast of four, condensing and improving the work enormously. Refining and detailing the narrative structure was also an important aspect of this part of the process, although much of this work would also happen on stage.

For purely practical reasons, the actors had relatively little input into the writing process; as all the action was to be filmed, time constraints meant that we needed to begin with a text that the actors could learn prior to filming. This produced a more literary text than either of us expected: the texture of the writing which has in my experience so often developed out of actor improvisations (as it did in our subsequent project *Kellerman*) was in this case lifted from British film and theatre of the late 1950s and 1960s, in particular Pinter and Joe Orton.

Despite its relatively eccentric staging, *Hotel Methuselah* reads pretty much as a play. The story unfolds through a series of dialogues and there is a kind of closure, but while Andrew Quick and I are the co-authors of this play, the making of the performance work was a collaboration involving a great many more people. The initial filming of the three bedroom scenes by Rodrigo Velasquez, which took place four months before the show opened, was hugely influential on how the text subsequently developed, and all four principal performers make the writing come alive, turning it into something much funnier, and much darker than it reads. Design and sound are both very important aspects of the audience experience.

At the point of writing this (in October 2010, five years after we first made the piece, which opened at the Nuffield Theatre, Lancaster University) *Hotel Methuselah* is still touring. We have performed at many of the principal small- and medium-scale venues on the British new performance circuit, many of these in or attached to universities. We have also performed in quite major theatres in France, Germany, Poland, Bulgaria, Armenia and Georgia. In November we go to Azerbaijan and there is talk of performances in Croatia and Ukraine as well as confirmed dates in a couple of British venues. *Hotel Methuselah* is now in repertory with two other shows, but shows no sign of running out of steam. We don't perform it that often (twelve performances in 2010) but it still feels fresh when we do.

Pete Brooks

Hotel Methuselah

*by Imitating the Dog
and Pete Brooks*

HOTEL METHUSELAH

BY IMITATING THE DOG AND PETE BROOKS

Written and directed by:
Andrew Quick and Pete Brooks

Original cast
HARRY   Simon Wainwright
AMY   Morven Macbeth
WEIRD MAN   Richard Malcolm
WEIRD WOMAN   Anna Wilson

Original performance
at the Nuffield Theatre, Lancaster, April 2005

Opening Sequence

We hear a phone ringing. Sound of whispering voices in many languages. Cut to an open copy of a French novel. The letters slowly fall off the page leaving some to form the title: Hotel Methuselah. Cut to a slow point of view shot (POV) that moves through an endless hotel corridor. We pass numbered rooms that give the impression of a colossal building.

VOICE–OVER (spoken by Harry) There's a time just after curfew when nothing moves except the rats, and when there's nothing to do except drink vodka and watch TV. No one speaks. No one knows why these things happen or why we're here, so no one talks of it or tries to understand. We are marooned in the no man's land of a city under siege, a Stalingrad of the soul, where our enemies have overrun the old tractor factory, and where we have only five rounds left each. It's winter now and somehow I know that this time the spring will never come and the trees will never bud and the snow will just keep falling for ever.

Cut to Harry in the woods. We hear the sound of battle and jets flying low overhead. Harry looks up and there is a loud gunshot. Cut to black and then cut back to a shot of a crow flying in the trees. Cut back to Harry: his nose is bleeding. The phone rings louder. Cut back to fast POV shot through the hotel corridor until the camera comes to rest on an empty reception desk. Cut to Harry at the reception desk. The phone is still ringing. He picks up the phone.

Scene 1: Reception Desk

HARRY Hello, hello.

A tall, stocky man enters. He is wearing a stained T-shirt. Unnamed in the performance, he is known as the Weird Man.

WEIRD MAN You're too late. You just missed her, Harry.

The Weird Man exits. Pause. A woman enters and moves towards the desk. She is wearing a tan-coloured coat and is carrying a suitcase.

Scene 2: Reception Desk

AMY I'd like a room.

HARRY Of course, a single or double?

AMY Single.

HARRY With bathroom?

AMY Yes, if you've got water.

Harry looks in the guest book.

AMY Just give me a room. Whichever is cheapest.

HARRY 14, then.

AMY I'll take it.

HARRY How many nights?

AMY Just tonight.

HARRY ID?

Amy searches for her passport in her bag. As she is doing this she puts a gun on the counter. Harry looks at the gun.

AMY Well, you know what they say?

HARRY No.

AMY They say a girl can't be too careful these days.

HARRY Sign here. And put your usual address.

AMY What do you mean, 'usual'?

HARRY Your home. (*Pause.*) I mean your permanent home.

AMY I don't have a permanent home.

HARRY Wherever you were before, then.

AMY It's none of your business.

HARRY I'm just trying to do my job.

Amy exits.

Your bag? (*Pause.*) I'll bring it up.

Pause. Harry fills in the hotel registry forms. Weird Man enters.

Scene 3: Reception Desk

WEIRD MAN Are you the new guy?

HARRY No, no, I don't think so.

WEIRD MAN I haven't seen you around here before. And I never forget a new face. Especially a pretty one like yours.

HARRY Sorry?

WEIRD MAN Nothing meant by it. Just fooling around.

HARRY Right.

WEIRD MAN You don't mind a bit of fun, do you? Having a laugh? Taking things to the edge. I mean, sometimes I like to take things a little too far just to see who blinks first. You blinked, Harry. Just then. See, you did it again. Blink. Blink. Blink.

HARRY How did you know . . .

WEIRD MAN Your name, Harry. Because I'm alert to the changing situation. What's in the air. What's floating in the fucking ether, Harry. Listening to the bush telegraph. To the beat of tiny drums. Tap, tap, tap, fucking tap. Are you a listener, Harry? Or are you more of a peeper?

HARRY No, no, I don't think . . .

WEIRD MAN Don't be defensive, Harry. We've all got our particular tastes. Vices. I like that word. Squeezes the life out of you, vice. You've got to loosen up a bit. Got any whisky?

HARRY No.

WEIRD MAN Beer?

HARRY Sorry.

Pause. The man and Harry look at each other.

Are you, are you the boss?

WEIRD MAN No, no, still looking for him. So many complaints have built up, Harry, over the years. I mean, look at this place. Aren't you ashamed, charging for this fucking sty? I wouldn't bed a fucking dog here. And there's not much I haven't bedded, if you know what I mean. Still, beggars can't be choosers. That's what I always say. We all have our cross to bear. And I cling on to the fact that one of the thieves was saved.

HARRY Who was saved?

WEIRD MAN Thieves, Harry. Nailed up along with Jesus. Christ, don't you read? I mean, there's a Bible in every fucking room. Words, Harry, like those. They just keep me fucking going. I'm hard for words, Harry. I get all moist on them. And you know what, I believe you do too.

HARRY I like to read.

WEIRD MAN Glad to hear it, Harry. Education. It's an important thing. Makes us think of the future, of a way out. So, what are you going to do about this shit-hole Harry? Or are your standards slipping like everyone else's?

HARRY I just do what I'm told.

WEIRD MAN But will you just be told, Harry?

HARRY Look, I just work here.

WEIRD MAN 'Course you do, Harry. It's not your fault. Nobody's anybody's fault any more. Nobody takes any responsibility. It's all pass the buck. Pass, pass, pass, fucking pass. And we call this service.

HARRY Can I help you, sir?

Pause. They look at each other.

WEIRD MAN You like reading, Harry?

HARRY Yes.

WEIRD MAN I read a lot. I get a lot of time for it, Harry. I've a wide range of interests. You'd be surprised what's on my top shelf. I'm a man with eclectic tastes. We're so alike, Harry. I think that's why we get on so well. You know, bonding. Like this. Of course, I'm not educated like you. More, er, self-taught. But I enjoy my intellectual pursuits. Take etymology, one of my favourite pastimes: 'the meaning and origin of words'. From the Greek *etumon*: 'the true sense of a word'. And I'm always after the truth, Harry. That's what we have in common. Finding out stuff.

HARRY I'm not sure . . .

WEIRD MAN And within the etymological framework, one of my favourite words is buggery. Not, you understand, because of what it signifies, although, of course, I'm not adverse to a bit myself, on occasions. No it's the history of the word that intrigues me. (*Pause.*) Well, Harry?

HARRY Well, what . . . ?

WEIRD MAN Well, aren't you curious? Just a little bit, Harry, as to the origin of the word buggery?

HARRY No.

WEIRD MAN Wrong answer, Harry. You mean yes. Well, Harry, seeing as you asked. Buggery derives from the word 'Bulgar', as in the occupants of the country known as Bulgaria. The thing is, Harry, the Bulgars were thought to practise the old rear-entry as a form of birth control. For them, it was a kind of sacred duty, a religious imperative, as it were. You know, not to engender any more little buggers, whose sorry fate would be to scrabble around in this shit-hole of a world. (*Pause.*) Why are the phones down?

HARRY They're not.

Harry picks up the phone, listens. There's no dial tone. He tries to get a dialling tone, without success.

WEIRD MAN Right. You're not a Bulgarian, are you, Harry?

HARRY No.

WEIRD MAN No, of course you're not.

The Weird Man exits. Harry puts the phone down and goes to the front of the desk; he picks up the suitcase and leaves to take the case to Amy's room. Cut to tracking shot of corridor. The camera stills on a doorway. We hear the sound of a woman crying. Cut back to Harry's reception desk. A woman enters. She is slight and dressed in a tight-fitting suit. Unnamed in the performance, she is known as the Weird Woman. She rings the bell.

Scene 4: Reception Desk

HARRY Sorry. I'm so tired.

WEIRD WOMAN Of course you are, all that crawling around and poking your nose in where you're always expected.

HARRY Pardon?

WEIRD WOMAN Always on the run, aren't you?

HARRY It's what I do.

WEIRD WOMAN Run, run, run.

HARRY Looking after the guests. It's my job.

WEIRD WOMAN Of course it is.

HARRY Look, do you need a room?

WEIRD WOMAN I already have a room. Don't you recognise me?

HARRY No, no, I don't think so.

WEIRD WOMAN Really, Harry.

HARRY How do you know my name?

WEIRD WOMAN Anyway, you just missed her.

HARRY Who?

WEIRD WOMAN That's your problem, isn't it? You're always just missing things.

HARRY Look, I do my best.

WEIRD WOMAN Not good enough. You see, if we choose to act on our desires, then we have to own up to the consequences. Be prepared to carry the baby, so to speak.

HARRY I don't know what you mean.

WEIRD WOMAN Well, you should, Harry.

HARRY I just do my job.

WEIRD WOMAN I know you do, if you get my meaning.

HARRY No, I'm afraid I don't.

WEIRD WOMAN You know. Make the first move. Follow your instinct and then take control.

HARRY I sign people in. And then take them to their rooms.

WEIRD WOMAN But every action has a reaction, Harry. If you look too much, you can bet you're going to get caught looking.

HARRY I'm supposed to keep an eye on things. To make sure that . . .

WEIRD WOMAN Nothing untoward is going on . . .

HARRY No, that everything is in order, is how it should be . . .

WEIRD WOMAN That things don't take an unsavoury turn . . .

HARRY Yes, I mean, no, not in that way.

WEIRD WOMAN What way, Harry? I think you're being a little bit naughty. Do you want to get naughty with me?

HARRY No.

WEIRD WOMAN Well it wouldn't be the first time would it? I mean, you're getting to be a bit of an expert. A bit of a wizard.

HARRY Can I help you?

WEIRD WOMAN Oh, I'm hoping that you can.

HARRY Like, get you a drink.

WEIRD WOMAN Trying to loosen me up?

HARRY It was an example.

WEIRD WOMAN I'll have a vodka. Just to oil the wheels, so to speak. (*Harry pours a drink*) So, what do you charge?

HARRY Sorry?

WEIRD WOMAN For the drink. Drink makes people talk. Loosens tongues. And I like a loose tongue. Why don't you join me, Harry, you seem a bit tense.

HARRY I don't drink on the job.

WEIRD WOMAN Then why are you so fucking irresponsible? You're just like all the other fucking men I know. Pant. Pant. Pant. And then empty it all out into the dust bag. Without a care in the world about what might happen next.

HARRY It's on the house.

WEIRD WOMAN What is?

HARRY The drink.

WEIRD WOMAN That's most kind. (*Pause.*) Would you like to touch me, Harry?

HARRY What do you mean?

WEIRD WOMAN I mean, touch me. You've touched a woman before, haven't you?

HARRY Yes, of course I have.

WEIRD WOMAN Well soldier boy, why don't you touch me?

Scene 5: Reception Desk

Amy enters. A 1950s French song is playing in the background.

AMY   Hi.

HARRY   Hello.

AMY   Listen, er . . . ?

HARRY   Harry.

AMY   Harry. Thanks for bringing my bag up earlier. I'm sorry, that was rude of me.

HARRY   It's OK.

AMY   It's not, but thanks for saying so. It's difficult at the moment, being a woman and travelling alone.

HARRY   It must be very difficult.

AMY   So, what's your story? On your own?

HARRY   That's a very personal question.

AMY   Well, Harry, things tend to get personal very quickly in a war zone. Is there any coffee?

HARRY   No.

AMY   How about vodka?

HARRY   Russian or Polish?

AMY   Whatever you got.

HARRY   Japanese. (*Harry pours out a drink.*)

AMY   Are you here for long?

HARRY   Not really. I mean . . . I don't know what that means.

AMY   I like this song.

HARRY   Do you? I think I've heard it before.

AMY   It's a very popular tune.

HARRY   Is it?

AMY   Are you all right, Harry?

HARRY   Not really. (*Pause.*)

AMY   Harry?

HARRY   What?

AMY   Would you sleep with me?

HARRY   What do you mean?

AMY   Come on, Harry, it's a simple enough question.

HARRY   You don't know me.

AMY   No, but I like it that way. I could write your lines and you could speak them with truth and conviction.

HARRY   And what would I say?

Scene 6: Amy's Bedroom – Night

Harry and Amy, in bed. They have just finished having sex.

HARRY How did that happen?

AMY It's what lonely people do when they think their world's coming to an end. (*Pause.*) What are you thinking?

HARRY That I should go.

AMY Is that all?

Harry, lost in thought, does not reply.

AMY (*lights a cigarette*) Penny for them?

HARRY Sorry?

AMY What's on your mind, Harry?

HARRY I'm wondering . . .

AMY Yes . . .

HARRY I'm wondering why this hurts so much.

Harry gets up and starts to dress.

AMY I'm not sure hurt comes into it any more.

HARRY So you don't feel pain?

AMY No, not really. Can't say that I do.

HARRY Love?

AMY Say what I want. What I need to hear.

HARRY Which is?

AMY You call me sweetheart and I would look into your eyes . . .

HARRY What colour are they?

AMY It's not important. It's a black-and-white film. It has to be. You would say everything with certainty, as if it were fact. You know, that confidence that only people in the movies have. An unflinching hold on a fucking bright future. I'd look into your eyes and . . .

HARRY I take it this is a romance?

AMY If that's what you want to call it. I always thought I'd rather love a man and never be loved back, than be loved and never know it. Now that I have loved and been loved and now that they have gone, I'd rather not know anything at all. Can you stop me thinking, Harry? Stop me being who I am? Can you be from a different film? I'll give you different lines. You can be taking all you can from life and giving nothing back and we can fuck, because we want release, not because we want love. Can you do that? Harry, can you do that for me?

Amy leaves.

Cross fade to:

AMY Pass.

HARRY So what's left?

AMY Not much. Alcohol, sex with strangers. People you know that won't be around for much longer. Memories. And stories. Stories you cling on to, just to keep yourself going. Lies mainly. Things that happened. Things that might happen. Dreaming up things that you want to happen. Realising that dreams aren't enough. Realising how quickly dreams turn into nightmares. Then knowing that life's a bloody living nightmare, where's there's no difference between being asleep or awake, where's there's no rest for the wicked. (*Laughs.*) You know the sort of thing.

HARRY And that's it?

AMY Change the subject, Harry. Talking only makes it worse.

HARRY What to? What else is there?

AMY Shall I tell you a story?

HARRY Does it have a happy ending?

AMY Probably not.

HARRY Is it a boy-meets-girl kind of story?

AMY Yes and no. There's a man, but he's not the main character.

HARRY The main character's a woman.

AMY Yes, the man's not much more than an onlooker really. It's the woman's story. She is in this hotel room. She arrives unexpectedly in a city under siege and in her handbag she carries a gun. Nobody knows who she is or where she's come from, it's a mystery. She sleeps during the day and at night she sits by the window smoking, her face lit by the flames of buildings burning in the diplomatic quarter.

HARRY Why is she here?

AMY There, Harry, it's there.

HARRY Yes.

AMY She's waiting.

HARRY What for?

AMY She's getting ready, preparing herself. She's very organised. Nothing's been left to chance. All the arrangements have been made. She's the sort of woman who knows her own mind. You know the type, vulnerable but determined.

HARRY Sounds like a film.

AMY It is, in some ways it is terribly like a film. You see, this woman has come to this hotel room because there is something that she must do. It's something that she knows is terribly, terribly wrong. But it's something that she must do.

HARRY Why?

AMY Because she has no choice. Because in the end, everything . . . everything . . . all the events in her life . . . have come down to this. You see, there's something wrong . . . how she feels . . . about everything. It's like she's been emptied out. Yes, that's it. You know, hollowed out. Like she's been sick so many times that there's absolutely nothing left. Energy, bile, hope, vomited out. You know. And now there's nothing left.

HARRY This thing she has to do, does it have something to do with the war?

AMY Yes, it does.

HARRY And do I know this woman?

AMY You think you do, but you don't. Give me your hand.

HARRY I've got to go.

AMY I haven't finished my story.

HARRY I know.

AMY Don't you want to know how it ends?

HARRY No. You've already told me it doesn't have a happy ending.

AMY I said probably.

HARRY I've got to go.

AMY Goodnight, Harry.

Cross-fade to empty corridor. Fade back to the bedroom. Amy is alone. She is speaking on the phone.

AMY Hello. No. I'm fine. I'm OK. It's just this hotel. There's not much to say is there? Listen, I'm having his things sent on to you. No, just letters and photos mainly. (*She starts to weep.*) Look, I'm OK. Fine. I'll be in touch.

She puts down phone. Cut to fast POV shot through hotel corridor until the camera comes to rest on the empty reception desk. Loud sound of gunshot.

Scene 8: Weird Woman and Weird Man Interlude

Flies swarm on the screen. The phone is ringing.

Scene 9: Reception Desk

The phone continues to ring. Cut to Harry arriving back at the desk. He picks up the phone.

HARRY Hello? Hello?

Weird Man enters.

WEIRD MAN You're too late. You've just missed her, Harry.

Weird Man leaves.

Scene 10: Reception Desk

Sound of the French song. Phone rings. Amy enters.

HARRY Hello? Hello? (*Pause.*) Fuck you. Fuck you.

He slams the phone down.

AMY Excuse me.

HARRY I'm sorry. We're having trouble with the phone system.

AMY Isn't everybody?

HARRY You want a room?

AMY Yes, of course I do, it's a hotel, isn't it? Sorry, I'm very tired. It's been a difficult day. What have you got?

HARRY I'm afraid we're very busy. We've got one room left.

AMY I'll take it.

HARRY Room 14, then. I can do you a good rate. If you're tired I can check you in later. I'll need your passport.

AMY Fine.

Harry takes the passport and glances over it. Amy lights a cigarette.

HARRY You're a translator.

AMY Sorry?

HARRY It says here that you're a translator. See, 'Occupation: translator'.

AMY Yes. That's what I did. And you?

HARRY Excuse me?

AMY You must have done something before. You don't look like a typical bellhop to me.

HARRY Night porter.

AMY Sorry?

HARRY I'm a night porter. We don't have a bellhop here.

Amy sees that Harry is reading a French novel.

AMY You read French.

HARRY Yes.

AMY *La vérité n'existe pas. Il n'y a que perception.*

HARRY You speak French too.

AMY It's Flaubert.

HARRY Is it?

AMY It was a long time ago. Look, I'll find my own way up to the room. If you can bring my bag up when you are ready, I need to wash.

HARRY Of course.

He suddenly remembers the water's off. Shouts:

There's no water. Damn.

Cut to:

Scene 11: Corridor

Side-on tracking shot of corridor. Weird Man and Amy meet.

WEIRD MAN Lost, are you?

AMY Excuse me?

WEIRD MAN A veritable labyrinth, this place. You could wander these corridors for days.

AMY I'm fine, thank you.

WEIRD MAN Oh, I know you are. Particularly fine.

AMY Excuse me, but I'd like to go to my room.

WEIRD MAN Of course.

AMY I'm in a bit of a hurry.

WEIRD MAN Excuse my bluntness, but does the idea of fucking him make you wet?

She slaps his face.

Oh, sorry, am I being a bit personal?

As she exits.

By the way, he's married. But then you'd know that, wouldn't you.

Corridor sequence. We pass doors.

Cut to:

Scene 12: Reception Desk

Weird Man approaches Harry's desk.

WEIRD MAN Tired, are we?

HARRY Sorry?

WEIRD MAN You must be the new guy.

HARRY No.

WEIRD MAN Always tired, the young. Always asleep. It's as if they are avoiding life. Giving up on all its opportunities. Don't you just want to grab it, Harry?

HARRY What?

WEIRD MAN The moment. And wring it dry, take it for all it's worth. No going back, no regrets. Take a big bite out of it Harry. This is no time to sleep. Slumped on your desk, dribbling like an old man.

HARRY I'm tired. Up all night. Taking calls. Checking people in.

WEIRD MAN Of course you are. It's an important job. I forget that. Tending to people's every need. Do you think you're good at it?

HARRY What?

WEIRD MAN You know, 'it'.

HARRY I don't know what you mean?

WEIRD MAN It, Harry. It. Needs. Knowing what people want. And how to satisfy them.

HARRY I don't know what you want from me, sir.

WEIRD MAN (*ignoring Harry*) You see, I count it as one of my strengths. Knowing what people want. If you know what people desire, Harry, then you also know what they fear. And if you know what people fear, then you've got a hold over them. Love and hate. *Odi et amo* in the old tongue. So closely related. The two emotions at full circle, at full tilt. Know any Latin, Harry?

HARRY No.

WEIRD MAN I bet you do. Those filthy words, they're all Latin. And they sound so . . . erect, oh sorry, correct.

HARRY I wouldn't know. I can barely speak French.

WEIRD MAN Oh, but I bet you do, Harry. Even if you don't know the words, you know the actions. On your knees, bent double, mouth open, tongue tonguing, legs open, arse in the air, counting the time before that delicious spasm. One, two, three, four, five, six . . . (*Does obscene little panting sounds as he says the numbers.*) *Un petit mort*: a little death, Harry. Isn't that all we want? Isn't that life's great rehearsal? The phut-phut of the engine's stammer. Before the great big light goes out?

HARRY I wouldn't know.

WEIRD MAN Of course you wouldn't, Harry. Asleep all the time, waiting for that phone to ring. But here I am, going on. And I only came in for a light. Got a light Harry?

HARRY Yes. (*Passes him the matches. Pause.*)

WEIRD MAN Do me the honour?

Harry strikes the match and a little nervously puts the match to the cigarette in the Weird Man's mouth.

WEIRD MAN Now that's what I call service. And breath like a peach.

HARRY What.

WEIRD MAN Like a ripe peach, Harry. Take a big bite of it. Remember, life's too short to be holding back.

Harry watches Weird Man leave. He waits a moment, then goes to front of desk and picks up Amy's bag. He exits. Side-tracking shot of corridor as Harry walks to her room. We see doors slowly pass by. Suddenly, we cut into a series of rooms where Harry glimpses figures that turn towards him as he begins to run past each of the doorways.

Cut to overhead shot of corridor floor. Cut back to the reception desk. Harry is writing in the guest book.

Scene 13: Reception Desk

Sound of the French song in the background. Weird Woman enters.

WEIRD WOMAN What do you have to drink? I'm so parched.

HARRY The water's off, at the moment.

WEIRD WOMAN I was thinking of something a bit stronger.

HARRY There's vodka.

WEIRD WOMAN Vodka. Vodka makes me so maudlin. And there's too much sadness in the world, don't you think?

HARRY Yes, I suppose there is.

As Harry pours the drink, Weird Woman sings along with the French song.

WEIRD WOMAN I like this song. You speak French, don't you, Harry? Almost makes me choke. What do you miss most, Harry?

HARRY I'm not sure.

WEIRD WOMAN You must miss your wife.

HARRY What?

WEIRD WOMAN Your wife, Harry.

HARRY But I'm not married. I've never been married. I don't even have a ring.

WEIRD WOMAN So easily slipped off, in my experience.

HARRY What do you mean?

WEIRD WOMAN The ring, Harry. Avoids embarrassment. Misses out all that awkwardness. Gives us a sense of freedom. To do what we want. Why don't you join me?

HARRY Join you for what?

WEIRD WOMAN A drink, Harry. If I didn't know you better, I'd say you were trying to lead me on.

HARRY Well, you don't know me. Have we met before?

WEIRD WOMAN But I get that sense that you want to.

HARRY Want to what?

WEIRD WOMAN Know me. I mean you've known other women, haven't you?

HARRY Yes, of course I have.

WEIRD WOMAN It's just that you're so nervous. Look at you, palms sweating, shaking like a little bird. It doesn't have to be that bad. Just two people taking comfort in one another. Taking our little bit of pleasure. I mean, it's not as if this is your first time.

HARRY Sorry?

WEIRD WOMAN Do you remember your first time, Harry? Was it sweet and gentle? And did you take your time, making that final push that had occupied your grubby little mind for so long? Or was it the grunt, grunt, grunt of the sty? Eyes closed and holding on for dear life from the moment that little piggy was let in through the door. I suppose the question is, if you don't mind me cutting to the chase, do you fuck, Harry? Or, do you make love?

HARRY I . . . I . . .

WEIRD WOMAN And what was it like, the last time, with your wife?

HARRY I told you, I don't have a wife.

WEIRD WOMAN Did you feel guilty, knowing you were leaving her?

HARRY I never left her. I've never left anyone.

WEIRD WOMAN Knowing that you would never see her again. And then, the baby?

HARRY Baby, what do you mean 'baby'?

WEIRD WOMAN Did you try that little bit harder? Were you a little less selfish? Did you think of her needs, Harry, just for once? I'm sure you did, I can see it in your eyes.

HARRY You said baby, what do you mean 'baby'?

WEIRD WOMAN Of course, you wouldn't know. It's not as if your type has ever worried about consequences. It's all a rush to the head, then that little release that you treasure so much. Pathetic really. There's more pleasure in a sneeze. All this forgetting, Harry, what sort of excuse is that?

HARRY It's not an excuse. I try to remember. You've no idea.

WEIRD WOMAN Oh, but I do, darling.

HARRY What do you . . . ?

WEIRD WOMAN And what about my longings?

HARRY Sorry?

WEIRD WOMAN How are you going to satisfy them? I'm a difficult woman to please. My needs, Harry. It's time to leave yours behind. No wonder your hands are all damp. There are tears in your eyes. Finish your drink. It'll calm your nerves for what lies ahead.

Cut to slow POV through the hotel corridor.

Scene 14: Corridor

Amy and Weird Woman meet.

WEIRD WOMAN I think this must be yours.

AMY Where did you get this?

WEIRD WOMAN You must have dropped it. He's very handsome. Is he your boyfriend?

AMY It's my husband.

WEIRD WOMAN Is he here with you?

AMY He's dead.

WEIRD WOMAN I'm so sorry, the tragedies of war. All alone then? And in your condition.

AMY I don't know what you mean.

WEIRD WOMAN No point in trying to hide it. Loosen the waistband, that's what I say. Let the world know another sorry soul is on its way.

AMY How did you . . . ?

WEIRD WOMAN Know. The bush telegraph, the constant whispering behind closed doors. I bet your husband would have been pleased. Men get so carried away by their little achievements.

AMY Thank you for your concern. I'd better be going.

Cut to Amy arriving at the desk.

Scene 15: Reception Desk

AMY Listen . . .

HARRY Harry.

AMY I have this feeling that we know each other.

HARRY Not that I remember.

AMY No, you wouldn't, would you? Have you heard from your wife?

HARRY I don't have a wife.

AMY Strange, somebody just told me that you have.

HARRY Did they? Well, I don't.

AMY Girlfriend?

HARRY Yes, sort of.

AMY What's her name?

HARRY I can't remember.

AMY You were obviously very close.

HARRY It's not like that.

AMY I know. Sorry, I was making a joke. A stupid joke. Is she pretty? Is she prettier than me?

HARRY No.

AMY Liar. But that's OK. Is there any coffee?

HARRY No.

AMY How about vodka?

HARRY Polish or Russian?

AMY Whatever you've got.

HARRY Japanese? (*He pours a drink.*)

AMY Listen, Harry, it's late and we're both tired. There's a war going on outside and sooner or later you're going to ask me how I ended up here and when you do I'm going to say that I'm running away. And you're going to say 'From what?' and I'm going to say, 'It's none of your business.' And then there will probably be an awkward silence and then I'll say, 'And you, what's your story?' And you'll say, 'No story, just an incoherent string of events.' And then I'll say, 'Let's cut the crap, Harry, do you want to sleep with me?' (*Pause.*) And then you'll say? Well, do you? (*Pause.*)

HARRY Yes.

Amy exits. Cut to POV corridor shot.

Scene 16: Amy's Bedroom

AMY Are you OK?

HARRY Yes.

AMY Do you wish that hadn't happened?

HARRY No.

AMY Why are you so sad?

HARRY Am I?

AMY Yes, I think you are, Harry. I thought it the moment I saw you.

HARRY That makes two of us, doesn't it?

AMY I suppose it does. What are you thinking about?

HARRY I'm trying to remember someone. Trying to remember her face and I can't.

AMY Your girlfriend?

HARRY I don't know.

AMY Why can't you remember things, Harry?

HARRY I think, I think, maybe I got hurt. That something happened. Sometimes I remember flashes, faces. Mainly I don't. I remember that before I worked here I did something else. I can read French. I get headaches. I feel like I've only just arrived. I can't remember before. Sometimes my body aches so much I have to hold myself still until the pain passes. At night I check for scars where I think they should be. There's no bruising, nothing, not a mark.

AMY Are you lonely, Harry?

HARRY Yes. But mainly I'm scared. I'm scared that things are always going to be like this. That they're never going to be normal again.

AMY (*laughs*) Normal. What does normal mean?

HARRY Normal means remembering what happened yesterday. Normal means having a home and a family.

AMY A wife?

HARRY Maybe, maybe, a wife.

AMY Or, a girlfriend? Would you like me to be your girlfriend? Do you think that would make things normal?

HARRY I don't know. What about you?

AMY What about me?

HARRY What would you like?

AMY I had a husband. He died.

HARRY I'm sorry.

AMY I know you are. What are you thinking?

HARRY I'm wondering why it's all such a mess. Why it's so . . . so difficult.

AMY Is it?

HARRY Don't you feel pain?

AMY Not any more.

HARRY What about love?

AMY Pass.

HARRY What does that leave?

AMY Memories.

HARRY That's it?

AMY I can't think of anything else.

HARRY It doesn't leave me with much, does it?

AMY I know. I'm sorry. Anyhow, it leaves you with now.

HARRY I don't think now is what I need. I'm not sure now's enough.

AMY That depends on the now. (*Pause.*) Don't leave, Harry.

HARRY I've got to go.

AMY Stay. Tell me what you like.

HARRY I like your back.

AMY What else do you like, Harry?

HARRY I like your hair. I like your skin. I like your breasts.

AMY Am I your girlfriend, Harry? Would you like that? Would you like me to be your girlfriend?

HARRY Yes.

AMY Ask me.

HARRY Would you be my girlfriend?

AMY Say please.

Cut to corridor tracking shot. Cut back to Amy's room. She's alone. We see her looking at the gun. She picks up the phone.

Please be there.

There's a knock at the door. She swings around with the gun and points it at the door. Cut to fast POV shot through hotel corridor until the camera comes to rest on the empty reception desk. Loud sound of gunshot.

Scene 17: Weird Woman and Weird Man Interlude

Flies swarm on the screen. The phone is ringing.

Scene 18: Reception Desk

The phone continues to ring. Cut to Harry arriving back at the desk. He picks up the phone.

HARRY Hello? Hello?

Weird Man enters.

WEIRD MAN: You're too late. You just missed her, Harry.

Harry puts phone down and Weird Man leaves.

Scene 19: Reception Desk

Sound of the French song in background. Amy enters.

AMY I'd like a room.

HARRY I'm sorry we're full.

AMY What about 14?

HARRY What?

AMY 14. The key, hanging there.

HARRY There's someone in 14.

AMY There can't be, the key's there.

HARRY People leave their keys when they go out.

AMY It's after midnight.

HARRY That's not late.

AMY There's a curfew. Could you just check?

HARRY I don't need to check. There's a woman staying in that room. (*He checks the guest book.*) I'm sorry. I was sure.

AMY It doesn't matter. Just a mistake.

Harry hands the key over.

If you could bring my bag up when you're ready.

Amy leaves.

Scene 20: Reception Desk

Weird Man enters.

WEIRD MAN Christ, are you still here?

HARRY I always work nights.

WEIRD MAN So you do, Harry, so you do.

Pause. Weird Man looks at Harry. Harry shifts uncomfortably.

WEIRD MAN Not much of a conversationalist are we?

HARRY No.

WEIRD MAN I mean, it's not as if people are queuing up to sample your searing wit and repartee.

HARRY I like it when it's quiet.

WEIRD MAN It's a lost art, conversation. Social intercourse, that's its proper name, isn't it? I like a bit of chitchat, Harry. Chewing the cud and all that. And sometimes I like to delve a little bit deeper, get my chops around the heart of the matter. Like the problem of time, Harry. It obsesses me. Can't get it out of my fucking head. Does it go backwards or forwards? Or does it move in little flurries? The little in and out of time.

HARRY I don't concern myself with such things.

WEIRD MAN 'Course you don't. You've got bigger problems on your plate. And you don't want to distract yourself with the fripperies of fucking philosophy. I mean, where the fuck does it get you, after all? I'll tell you. Fucking nowhere. Too much thinking, Harry, freezes your balls, and I like it when they're hanging really loose. (*Pause.*) So how are yours feeling, Harry, at this precise moment?

HARRY What?

WEIRD MAN (*very close to Harry's face*) Balls, Harry. Relaxed in their sack, or clinging like limpets to a rock in a storm?

HARRY (*leaning back*) You're . . . too . . . close.

WEIRD MAN Oh, sorry. Am I crowding you, Harry? Invading your personal space? I hate that, Harry, I fucking do. When a man gets too close. It makes me gip. Brings the bile up. Makes me want to lash out. Do something I might regret. And you're too close, Harry. A bit near the knuckle. So what exactly are you after? I mean why the fuck am I standing here talking to the fucking likes of you?

HARRY I just stand at this desk. People arrive and I check them in and I take them to their room. I serve drinks and I hand out towels. It's no big deal.

WEIRD MAN Oh, but it is Harry. It's a big fucking deal. I mean, you haven't told the complete story, have you? And I can't abide a man who lies, who isn't straight with me. Who fucks me around. It gets my blood up. And I hate it when I lose control. When things get too messy. I mean, what I find really fucking galling is the cleaning up. I mean, it's so fucking demeaning. Mop, mop, scrub, scrub. Disinfectant, to cover over the smell of it all. Trying to hold your breakfast down. Trying to keep it together. Of course, you know all this, don't you? It's not as if you are above a bit of cleaning up yourself. Especially after the mess you have so fucking obviously made of it all.

HARRY I don't know what you're talking about.

WEIRD MAN This, Harry. (*Pause.*) This complete fucking mess you're in. (*Pause.*) I mean, who's going to wipe your fucking arse when it's over? Let me tell you. I'll do almost anything. Truth be told, I've done almost anything. But I draw the line at that, Harry.

HARRY Who are you?

WEIRD MAN Think of me as the cleaner, Harry. As the poor fuck who scrubs away and hoses it all down when the dust has settled. We crate it all up and send it off and wait for the next arrival.

Pause.

HARRY What, exactly, do you want?

WEIRD MAN Not much, Harry. A little bit of resolution? Is that too much to ask for? Then again, you'd know all about that, wouldn't you?

Weird Man exits. Telephone rings.

HARRY Hello? Hello? Can I help you?

He puts the phone down. Leaves desk, picks up case and takes it to Amy's room. Cut to side-on corridor tracking shot. Cut to graphic scene of Weird Man and Woman having sex. It's as if Harry is looking on.

Cut back to desk. Harry is waiting at the desk. Weird Woman enters.

Scene 21: Reception Desk

Harry draws in the guestbook.

WEIRD WOMAN You'll go blind.

HARRY Sorry, I must have dropped off.

WEIRD WOMAN All those little words. Making your eyes struggle in the dying of the light. First it'll be glasses, then glaucoma, then, well, 'endless frozen night' springs to mind.

HARRY It passes the time.

WEIRD WOMAN Does it, really?

HARRY No, not really. I find it difficult. I don't have a dictionary. Sometimes I seem to read the same sentence again and again.

WEIRD WOMAN Still, it's good to keep the mind active, isn't it? Escaping into the words of others, even if they're the same old letters swirling about the page, like flies. There's something so comforting about repetition, don't you think?

HARRY I don't find it comforting.

WEIRD WOMAN No, well, you wouldn't. A guilty conscience never gives us any rest.

HARRY I've done nothing to feel guilty about.

WEIRD WOMAN Now that's not quite accurate is it? But still, let's not dwell on the past. I'd like to focus on the future.

HARRY Is there something you want?

WEIRD WOMAN Now you're talking. I'm an expert in wantonness. But what are you an expert in, apart from prowling around and fucking people you shouldn't?

HARRY Now that's out of . . . .

WEIRD WOMAN Not that I'm being moral, God forbid, anybody accusing me of that. But it does put me in a quandary.

HARRY What do you mean?

WEIRD WOMAN A dilemma, Harry. Whether to let you fuck me or not. You see, I've never been one for seconds.

HARRY But I don't want to.

WEIRD WOMAN Of course you do, soldier-boy.

HARRY Why did you call me that?

WEIRD WOMAN What?

HARRY Soldier-boy.

WEIRD WOMAN You're in uniform, aren't you?

HARRY It's a hotel uniform.

WEIRD WOMAN Is it?

HARRY Yes, it's blue, it's got brass buttons. Soldiers' uniforms are brown or green or some fucking colour that doesn't show up. Soldiers don't wear blue uniforms. Not since Napoleon's time. This is a hotel uniform. It's a night porter's uniform. Look, I read French. I don't work here full time. Look, the uniform doesn't even fit properly. I'm just doing this for the money, until it's all over, when the fighting stops and we can all get back to normal. It's just to get by, until I fix myself up with something more permanent.

WEIRD WOMAN Look, are you going to fuck me or not?

The telephone rings, interrupting Harry's disjointed flow. He picks it up and slams it down again without listening.

WEIRD WOMAN That'll be room 14.

HARRY What?

WEIRD WOMAN The girl in room 14. She wants you.

HARRY She's only just arrived. I don't even know her name.

WEIRD WOMAN She knows you.

HARRY What do you mean?

WEIRD WOMAN She showed me a photograph, you and her, and it looked like it was from before. (*Pause.*) Run, soldier-boy. It's already too late.

Harry waits a moment, then goes to front of desk and picks up Amy's bag. He exits. Side-tracking shot of corridor as Harry walks to her room. We see doors slowly pass by. Suddenly we cut into a series of rooms where Harry glimpses figures that turn towards him as he begins to run past each of the doorways.

Cut to Harry arriving at Amy's room.

Scene 22: Outside Amy's Bedroom

HARRY It's the porter.

AMY What do you want?

HARRY I thought there might be a problem.

AMY There isn't.

HARRY Are you sure you're OK?

AMY Yes, I'm sure.

HARRY I'm sorry, I'll go.

Harry starts to leave.

AMY Have we met somewhere before, Harry?

HARRY I don't know, I mean, I wouldn't know. You see, I have this problem with my memory. I don't remember things too well.

AMY Is it something that happened to you because of the war?

HARRY I think so. Probably.

AMY It's just that you seem familiar.

HARRY Maybe you stayed here before.

AMY It's not very likely. And anyway I would remember.

HARRY Of course you would.

AMY Maybe I know you from before.

HARRY Before all this?

AMY Yes. (*Pause.*) I couldn't sleep.

HARRY It's the noise.

AMY No, it's not that, I can never sleep. I don't like being alone. I had a husband. He died. He was a soldier. He got shot. These things happen. I suppose you can say it was an occupational hazard.

HARRY I'm sorry.

AMY I know you are. I'm sorry too. Everyone's sorry, but it doesn't make any difference.

Harry starts to leave.

AMY Don't go. Have a drink.

HARRY And what?

AMY Pretend.

HARRY Pretend that we are other people. Pretend that none of this is happening. I'll pretend I have a past and we can both pretend we have a future.

AMY Yes, if you want.

HARRY We could be man and wife.

AMY Or a couple on honeymoon.

HARRY A soldier and his bride.

AMY Making love in a hotel on the night before he goes off to war. (*Pause.*) Would you like that, Harry?

Cut to Harry and Amy having sex in her room.

Cut to:

Scene 23: Amy's Bedroom

Harry and Amy in bed after sex. She sits naked with her back to him.

HARRY It's always a bit strange isn't it, after . . . ?

AMY After what, Harry?

HARRY After . . . you know . . . after . . .

AMY Fucking . . . .

HARRY After . . . Yes.

AMY Shall I tell you a story, Harry?

HARRY A story? Does it have a happy ending?

AMY Is that important?

HARRY It helps, sometimes.

AMY Well, I'm pretty certain this one doesn't have a happy ending. None of the best stories ever do.

HARRY How does it begin?

AMY There's this woman and she is in this hotel room.

HARRY I think I've heard this story before.

AMY Yes, you've heard it before.

HARRY And do I know this woman?

AMY You think you do, but you don't.

She takes his hand.

HARRY I have heard this story. It's a boy-meets-girl kind of a story.

AMY Yes, it's that kind of story. Only, it's not really about the man. He's only a bit part.

HARRY I see.

AMY This woman and this man, they meet in a hotel.

HARRY What kind of a hotel?

AMY Well, it's seen better days. It used to be the best hotel in the city. It was famous for its cocktails and dances. Now it's faded and you can get a room for a very cheap rate. You know the kind of place, Harry.

HARRY And what does he look like?

AMY Who?

HARRY This bit-part of a man.

AMY Let's see. He's around six foot tall. Thin. He has blond hair and pale skin. Looks like he's spent his life indoors. He's not strikingly handsome, but there's something rather beautiful about him. He looks gentle. You know, lost and a bit sad.

HARRY Does she like him?

AMY I'm not sure like comes into it, Harry. She trusts him. When she starts talking to him she . . . for a moment . . . she doesn't feel frightened any more.

HARRY What does she have to be frightened of? Is she on the run?

AMY No, she's not on the run.

HARRY Then why should she be scared?

AMY We never really find out. Only, when she starts talking to this man, she suddenly realises what it is that she has to do. And there's no going back. He's not the reason, he's more the . . .

HARRY Trigger, he's the trigger.

AMY Yes, that's right, he's the trigger.

HARRY And do they know each other?

AMY They think they do, but they don't. Then again, they think they don't, but they do.

HARRY Sounds like a film.

AMY It is. It's just like a film. There's something wrong with this woman, although we cannot tell what. And it's obvious that they haven't met in the hotel by chance. Something has brought them together. What's not clear is why and what will happen next.

HARRY Do we know anything about them, before they meet in this hotel?

AMY That's the thing. There is no before, or after, for that matter. There's no explanation. Just this one scene and it keeps playing over and over.

HARRY I'm not sure I'd like that.

AMY No, you wouldn't, Harry, you wouldn't.

HARRY So what happens in this scene?

AMY What happens is that they meet. They start talking. They have a couple of vodkas. And then for some reason the woman invites him to her room and they have sex and for a moment she thinks that perhaps she knew him before, or that maybe she knew him in another life, and at that moment she thinks that maybe he can save her from what she has to do.

HARRY And does he?

AMY We never find out.

Cut to corridor outside Amy's room.

Cut back into Amy's room. She's alone. She is speaking on the phone.

Please, is somebody there?

There's a knock at the door. She pulls out the gun and points it at the door. The phone rings. Amy puts the gun in her mouth and she pulls the trigger. Blood splashes on the wall. We see Amy sprawled on the bed. Harry rushes in and looks at the body. He then picks up the phone. He hears his own voice through the earpiece: 'Hello? Hello? Can I help you?' He puts the phone down. He sees a photograph on the bloodstained sheets. He picks it up and looks at it. Close-up on the photograph. We see a picture of Harry and Amy as a married couple.

Cut back to opening sequence of Harry in the forest. The camera circles around Harry in his soldier's uniform. His nose is bleeding. Cut to:

Scene 24: Reception Desk

Weird Man enters and we see Harry at the desk with the phone in his hand.

WEIRD MAN You're too late. You just missed her, Harry.

The Weird Man exits and Amy enters as in the opening hotel sequence carrying her suitcase. Harry slowly puts the phone down. He does not acknowledge her. Slow fade to credits.

Trans-Acts

created and performed by
Julia Bardsley

Author's Notes

Julia Bardsley

'Bardsley is a really fascinating artist . . . She could have been running the National Theatre by now, but instead quite deliberately chose a different career path. In recent years she has been making inspired and unsettling work on the cusp between the theatre and the gallery.'

Lyn Gardner, *The Guardian*

Trans-Acts emerged out of a critical transition period filled with doubt, questions and a desire to create a type of work that brought into dialogue my visual art/installation practice with performance. It articulates a moment of struggle to do with my identity as an artist and to find, through the creative process, practical means to make a form of theatre that felt appropriate for me. Although the work is deeply rooted in a very personal investigation, there is always an attempt to transcend the personal and translate these very private preoccupations into an experience that escapes a closed or fixed reading.

I'd been interested in this notion of 'trans' for a while, interested in how this idea is deeply embedded in all things creative – the place of one thing becoming another, of shifting states, of a straddling between worlds, caught between knowing and not knowing, reality and fiction. At the same time, without having a real idea where it would lead, I'd instigated regular dialogues with the actress Anastasia Hille about her experience of being an actress. Somewhere in my mind I was thinking of creating a piece for three actresses that interrogated the process of performing and the experience of the actress within the theatre frame. Anastasia's characteristically candid and raw divulgences about the performer's inner vocabulary, strategies for survival, confrontation and embracing of fears, left me with a rich reservoir of materials. In particular, I was struck by her take on humiliation and its relationship to the horizontal. These became core thematics of the piece that eventually became *Trans-Acts*.

Whether out of necessity or selfishness I ended up taking the three roles that existed within the third part of *Trans-Acts*; that of the mute Director, the Actress trapped within the confines of a TV screen and the transcendent Understudy. The piece became a dialogue with myself about my relationship with the theatre, an acting out of traditional power dynamics in an attempt to confront something of the past, shed habitual working methods and free myself to emerge simply as a creative being.

Act Three of *Trans-Acts* is preceded by *Act One: Transgression*, where the artist (myself) is seen in the guise of three necessary transgressors – necessary for the creative process – the Dunce, the Fool and the Devil. This act is manifest as an installation of large black-and-white pinhole photographs, a video projection of foolish suicide attempts, a flick book and a box of 35mm photographs. It was here that I planted the seed of Eve as the ultimate transgressor – the first sinner, the one to blame for everything, the one who stumbled and fell, who humiliated herself and ended up horizontal. *Act Two: Transformation* took the form of a photographic frieze with three peep boxes mapping the transformation of the Artist into the personas of The Director and The Actress. On a stool, surrounded by the actual garments seen in the photographs, the live Artist transforms into The Director for the assembled audience of twelve, who are then led into the ultraviolet room for *Act Three: Transcendence*. The twelve sit round a large table and in this intimacy and proximity, witness the piece.

The main structuring device for Act Three of *Trans-Acts* was the Passion – the last three days of Christ: Day One – Crucifixion, Day Two – Burial, and Day Three – Resurrection. Obviously the twelve sitting round the table echo the apostles and the Last Supper, but hopefully this realisation only dawns later. I often look to an existing framework from which all the ideas of a piece can grow and mutate, leaving the point of origin buried or at least heavily veiled. This point of origin is a point of departure but also acts as a safety net, to be returned to when lost or needing a prompt. *Trans-Acts* is now one of three pieces, including *Almost the Same (feral rehearsals for violent acts of culture)* and *Aftermaths: A Tear in the Meat of Vision*, that make up 'The Divine Trilogy'. All use biblical stories as their sub-structuring devices.

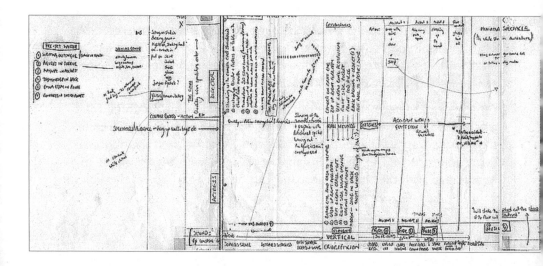

The text itself evolved over a number of months and is made up of fragments, small thoughts, sentences, dreams and subverted quotes from films.
My process often starts with simultaneous reading research and note-
taking on any number of seemingly disparate threads. In the case of *Trans-
Acts* I was interested in exploring falling, humiliation and ascent as a fall in
reverse; the accident as an opening for possibility; tongues, ventriloquism
and who owns your voice; sacrifice, mimetic desire, imitation and the
scapegoat; identity and the loss of self through repetition; what is revealed
and what remains hidden. I then start to make transgressive marriages between these ideas, moving from my head into my hands, making objects,
photographic and video tests, developing the visual language of the piece,
the spatial and physical dynamics. This then moves into creating a performance score, which starts to organise the material on a temporal level.
This score acts as both a practical and a creative tool. The final text as it
appears in this anthology seems more like a film script, with descriptive
passages to give the reader as clear an idea as possible of the live performance. All the spoken text is delivered by The Actress and is pre-recorded,
as The Actress exists only on video. When the Miniature Director comes
into play, this too is pre-recorded. The Director speaks only through her
actions, the chalked texts she makes on the table and, fleetingly, through
the ventriloquist puppet version of herself.

I should say a bit about the garment that I designed for The Director. I knew
that it needed to be green, green being the colour of envy, and envy is
certainly what characterised this director's relationship with The Actress. It
also needed to be a suit, to have a certain masculine formality, a strictness but
feminised by a skirt rather than trousers. It also required a grid pattern – the
Grid appeared as an image throughout *Trans-Acts*, a device for registering
and containing scattered debris of the body moving in space. The Director's

Below: first version of performance score for Trans-Acts.

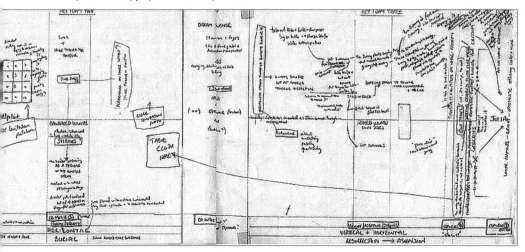

garment included a number of 'animal' elements: a horn coming out of one elbow, a small stoat's tail which protruded from a red velvet vagina-like opening, the back panel of the jacket unzipped to reveal its lining of rabbit fur (the same fur lined the inside of her red stilettos). In one sleeve there was a zipped opening, a wound, that contained miniature figures of The Director and The Actress. The costume becomes a physical manifestation of the themes of the piece and a psychological garment revealing the true nature of the

persona of The Director. This garment was eventually made with meticulous precision and care by Sonja Harms.

The sonic dimension of *Trans-Acts* consists of pieces made by my long-term collaborator, the composer Andrew Poppy. Almost all the sonic material came from previous theatre shows that we had made together. There are historical reverberations at work which lend a depth to the piece of which maybe only Andrew and I are aware. But the existence of these fragments from our theatrical past in this new work is a comment on both legacy and renewal.

The pleasure of making solo work is that you can dispense almost totally with rehearsals. The work starts to manifest itself, comes into focus and is played out in your head and is then worked on and refined in front of the audience. The only need for rehearsal is on a practical/technical level. The detailed work of performance comes in the repetition of performing live, with those witnesses contributing to the work through their presence and concentration, helping you understand what the piece is while you're performing it. As all the dialogue in *Trans-Acts* is pre-recorded, it has never changed. This fixed parameter allows a level of both meticulous discipline and pleasurable freedoms within the live performance context.

The role of and relationship to the audience have become key considerations in the pieces that make up 'The Divine Trilogy'. *Trans-Acts* allowed me

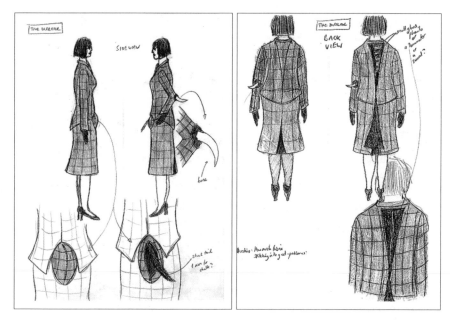

Left and above: garment drawings for The Director.

to address my dissatisfaction with the fact that so much theatre seems to exist, spatially at least, so far away, in the distance. I was interested in re-configuring the proximity of the audience not only to the performer but also to the environment and the objects that are equal players in the piece. So much theatre plays with clumsy approximation on a visual and material level. I wanted the objects introduced into the theatre of *Trans-Acts* to be given as much consideration and care as a visual art object, pieces that exist and have potency in their own right. The proximity of the audience to the objects and the performer allows for a filmic level of close-up to exist, with visual detail informing the experience of the spectator. All the elements of the piece co-exist with equal status, with no one part dominating the whole. Of course, certain elements are foregrounded for specific effect at parti-cular moments, but there is an attempt to democratise the theatre arena, away from the traditional dominance of spoken language, vocal narrative and the presence of the actor over all other elements. There is a way that narrative can exist in other forms, through the sentences of objects in space, through a grammar of materials or implied through spoken language but never totally seen through in a linear way. The audience piece together the fragments that are offered and construct multiple meanings through the filter of their personal perception.

Trans-Acts was created and performed by Julia Bardsley with music by Andrew Poppy. All other production credits and acknowledgements appear at the end of the performance text.

Trans-Acts performances:

CBA studios, London, 2004

NRLA (National Review of Live Art) Glasgow, Scotland, 2005

TROUBLE Festival #1, Brussels, Belgium, 2005

SPILL Festival of Performance, London, 2007

KARNART, Lisbon, Portugal 2008

Trans-Acts was developed with financial assistance from a NESTA Fellowship (National Endowment for Sport, Technology and the Arts).

Trans-Acts

act one: transgression
act two: transformation
act three: transcendence

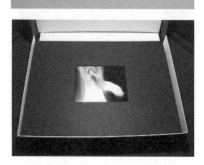

EVE SLIPS UP IN THE GARDEN

Act One: Transgression

an exhibition prologue of pinhole photographs, flick book, projected suicides
and 35mm photos in a box – the artist in the guise of necessary transgressors:
the Dunce, the Fool and the Devil.
This is scapegoat Eve – sad, mad and bad.

DUNCE (sad Eve)

9 PLACES of HURT:

pinhole photographs/digital inkjet prints,
all images produced 'in camera' with no post-production manipulation

TEARS
PISSING
MATHSPELL
SLEEPWALKER
DIVIDED
DAD
BLOOD
MOTHER
SURRENDER

FOOL (mad Eve)

9 PLACES of HUMOUR:

digital video grabs/inkjet prints

EVE SLIPS UP IN THE GARDEN

flick book: digital video grabs/inkjet prints

EVE PERFORMS SUICIDE ATTEMPTS

digital video projection

DEVIL (bad Eve)

9 PLACES of SIN

black archive box, 9 35mm/digital video grabs/inkjet prints

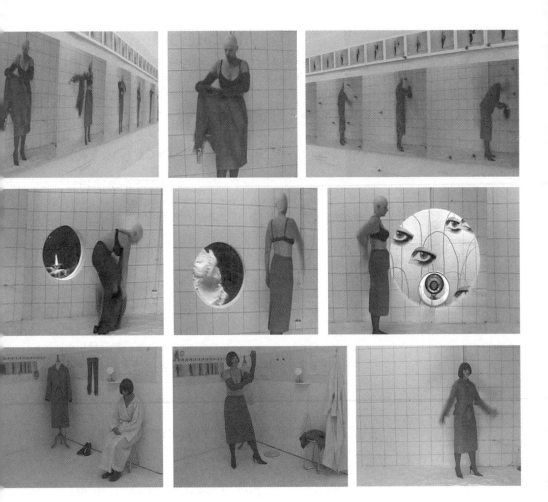

Act Two: Transformation

Exhibition prologue continues with photographic frieze,
object embellishments and three peep-box interruptions.
At the end the artist undergoes a further transformation,
assuming the role of The Director:
part animal, part human, part male, part female.
The mute hostess moving towards a zone between
the object and the final act of performance.

Act Three: Transcendence

A battle between The Director, The Actress and The Understudy,
the desire for the horizontal and the seduction of the curtain,
accidents and miracles, displays of wounds, dreams of damage
done by the tongue and the gun, a shadow with 'magic'
written on its eyelids and falling in reverse.

An accident at the crossroads between video and live presence.
A smash-up at the intersection of performance and the script.
A Director and Actress splayed across the dissecting table,
waiting for The Understudy to walk on and corpse.
A last supper for an audience of twelve intimates.

Personas

The Director
The Actress
The Understudy

A note on the notes

A suggested approach would be to read the whole text through once, ignoring the notes. Then read through a second time, referring to the notes if desired.

1. The Twelve Apostles, the Last Supper and Betrayal. 'You will all fall away because of me this night. You will deny me three times . . . after three days I will rise again' (The Bible).

The significance of the number 3 – various trinities: the Dunce, the Fool and the Devil; The Director, The Actress, The Understudy; the three acts of *Tran-Acts* and their place in Julia Bardsley's 'The Divine Trilogy'.

2. What is the accident? An extreme event, a necessary event, an event that leads to a precise moment of clarity – a place of shift, alteration, of becoming anew. The accident as the possibility of resurrection?

3. The flock – 'Feed my lambs, tend my sheep . . . ' (The Bible).

The Performance Text

Act Three: Transcendence

The audience of twelve[1] enter an ultra-violet, white-curtained chamber. There is a long black table with benches where the audience sit. At one end of the table is a TV monitor (this contains The Actress) and at the other end is The Director's chair. In the corner of the space is a small curtained stage.

The Director takes a piece of chalk from her mouth and writes: DIRECTOR *on the table. At the other end of the table, under the TV monitor, she writes:* ACTRESS. *She puts in the Day One video tape. The image of The Actress appears on the TV screen. She has a visible wound over one eye. Text delivered in shock and distress.*

Day One: (Accidents)[2]

Accident One

ACTRESS: I was in my car, driving pretty slowly. I had a splitting headache and all I wanted to do was get home and lie down. In front of me was a truck, transporting animals, sheep I think. My mobile rings and I go to pick it up off the passenger side. Then suddenly there's this screaming sound that seems to go on endlessly, then quiet. The next thing I know I'm being brought round by a medic or someone. They found me flat out, in the road, like this.

She demonstrates the position.

ACTRESS: I hurt all over. I mean, I was in a real bloody mess.

Actress, looking at The Director, out of acting mode.

ACTRESS: Was that the sort of thing you were after? (*Pause.*) I'd like to try it again.

The Director stands up and unzips the bulge in the front of her skirt. She pops out a little furry tail and pulls out a red velvet pouch, tipping the contents out on the table. They are tiny sheep.[3] During the next speech, she plays with the sheep on the table, arranging them.

Accident Two

The Actress is seen on the TV monitor, smoking. She delivers the lines in a deep, husky, seductive voice.

ACTRESS: I was in my Renault, driving pretty slowly. I'd just finished shooting and I had a splitting headache. It was my time of the month and I was feeling pretty awful. All I wanted to do was to get home and lie down, lie down in the dark. In front of me was a truck, transporting animals, sheep I think, or lambs. Strapped to the top was a metal fence or iron railing. Anyway, my mobile rings and I go to pick it up off the passenger side and it slips out of my hand and in that split second, it happens. There's a penetrating, screeching sound and then silence, everything in slow motion. Intense white light and then darkness. The next thing I know, I'm being bought round by the shepherd who's been driving the truck in front. I'm surrounded by bloody lambs and sheep bleating away. I'm splayed out in the road and it hurts like hell.

Blood gushing everywhere from my head, my arm, my side and my elbow, even my back. I'm in a real bloody mess.

Actress, looking at The Director. Out of acting mode.

ACTRESS: Look, do you think I could try it without the cigarette? The thing is, I'm not a smoker and they can always tell if you don't smoke . . .

The Director gathers up the sheep. During the next speech she puts them away in the red bag.

Accident Three

The Actress is seen on the TV monitor, with a glass of red wine in her hand. Extreme delivery – acting The Actress.

ACTRESS: I was in my new Mercedes Sports. I'd just finished shooting and I'd got an atrocious migraine. All I wanted to do was to get home, have a drink and lie down. In front of me is a truck transporting animals, sheep I think, or lambs, I don't know, bloody animals anyway. And my mobile rings. I go to pick it up. Now it's the time of the month so I'm not feeling my usual

4. 'I will strike the shepherd and the sheep of the flock will be scattered' (The Bible).

5. The Lamb = the sacrificial animal.

6. 'They shall look on him who they have pierced' (St John's Gospel).

7. The substitute, the stand-in, the carbon copy, the scapegoat – ripe for sacrifice. For more about the idea of the scapegoat see René Girard, *The Scapegoat* (Johns Hopkins University Press, 1986).

8. The sponge soaked in vinegar to quench the thirst of Jesus on the cross.

self, not feeling myself at all, and the bloody phone slips out of my hand and drops on the floor. I'm scrabbling around keeping one eye on the road and the other looking for the phone and in the back of my mind, part of me is thinking, this isn't going to have a happy ending. And at that moment there's this hideous screeching, a terrible scream that seems to go on endlessly, then utter silence. I feel like I'm floating, maybe even flying and there's this incredibly intense white light, then total blackness. The next thing I know, I'm being brought around by the fucking shepherd who'd been driving the lorry in front. I mean, he's standing over my broken body and says, 'I will strike the shepherd and the sheep of the flock will be scattered,'[4] or some such cryptic shit. I'm lying on the pavement, surrounded by bloody dead lambs[5] squashed all over the road, with sheep bleating in my ears, and I'm impaled by the iron railings. I mean, bloody great spikes piercing my flesh, making these enormous gaping wounds.[6] And then my understudy turns up out of the blue.

She picks up the glass.

ACTRESS: Thank God for body doubles.[7]

She drinks.

ACTRESS: Oh Christ! This tastes like bloody vinegar.[8]

She goes to put the glass down and it falls over.

ACTRESS: Oh, shit!

Sound of breaking glass, a car smash-up moving into sine waves, suspended mode. The image of The Actress on the monitor is in slow motion as the glass smashes.

The Director gets out the Falling Glass sequence, placing each part of the sequence on the table. She then chalks up ACCIDENT, with an arrow down one side of the table in the direction of the falling glasses and MIRACLE with an arrow on the other side in the direction of the glasses repairing themselves. She gets a real glass of wine, takes a sip and completes the image of the backward motion of the falling glass with her own glass of wine by placing it on the table to complete the 'miracle' sequence. The Actress ends up sipping her wine again.

ACTRESS: Sorry, where was I?

9. It could be another trinity – a female trinity: Grace, Eve or Mary.

But this is about a fall from grace.

10 and 11. The Five Wounds of Christ: two in the palms, two in the feet and one in the side. In this instance there is one under the eye, one on the elbow, one in the side, one in the forearm and one in the back.

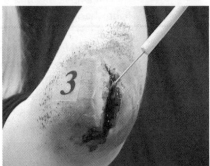

12. A reference to Lacan and the mirror stage of a child's development, relating to identity and the mirror; or it could be a reference to an actual stage that has a mirrored floor – like the one in Julia's production of *Hamlet*? (Young Vic, London, 1994).

Looking at her script to find her place.

ACTRESS: Look, what you just did there . . . Was that an accident or a
miracle? Well, I suppose you'd say it depends on direction . . .
and timing . . . time and space . . . You know, I always wanted
to be called Grace . . . [9]

*The Actress feels the wound points on her body, which are overlaid with forensic
stills of the wounds' entry-points.* [10]

*The Director puts the Falling Glass sequence on a shelf to the side of the table. She
gets a red arrow magnet, lifts up a disc out of the table. On the underside, written
in chalk is: 'Was there any damage to your hands and feet?'* [11] *She knocks on the
table to get The Actress's attention.*

ACTRESS: (*shaking her head and answering the written question*) No . . .
just one of those happy accidents I suppose.

She carries on drinking the wine and looks at the palms of her hands.

Transition:

*The Director goes to put on Miniature Spectacle CD. She starts to set up the
Miniature Spectacle. She turns off the main Director's light, brings over the
Anglepoise and switches it on. She uses a sucker tool to take out a circular mirror
from the table. She gets a small, revolving-mirror stage out of the drawer. She puts
the mirror on top of the stage, red velvet side up. The Actress watches The Director.*

ACTRESS: Look, is there a part in this for me? (*Pause, waiting for an
answer.*) I know all about the mirror stage . . . [12]

(*Still no response.*) Do you know who I am?

*The Director moves towards The Actress. The Actress follows, The Director switches
off the videotape. She turns up the volume on the CD and returns to the table for:*

The Miniature Spectacle

*The Director sets up a performance in miniature. She takes out a stand and puts it
on the table. She puts title cards on the stand and sets up the camera on the title
cards.*

13. An accident as part of the creative process.

14. The Director as Magician (again). Another reference to Julia's production of *Hamlet*, where The Director (Julia) played the role of a Magician – conjuring the piece into existence. An example of the willing suspension of disbelief.

15. The Angel as a body released through death – transcending the mortal, shedding the weight of the flesh, into weightlessness.

We read:

The Miniature Spectacle *on the TV monitor.*

She changes the card. Next card reads:

Day One: The Happy Accident[13]

From the drawer, The Director takes out medical scissors and a mouthpiece studded with pins. She uses the scissors to unzip an opening in her sleeve and pulls out a miniature figure of herself, a miniature Director with a video camera at her eye. She puts the figure on the stage. She puts the mouthpiece in her mouth and takes a miniature Actress out of her sleeve. She puts the pins into the red plasticine in the miniature Actress's body, mimicking the wound/entry-points described in the accident stories. She puts the Actress figure on to the stage and starts the revolve on the miniature stage. She trains the camera on the two miniature figures and films them. The close-up images are seen on the TV monitor as they turn on the stage.

The next title card reads:

Day Two: The Burial or The Horizontal

The Director puts the camera down and trains it on the next card. She stops the revolve, takes the miniature Director off and puts her in front on the table. She puts the Actress figure in the drawer. She turns the disc over with mirror side up. She takes a miniature table out of the drawer, pulls a miniature reclining Actress figure out of her sleeve and lays her on the table. She then pulls out a miniature white tablecloth and lays that over the body. She then uses her powers to make the table levitate.[14] When the table finishes levitating, she throws everything into the drawer.

The next title card reads:

Day Three: The Miracle or The Rising

The Director figure and the mirror are moved on to the table. The revolve stage is put in the drawer. The light is turned up and put under the table, throwing light up through a hole in the table. The Director pulls out a miniature glittered ladder and places it at the top of the hole in the table. She gets the camera and films herself pulling up a silver chain. On the end is a miniature angel figure[15] that ascends the ladder and flies through the air towards The Director. She puts the camera down and the angel sits on her hand. The Director goes into a reverie. Applause on the

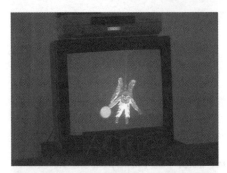

16. 'The body wrapped in a shroud and laid in a new tomb . . . ' (The Bible).

17. The power of the horizontal – a neglected or shunned plane. The view is more interesting down here. Perhaps an enforced fall from favour is a blessing in disguise?

18. For more about Eve see Pamela Norris, *The Story of Eve* (Picador, 1998).

19. 'Maybe humiliation brings wisdom. It enables us to see the world at grass level, in the dirt, on the horizontal. There is no place in this state of humiliation for vanity or judgement. And it is only when someone falls that someone else can learn to catch' (Anastasia Hille, from conversations with Julia Bardsley about acting, 2001).

20. The fight for the Fall. 'The fall is what is most alive in the sensation, that through which sensation is experienced as living. The intense fall can thus coincide with a spatial descent, but also with a rise.' Gilles Deleuze, *Francis Bacon: The Logic of Sensation* (Continuum, 1981).

21. Rewritten from Lucan, *Civil Wars*, Book VI, 563–8.

22 The Actress and forced speech, having to recite text and script that are other people's words, not her own.

Speaking in tongues = glossolalia. 'They will speak in new tongues . . . ' (St John's Gospel).

soundtrack breaks her out of her reverie. She shoves the angel into the drawer, gets the light from under the table and puts it back on the trolley. She staggers over to the VHS player and puts in the Day Two tape. She goes back and controls the volume as the video audio kicks in and the voice starts. During the next section of text, The Director clears away the rest of the Miniature Spectacle objects into the drawer.

Day Two: (Burial/Horizontal)[16]

The Actress is on the TV, feathers are falling. She falls into shot. She is lying on a red velvet cushion. She is half-asleep, in a dream world, horizontal.

ACTRESS: I keep wanting to lay down, to be horizontal,[17] it doesn't make sense, but maybe it's because I can't see the whole picture. Perhaps it's connected to humiliation – wanting to fall over for everyone to see, be in the dirt like Eve and then blamed for everything.[18, 19] The thing is, did she jump or was she pushed? Maybe it wasn't an accident after all. I have this sensation of falling, I want to fall, I can see things clearly. I'm horizontal again, it seems a good plane to be in . . . [20]

The Director gets up and starts to take piles of images out of four drawers in the table.

ACTRESS: I'm at a party. At the end of a long corridor is an old-fashioned elevator. I go up to the top floor, the doors open and I enter a dark bedroom. A man I know is asleep in a single bed. Suddenly I start to piss – great floods all over the floor. I desperately try to mop up the pee with towels but there's just too much of it. All I can think is that I mustn't forget to feed the animals.

            I'm at a friend's funeral and a woman bends over the dead body and while she's planting kisses on our dead friend's face, she mutilates the head and with her teeth opens up the tight closed mouth and bites off the tip of the tongue.[21] She pours mumbled secrets into the icy lips, she turns, the tip of the tongue still hanging from her mouth, she smiles and I see that the woman is me . . . I look at the body in the grave and see that the body is mine. I scream in a tongue not my own, speaking in tongues not my own.[22]

23. 'Spectacular corporeal displays; prostrations, convulsion, foaming at the mouth, the vomiting of pins and nails, levitation and ventriloquial forms of utterance.' From Steven Connor, *Dumbstruck* (Oxford UP, 2000).

24. 'Demonic possession came to replace religious ecstasy as the principal mode of access to spiritual transcendence.'

'It gives disease not only a name but a tongue, making it possible to converse with the disease itself' (from *Dumbstruck*, as in note 23).

25. Doubting Thomas – called the Twin (one of the disciples): 'Unless I see in his hands the print of the nails, and place my finger in the mark of the nails and place my hand in his side, I will not believe.' St Thomas's faith was renewed by entering through the wounds of Christ.

26. *'I'm Jealous of Jesus'* is the title of a song written by Angela Clerkin which featured in her show *The Dream Killers* (Drill Hall, London, 2004).

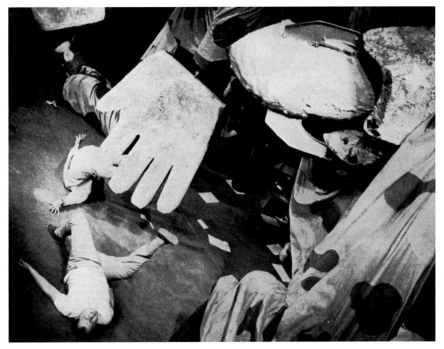

Above: the fall of the dummy soldier at the end of Act One of *US*.
Photo: Morris Newcombe / ArenaPAL.

Below: conjuring the spell in *A Girl Skipping*. Photo: Bob van Dantzig.

Above: *Hotel Methuselah*. Photo: Richard Malcolm.

Left and below: images from *Trans-Acts*
Photos: Julia Bardsley (left), Andrew
Poppy (below).

'What he wants of her / What she wants of him'. Scene from *Don Juan. Who? Don Juan. Kdo?* Photo: Žiga Karitnik.

Above: the recurring image of the 'accident pose' from *Miss America*. Photo: Lori E. Said.

Below: from the 2011 production of *48 Minutes for Palestine*. Photo: Taryn Burger.

There is some backwards talking on the soundtrack, which The Director mouths to. She starts to hang the separate parts of the levitation image on to the wall.

ACTRESS: I'm feeling free and liberated, in a short white summer dress, no shoes – there is a sandpit or dune. I run down into it and just lay in the sand feeling good. There are some parents and children playing in the pit. One boy comes up to me and rubs his muddy hands on my face and arms. I don't mind, I can wash it off. Something changes. I'm in the same sandpit, this time the child comes up and rubs something on my face and arms, it's not mud this time, it's dog shit. I have to find a way to clean it off. I remember my sister lives near by. I go back to her flat. She's hosting a party for Japanese businessmen. There's a camera crew and a stage management team. I just want to find the bathroom to wash the shit off. I go to the downstairs toilet. There are three girls in there, they say, 'Don't we know you?' I say, 'No.' I don't know what they're waiting for. They tease me, say they might have a bath or they might not. Then they say, 'Don't we know you?' I say, 'No.' Then one of the girls starts shaking, foams at the mouth and then vomits up pins and nails.[23] The second girl falls back on the floor, then levitates and utters, 'I am your disease, I have a tongue and can talk back.' The third girl says, 'Don't I know you?' I say 'No,' and go to the bathroom upstairs.[24]

The Director has finished the levitation image and comes to the end of the table. She works with the text, relating it to the room and the pocket in her jacket.

ACTRESS: I'm in a shop, I ask the assistant where I'd find the wine glasses. She warns me, says they're very expensive and then points to a hole in the wall. I'm in a circular room draped in heavy red curtains. There is an old woman with long nails sitting in some mud, saying, 'I don't believe it, I can't believe my eyes,' and a small boy called Thomas with blood on his hands, stroking her side.[25] I pull back one of the curtains and look behind it. I think I see my understudy. I can't be sure, but something from the dark emerges, a shadow with magic written on its eyelids. In the corner is a small stage and I see an angel, singing a song called 'I'm Jealous of Jesus'.[26] I say to her, 'Those side stages are a place for a sad song or a saint's humiliation.' Then a performance begins.

27. Is this a desire to return to a state of not knowing, of a lack of self-consciousness, away from the critical, self-seeing eye – to be free of the disapproving conscience?

28. See notes 10 and 11.

29. An alternative image of the crucifixion – a piercing of the tongue, to wound the tongue and render it unable to speak (the truth) and deliver the Word. The tongue seen as a weapon of some kind.

30. The linen shroud that covers the body in the burial – the horizontal curtain.

I was caught between two stories, listening to a force that seized me. I wish I was there again. Where did that moment go? I want to return to the imaginary stage.[27]

On the video we see The Actress on a small side stage, showing off her wounds. The Director goes to the CD player and changes the CD ready for a performance.

The music cuts in loud. The Director turns on the stage spotlight and enters the corner stage. She turns on the mirror ball and opens the curtains.

She starts her performance. Showing off her wounds.[28] She turns and pulls down the zip on her back. The back panel is lined with fur and houses a metal spike. She pulls out the spike and takes an image of The Actress. She puts the spike through the face of The Actress. She then performs 'The Spike through the Tongue' routine.[29] Applause ends the track, she turns off the mirror ball and staggers off the stage. She turns off the spotlight and turns down the music volume.

ACTRESS: I'm making a show, sitting in an auditorium. A spotlight comes on and follows a baby crawling across the stage. I think, what a fantastic moment. Everybody claps. Offstage, babies are crying. Suddenly they stop. I know this is my cue. I pull a rope and thousands of objects fall from the flies. They are babies' heads. I recognise every single face. The last head comes towards me with an open mouth.

The Director goes to the end drawer and takes out a white tablecloth.[30] She lays it along the top of the table and throws cords attached to the cloth down to the other end of the table. During the next piece of text, sitting at her seat at the head of the table, she pulls the tablecloth towards her until it covers the whole table.

ACTRESS: We've been given free tickets to a show called *Raid Me*. It's happening on a TV set, not in a theatre. The set is very modern, plastic, moulded and clean. An older rough guy, a bad actor with a dog, is eating dry Rice Krispies. The Director is telling him off. The set is a kitchen with a sliding door and there's a theatre trick with the stairs. I think it's not very good, Christian says it's terrible, typical small-scale touring. We help strike the set, but don't know if the bins are part of it. Should we empty the rubbish or is it a prop? It's difficult to know what to throw away and what to keep.

31. An observation. There is more Judas in my name than Jesus.

```
1 2    4
J U D A S
1 2    4
J U L I A
1      2
J E S U S
```

32. The Camera as: the Eye, the I, the Ego, a Hole, a Wound, a Vagina, a Mouth, a Weapon, a Gun or a Tongue.

33. The Mirror: an object central to the realm of transformation – for use as a self-portrait – reflecting back the image of The Director. Used to examine the self or in this case as a shield or defence against the camera/gun.

I'm in a rectangular room lined with fragile white curtains. In the middle of the room is a long banqueting table laid with bread and wine and there are twelve people sitting at the table and they look at me and they point at me and they all say, 'Are you Judas or are you Jesus?'[31] They expect something from me. I'm standing in front of them, naked, but I've forgotten my lines. I try and speak, to explain that I'm not an actress but nothing comes out. I have things to say but my throat is dried out.

The video cuts to a view of The Actress from her feet. She looks up and talks to the camera.

ACTRESS: Look, whose dreams are these? They're certainly not mine. I think they're yours. You're meant to be helping me, for Christ's sake, not projecting your own neuroses on me. I've got enough problems of my own without having to deal with yours, thank you very much.

The video cuts to overhead view of The Actress.

ACTRESS: You know, the only reason that that cloth isn't called a curtain is because it's flat, horizontal, not vertical. The plane is the difference between the same object being understood as one thing or something else. As one thing or someone else.

The video moves into the film sequence:

'WHAT'S BEHIND THE CURTAIN?'

The Director and The Actress meet each other in a white-curtained room. They embrace and kiss.

We see The Director with a camera[32] and The Actress with a mirror.[33]

34. A repetition of the wounds – the wounds of Christ echoed, repeated.

35. The ritual murder of the self – the destruction of the familiar identity in order to be free to move somewhere else.

36. A reproduction of the levitation image of the pinhole photograph constructed on the wall in the previous section, and as seen in Act One: Transgression. Levitation as a miracle and an act of healing – The Director plays the role of God?

37. A reference to René Girard, *A Theatre of Envy* (Oxford UP, 1991).

38. Haptic: to touch, the possibility of seeing or a type of vision distinct from the optical.

39. The piece has a dual function. The Director wants to make the audience see something, to construct an experience for them, and at the same time wants something to be made clear or verified for herself.

Then *The Director's camera turns into a gun. She shoots The Actress and we see blood in her eyes and bullet wounds in both the palms of her hands.[34] She falls to the ground.[35]*

The Director appears and performs a levitation on The Actress, who rises,[36] but at the same time is transformed into The Understudy (Julia). The Actress and Director have disappeared, leaving The Understudy, who exits from the scene.

During this, The Director has folded up the tablecloth and moved towards the TV. At the end of the video sequence, she tries to capture the figure on the screen with her hands.

She then puts on the DAY THREE *videotape. The image of The Actress comes up, looking directly to camera. She is angry. The Director takes a knife and fork from the drawer, turns over the mirror and starts to look at herself in it.*

Day Three: (Ascent)

ACTRESS: Can I ask a question? (*No reply.*) Is this a theatre of envy?[37] The thing is, I've got no idea what I'm involved in here. You've got to fill in some details for me – you know, is it a film, a play, or am I just making an exhibition of myself? If you ask me, I think you've lost the plot. Who dunnit? I don't give a toss. I was framed and you're to blame.

(*Indicating to the audience.*) I know what you're trying to do. You want to make them see something.[38] At the same time you want something to be revealed for yourself.[39] You're so selfish! What about me? I mean, why am I stuck in here and you out there? Is it because you've given yourself a more interesting costume? Yes, that's exactly it. God, I don't even get to have the best costume any more. Your vanity's getting the better of you. You should have caught me, but you were distracted by the light and couldn't see to save me. Which side of the veil are you on anyway? Speak up, I can't hear you.

The Director puts the mirror up to The Actress.

40. This is a notion plucked from Wittgenstein. My interpretation is that it's about moving away from the simplistic 'either/or' mechanisms of discourse. In this context it relates to not having to make a choice between being one type of artist in opposition to another – allowing the possibility of being many things, working in multiple forms.

41. 'We have seen ventriloquial women. As they sit, a little voice is heard to issue from their genitals and respond to questions . . . they give rise to terrible errors and incredible calamities' (*Dumbstruck*: see note 23).

42. 'You should be suspicious of happy endings.' This is a quote from Fay Weldon, heard while listening to the radio.

ACTRESS: I don't even trust that that reflection's reliable any more.
              Look, it's simple, all I need to know is if this story's about an
              angel or a devil, an ascent or a fall?

There is the sound of laughter. The Director trains the light from the mirror along the wall, to the corner, out of which comes a voice.

PUPPET DIRECTOR: The title of the piece is, 'Transcendence'.

The Director moves towards the corner.

ACTRESS: Then it's about an angel?

PUPPET: Not necessarily. An ascent is just a backward fall, a fall is just
              an ascent in reverse. We can't know what it is until we've met
              it face to face. And even then it's not necessarily a question of
              'either'/'or'.[40]

The Director pulls back the white curtains and reveals the Puppet Director. She takes The Puppet down from the wall, brings her to the table and sits her on her knee. The Director manipulates the Puppet Director, as in a ventriloquist's act.[41]

ACTRESS: Does it have a happy ending?

PUPPET: You should be suspicious of happy endings. Someone once said
              that all that consoles is fake.[42]

ACTRESS: I think fake is underrated. I don't see the problem if it makes
              you feel better.

PUPPET: It's over.

ACTRESS: What's over?

PUPPET: The audition.

ACTRESS: And did I get the part?

PUPPET: No, you didn't in the end.

ACTRESS: Well, who did?

PUPPET: Your understudy.

43. The shadow = the understudy.

44. 'The disembodied voice lets slip things we don't want to reveal about ourselves' (from *Dumbstruck*: see note 23).

45. Referring to the images and objects in Acts One and Two, made and presented by Julia Bardsley.

46. The stigmata of repetition – either through the rehearsal period and/or during a long run of a play.

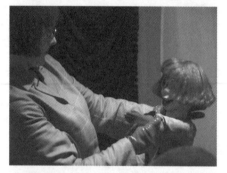

ACTRESS: My understudy?

PUPPET: Yes, she did the most illuminating reading while you were
              gone, full of life and truth. So authentic. It captivated me in a
              way that no other performance has done. A rare moment of
              light and beauty that went beyond the ordinary, into a magical
              place where we willingly suspended our disbelief. I was
              entranced, under a spell. She rendered visible and provoked
              sensation with a force so overwhelming it took my breath
              away. She screamed at death and shattered the glass, so chaos
              was let loose, but slaughter turned to laughter and the shadow
              smiled.[43]

ACTRESS: What are you saying? I could have done the same if I'd been
              given a little help, some encouragement, some proper direction
              and insight into the role. I mean, look at the obstacles you put
              in my way, you sabotaged my chances with this cheap wig. All
              I needed was a decent wig and bloody nails and eyelashes that
              stayed stuck on. How could an audience be fooled by this
              charade? Even this is fake, a piece of costume jewellery
              (*indicating her bracelet*). How could I ever be convincing under
              these conditions?

PUPPET: Believe me. I'm as sick of this as you are. I want to give up,
              disappear, surrender to something outside of myself, get some
              chaos in the equation.[44]

The Puppet turns to The Director and directs everything now to her.

PUPPET: (*laughter*) Give me your mouth, kiss me, kiss me. I am your
              mirror, you broke the glass. Violence will have an object and
              the object will speak back. (*Laughter.*) You're responsible, you
              made those filthy images of lips with metal and animal pushing
              through the folds. You displayed shards of bone and ripped
              flesh.[45] You put words into her mouth (*referring to The
              Actress*), made her say those things against her will, do those
              things night after night. Repeating, repeating, leaving her body
              battered and bruised.[46] She sacrificed everything for you, you
              warped, sick, sad fucker!

47. The mouth as an anus – a dirty mouth delivering profanities.

48. The Director silences The Puppet. 'Violence enacted on the dummy (puppet) is a violence enacted on the performer himself. The dummy is in fact a prosthetic part of the performer's own body. Disobedience of the dummy demands punishment, to be locked away. But it is not enough to punish, to discipline, the dummy must be annihilated.' On the film *Magic* (from *Dumbstruck*: see note 23).

49. I did indeed want to have a live animal in the piece originally. I thought I could borrow a goat from Surrey Quays City Farm but the practicalities of this made it difficult. Perhaps I should have been more tenacious, followed my desire and just dealt with the consequences.

50. 'Art I suppose is only for beginners or else for those resolute dead-enders who have made up their minds to be content with the ersatz of suchness, with symbolism rather than with what they signify, with the elegantly composed recipe in lieu of actual dinner' (Aldous Huxley).

51. The stab in the back – mimesis and mimetic desire – jealousy and envy. The ritual sacrifice of the substitute.

For more about mimetic rivalry see René Girard, *Violence and the Sacred* (Athlone Press, 1988).

52. 'Actresses never die!' – a quote from The Writer in the film *All About Eve*, a classic take on mimetic desire and mimetic rivalry.

53. As an Actress, she is never herself, she is always other.

(*Putting her red-gloved puppet hand to her mouth.*) Oh, dear. I've been a naughty foul-mouthed girl.[47] Wash my mouth out with soap, stand me in the corner, hold out my hand, pull down my pants and over your knee.

(*Shouting.*) Go on! Punish me! Punish me! What are you afraid of?

The Director puts her hand over The Puppet's mouth to stop her talking and throws her on the grass circle that's on the floor in the corner. She takes the knife from the table and starts to cut at The Puppet, cutting out her tongue.[48] (The tongue is a real piece of meat – an ox tongue.) She takes the tongue to the table and slaps it down on the mirror. She starts to carve it with the knife and fork.

ACTRESS: I know you wanted a live animal in this show, I read it in the original script.[49] You wanted a goat or a lamb but you couldn't cope with all the piss and shit that would create, so you found a substitute. Real, dead, flesh. You're just using that for effect, tying to be shocking in a desperate attempt to be authentic. Well, it doesn't work. We've seen it all before. You can't just slap down a piece of meat and expect everyone to be jolted into some sort of appreciation of The Real. It doesn't even look real. Inject some colour into it, get props to juice it up, spray on some glycerine and you might even get them to think that that lump of flesh is crying real tears![50]

(*Laughing.*) What you're looking for isn't dead you know. It's just very, very quiet. (*Laughing.*) Turn the volume up, you fucker!

The Director takes the knife and runs round to the back of the TV and stabs The Actress/TV. The Actress gasps and falls forward with the knife sticking out of her back.[51] The Director stabs the tongue with the fork and puts it in the fish bowl, laughing. She goes back to the table, looks at her reflection in the mirror. On the TV The Actress, with the knife in her back, lifts up her head, smiling.

ACTRESS: (*laughing*) Actresses never die![52] I'm not feeling quite myself at the moment.[53] (*She moves the wig about on her head.*) The audition is over! Actresses never die! (*More hysterical laughter.*)

54. Is The Director (Julia), who represents spectacle, having a battle with The Actress (also Julia) to become the shadow or The Understudy, who represents sensation? May this represent the violence of spectacle versus the violence of sensation? Based on an idea of Gilles Deleuze in *Francis Bacon: The Logic of Sensation* (Continuum, 1981).

Is this a struggle with oneself about who one is expected to be, who one wants to be, or thinks one wants to be, and a true, authentic version of oneself? The Director wants (desires) to be The Actress. The Actress wants (desires) to be The Director. The Understudy wants (desires) it all and gets it all.

55. A suicide or a murder – obliteration or disappearance is the desired outcome and seems necessary to prompt change, to transcend.

During this The Director pulls off her glasses, tugs off her gloves and takes off her jacket and shoes. She grabs the chalk and starts to write on the table:

DAY 1 — CRUXI-FICTION

DAY 2 — BURIAL

DAY 3 — ASCENT

She takes off her skirt and climbs on the table, drawing around her body with the chalk. She gets off the table and puts crosses on the chalk body where the five wounds are — the eye, the elbow, the back, the side, the crotch. She writes an equation with a triangle — D, A, U at each point of the triangle and TRANS across it.[54] She puts her red shoes, red PVC gloves, jacket and skirt on the table, in the shape of a body. She goes to the end of the table and in chalk writes:

BLOOD = WINE

BREAD = FLESH

She then chalks 'I, EYE' and an arrow in the direction of the circular mirror that's on the table. She sees herself in the mirror and starts to pull off her wig. Tears start to fall down her cheeks as she sheds the final traces of The Director from her body.

She looks towards the TV. The Actress has transformed into the image of the angel in white that we saw in the Miniature Spectacle. This is The Understudy (Julia) who is reaching towards The Director, and The Director is finally released.[55]

She looks round the room, at the Puppet lying in the corner, the ripped photo of The Actress, the tongue in the fish bowl, the levitation image on the wall. She walks backwards and leaves the room through the white curtains. On the TV, the room in which everything for Trans-Acts was filmed and made is revealed.

for
Stuart Bardsley
1926 - 1978

The end credits roll:

Performance, text, filming, editing, objects and images by Julia Bardsley

Music by Andrew Poppy

The Directors' costumes made by Sonja Harms

Table and benches made by Allscene, Allprops

Miniature figures made by Aldona Cunningham

with special thanks to: Andrew Poppy for audio advice, backwound assistance and support throughout the project, Wayne Lucas and CBA Studios, Melanie Smith and NESTA, Gus at Photo Fusion, Al Binks for ventriloquist's dummy, Anastasia Hille and Angela Clerkin for inspiration, Simon Vincenzi for advice and moral support, and the Bardsley Family.

For STUART BARDSLEY 1926–1978

The Understudy (Julia), dressed in white (like the angel in the Miniature Spectacle) comes into the space carrying a tray of glasses filled with red wine. She gives a glass of wine to each of the twelve members of the audience at the table.

THE END

With thanks to my first audience, who feature in these photographs:

Simon Vincenzi, Sonja Harms, Ann Gent, Martin Gent, Aldona Cunningham, Chrissy Stewart, Lee Robson, Wayne Lucas, Anastasia Hille, Glyn Perrin, Geraldine Pilgrim and Andrew Poppy on camera.

Touchstones for *Trans-Acts*

Visual Artists:
Cindy Sherman, Matthew Barney, Joel-Peter Witkins, Francis Bacon,
Cathy de Monchaux

Film-Makers:
Hans-Jürgen Syberberg, David Lynch, Ulrike Ottinger, Federico Fellini

Films:
Persona, All About Eve, Magic

Fashion Designers:
Hussein Chalayan, Junya Watanabe, Rei Kawakubo

Performance Makers:
Robert Wilson, Elizabeth LeCompte, Jan Fabre

Writers:
René Girard, Gaston Bachelard, Gilles Deleuze (on Bacon), Lewis Hyde,
Mikhail Bakhtin, Julia Kristeva

Further Reading:
'The Skin of the Theatre: An Interview with Julia Bardsley by Dominic Johnson',
Contemporary Theatre Review, Volume 20, No. 3, August 2010

'Genre-bending Performance', review of *Trans-Acts* by Jennie Klein, *PAJ:
A Journal of Performance and Art*, Volume 28, No. 1, 2005, pp. 58–66 (p. 64)

Digtal Resources:
Foolish Suicide Attempts from Trans-Acts (DVD)
SPILL Festival of Performance 2007 (DVD)
NRLA Thirtieth Anniversary Boxed Set – Books and DVDs
Featured in SPILL Festival of Performance: On Agency
all available from: unbound (www.thisisunbound.co.uk)

Web Links:
www.thisisliveart.co.uk/resources/Study_Room
www.juliabardsley.net
www.myspace.com/juliabardsley
www.vimeo.com/popbardprojects

*Additional material available at the Live Art Development Agency
study room*

Don Juan. Who?
/
Don Juan. Kdo?

a co-production
of Anna Furse, Athletes of the Heart (UK)
and Mladinsko Theatre (Slovenia)

Don Juan. Who? / Don Juan. Kdo?

FROM CYBERSPACE TO THEATRE SPACE

Like so many things we make, this project began with the smallest of ingredients – a word and a hunch. 1997: in conversation with Željko about men and war and sexual politics, I learnt the word *inat*, that translates among other things as 'pugnacious male stubborn pride' – the stuff of warmongering. Our dialogues subsequently continued in the cyberspace that was beginning to take root in all our ordinary lives. I was then struck by the effect this virtual space might have on our sense of who we are as presences for each other, and how ideas of gender might shift as we evolve with new technology. The idea for *Don Juan. Who?* took root.

The next step was the creation of our private cyberstudio, intended to mimic all the requisites of an ideal theatre base: studio, reflective space, and research archive. I cast and then invited the geographically dispersed company to meet here regularly to explore themes of men and masculinity via the different range of archetypes. Each week I would set a theme and writing structure, then sit back and enjoy the dissolution of my directorial guidance – for the most part, only occasionally stepping in and identifying myself to refocus the work. There was a certain pleasure (that Hélène Cixous has called *jouissance* – an untranslatable word combining joy and orgasm) in this collective, anonymous writing process. As words tumbled in front of our eyes, we learnt to hide in the screen, to nest, to flirt, to challenge, to argue, to flaunt, to cry and laugh 'out loud', to cheat, to lie and, most vitally, to masquerade and mimic each other in an environment in which there was, by design, no gender stability. Most of us admit to metaphoric cross-dressing. Many have now forgotten our individual authorship, such was the writing-pleasure-trance that we plunged into, losing ourselves as cyborgs for a brief hour or two each week. We collaborated in building our text, its poetry and its rhythms by removing censors and allowing ourselves to be interrupted by the unpredictable timing of words becoming visible as dictated by our on-screen tool. We learnt to play with interruption. We became, accidentally, a chorus.

In the summer of 2006 we met for the first time as a company and read some raw material out loud. Surprise! We'd written words worth speaking, words that had theatrical potential. In the end we had 500 pages to press into dramaturgical shape. We eventually began rehearsals in a unique way, holding in our hands a text we had voiced together, perhaps a new version of collective creation. But this was a text without characters, plot or narrative arc. That had to be sought in rehearsal. And so this text was in fact not a performative text at all but a trigger for embodiments, interaction, *jeu* – that French word for the game you are playing in theatrical action.

The text you can read here is therefore the eventual score we made of this combination of words on the page and how action and physical scenography evolved from it, in a process of imaginative logic. You will note that there are no stable Don Juans in the text, nor his conquests; because the piece is exploring how he is working through everyone on stage – 'the Don Juan in our minds' and, ergo, our bodies.

If we began with an idea for a work that would be about (Balkan) Men/Warriors, what did we come to? Something else of course. Our performance was certainly more generic, more messy, intimate and personal. A piece made of pieces of all of us, of the self-conscious exploration of our experiences and fantasies of Don Juanisms – not only seducer and *puer aeternus* but existential anti-hero. I was inviting us to confront: What is the mechanism of the Don Juan narratives? What's he made of? What's he jumping away from? What is freedom? How do women feel about men today and vice versa? We wrestled with this from all sides, culturally, imaginatively, confessionally, psycho-analytically. 'How can I have an authentic feeling in this culture?' one of us complained online – and that provoked Damjana Černe to create a scene of powerless frustration that ends with her biting her own arms in rage. If we are made of so many received and mediated ideas, are we also, maybe, making love? . . .

In the final, staged version, we return to The Scene more than once: a silver-screen cliché of seduction and abandonment set round a restaurant rendezvous. Around this are coiled other emotions and conflicts within ourselves and with the opposite (sex). For our Don Juan actually doesn't exist and nor does She. As He says in the end, he's a construct, but a construct nonetheless that, despite any sexual-political changes in the last decades, manages to survive in millions of website fantasies and, as we've discovered, lurking somewhere perhaps in all of us. The rest is a history germane to a co-production across two countries each with distinct theatrical traditions, political backgrounds, cultures, funding systems, audiences, artistic formations, rehearsal approaches, and of course language (on stage in Slovenia actors have to speak the formal version of the language and the theatre employs a consultant for this). Our collaboration survived many obstacles, not the least funding pressures. We never lost our nerve, or the integrity of how this project needed to evolve, over time, with the right kind of laboratory conditions in both cyber – and real – space.

The entire project was an experiment in collaboration today. I was privileged to work with an ensemble of outstanding performers – brave, physically inexhaustible, imaginatively alive, intellectually rigorous – who took responsibility for themselves and for the creation as a whole. Crucially, our cyberspace tool afforded a long gestation both in research (we wrote for eighteen months) and devising, an opportunity theatre artists crave and that is imperative for experimentation .

Our governments are withdrawing support for culture to an alarming degree. As I write this Arts Council England is talking of which puppies to drown. Theatre is seriously threatened. Forced to reinvent ourselves, co-operation such as ours might become not only desirable but also imperative. We have much to learn from working together, for it is in the pragmatics of everyday production that we discover the precise details of our differences and how to grapple together for a common purpose.

I wish to thank every individual artist, manager, translator, dramaturg, producer, administrator, technician, seamstress and cleaner in both countries who participated in bringing *Don Juan. Who?* to life. And I hope that as a reader now of our text you might find even a small part of yourself and the Don Juan in your own imagination in our work.

Anna Furse, London 2010

A WORKING MANIFESTO FOR THE COMPANY

- Theatre is poetry
- Physical theatre is a state of mind
- The terms 'dance' and 'theatre' become meaningless distinctions when the performer is embodied, expressive and scenographic
- We will thus call our work 'theatre' though to some it will seem more like dance or dance-theatre and we will not care for the definitions
- The actor is a creative artist
- Language is visceral
- Characters are formed on stage in front of the audience
- We have to manifest our differences
- We have to manifest our similarities
- The Chorus is a perfect strategy for ensemble ethics
- The Chorus of individuals struggling for consensus is a model of democracy
- We are always representing and showing that we are playing at pretending
- No theatrical illusion that isn't at the same time prepared to reveal its mechanisms
- No decor, only scenography
- From the functional and the essential the poetry of the theatre is forged
- Resist the literal. Look instead for how our minds are really working
- Be prepared to sweat, jump, run, fall, cry, be naked
- Love irony
- Strategy: seduce the audience, letting them know all the while that you know and they know what's going on
- Let the body reveal the subtext
- Let the imagination run riot
- Find the passion
- Enjoy the joke
- Play the game
- Learn the cha-cha

Anna Furse, May 2007

THE VIRTUAL GYM

Through the numerous conversations with Anna about the project *Don Juan. Who?* it soon became clear that it would have two phases, the virtual and 'the real'. The virtual space had to be a space where we could meet regardless of the geographical dispersal of each member, because the ensemble would be international. So I worked on the logistics for the construction of this virtual gym, which consisted of three elements: an open-coded program called upstage; a kind of virtual stage that enables the ensemble to meet either in the form of avatars, which move on the 'stage'–screen, or to be present only in the dialogue box and completely anonymous. In the beginning we also considered using webcams, but as it turned out they were unnecessary. The second element to make up our password-protected virtual space were the wiki pages, where everyone could publish their written contributions, commentaries, add internal or external links – basically a space intended for work in between our live sessions. The third element was a sort of a common limbo, an archive where we stored the saved material from all our live writing sessions, including visual material, reference articles and documents in their uncut form. This virtual studio was completed in the autumn of 2005. Our first sessions were exciting and invigorating. We were like a bunch of kids in a strange new playground for which the laws and rules had yet to be invented. The ensemble's computer skills varied greatly, but with time everybody improved.

The core of our research together was without a doubt upstage: initially the onscreen space in which we entered as avatars (which one chose or created oneself and where one could change the background and props), in which we sometimes found ourselves all together, and that was a lot of fun. But it actually turned out that the most important medium for us was the dialogue box, where each of us could be present in word form. The word is my body as I enter into the screen. The word signals my point of view, my emotional state, my view of the world.

> *as I touch the keys, I jump into darkness*
> *as I touch the keys, I feed myself*
> *a new form of a lonely nearness*
> *when I touch the keys, I am not I*
> *my flesh melts, evaporates and I am only words*
> *when I touch the keys, I realise, that through them I can only*
> *express fragments of my thoughts and emotions*
> *to touch is to echo, the touch is a word and different from a word*
> *it tells stories, feelings, longings . . .*

From the twenty-fourth live writing session,
29 September 2006

Words flowed through the screen, sometimes frenetically, sometimes recklessly, sometimes just poised on the lookout, when only the cursor pulsed into nothing and announced the next torrent of words. The emotional charge one could feel from the rhythm of repeated words or the 'silence' – that is, the absence of words – was incredible. The stream of words was the collective result of our presence, without a guide to guide us. Everybody had to be prepared for constant adaptation and had to let their thoughts be forced into another direction, contrary to their original intention. This openness and readiness to subsume your ego for the collective together with the technology of writing itself (where words fall into a common stream with a slight time-shift, forming unexpected meanings) produced a new alloy composed of ten points of view.

For everybody involved it was a remarkable experience and a test. It wasn't always easy because none of us had ever ventured to write a play online before. And not everybody stayed the course . . . By the end of the eighteen-month research period we ended up with a mountain of words. Five hundred pages of a verbal diarrhoea amid which diamonds shone. Even during the group sessions Anna and I were sifting the material. An analogy with sifting river mud in gold mining seems appropriate. The mountain was shrinking: from the first sifting we got to 327 pages of material with great potential. The second sifting yielded 202 pages of a structure without dialogue. In the final phase of the working draft we held in our hands seventy-five pages of text. This was our starting point when we entered into the 'real' space. We knew that the text would have to be cut no matter how painful such an operation might get. After seven weeks of rehearsals, we held in our hands, but already in our minds, forty-seven pages. Approximately 10 per cent of everything that we wrote. A 10 per cent outcome, then. Not bad, not bad, as Don Juan would say.

The process of co-mingling in virtual space as we wrote together, in a very special way, connected all the participants. The virtual space was a global reference area, the beginning of a dynamic dramatic process, the search for a word that might articulate your thoughts, the possibility of becoming someone else, to use masks and mimicry: the basic tools of acting used through the microcosm of the word. This collective experience has continued *via* different means in the search for a theatrical form in 'real' space, where physical action substitutes for psychology as a foundation from which the word can spring.

Željko Hrs, Ljubljana, July 2007

COMING TOGETHER WITH DON JUAN

In Japanese Buddhism there is an expression, *itai doshin*, that embodies the central aspiration for the creation of a truly democratic society. It roughly translates as 'many in body, one in mind'. The many in body celebrates the unique individuality that we all possess, the one in mind – that we might also, by respecting each other's uniqueness, search together for the central life-affirming values that we can all celebrate. It is a direct challenge to the duality that still dominates so much of Western philosophy – the split between the 'existential' and 'essential', the individual versus society, Good versus Evil, and Us versus Them.

The dream of all this 'coming together' is what in theatre we call ensemble. When ensemble occurs, the model of life for all of us is revealed and the dualities fall away. And somehow our hearts are touched. Of course it is rare, and difficult to attain. But the challenge is there. How do we come, without sacrifice or compromise, to one mind? As I'm a playwright, you'd expect me to say the initial creation of a 'text' is the heart, the magnet, the central inspiration, which it is hoped will draw the company together. And of course I will! But an equally challenging way to work is to enter on the epic journey of the collective piece. The project *Don Juan. Who?* set off with the most challenging of desires: to build bridges between artists across the cultural and linguistic divides, and to focus on one of the most provocative of our common myths – that of the priapic man himself – the expression of a force that permeates all our histories. And, courageously, to leave open what the final meaning might be, to enter into unknown territory. Literally. The group dived into the myriad possibilities of cyberspace, exploring the dangerous freedom of a medium where players could hide, and risk, create and re-create themselves – the modern equivalent of Don Juan's masque balls. There were the first sightings of a text of great integrity and wit, and then, in the next stage, the courageous meeting face to face, words fusing with a newfound physicality of expression as gradually fragments of potential meaning or rather pulses towards deeper imaginings began to surface. A process at all times of uncertainty, since initial certainty would not have been a true journey, holding out the possibility of only fixed traditional destinations.

Don Juan is a significant journey for all of us, including most centrally we the audience. What this work has envisaged demands to be shared. And in that desire there lies at heart a belief that we can communicate with each other, that there is hope – and that perhaps even, if only for a time, we, makers and witnesses, can become one together. And perhaps that old devil Don Juan can take us all on his legendary horse and gallop us into unknown hills, and unimagined cities.

Stephen Lowe, Nottingham, July 2007

THE PERFORMERS ON THE DON JUAN PROJECT

In my body and voice I am Doña Juana, I speak, feel and seduce as Doña Juana. I'm a double personality: simultaneously the seducer and the seduced. It seems to me that it is sometimes useful to look through the eyes of our specimen, and then maybe we can comprehend and see what they see.

Damjana Černe

Here we are thankfully far from the established paradigm of twenty-first-century theatre where it is assumed that 'good text/good actors' are enough and where direction and experimentation are doomed. We continue to persist instead, as Nietzsche would say, 'to have the courage to be unfit for one's own time'.

Marko Mlačnik

'The Don Juan in my mind' revealed herself/himself ripe in contradictions, challenging my 'politically correct' self-held notions of sexual relations: desire versus reason, control versus surrender, freedom versus responsibility. Don Juan: a demonic threat to status quo, an enemy to the possessed and the possessor, an irritant to people like myself seeking security in the known? How do I make this story of Don Juan my own? I begin to see how the clichés lie locked in my own physicality.

Tanya Myers

For me every man is Don Juan, 'until he is proved innocent'. What does this quote from our text mean? Am I guilty just by being? Do I have to fall in love with every woman that happens to slip into my bed? What about those who walked out on me? This happens. It's happened sometimes, to me and to my friends. Do those women have to prove something as well? All different, all equal. 'Stop the heart!'

Matej Recer

Don Juan. Who? represents for me the dilemma of the settled versus the nomadic instinct in the human being. Our Don Juan's 'crying for beauty' is the painful perception of the volatility of perfection and his consequent escape from it as soon as it manifests itself, before it decays, obsessively galloping towards the next desperate evasion from the life cycle: mutation, death, transformation . . .

Giovanna Rogante

I interpret Don Juan as the free spirit of anarchy, desire, radicalism that exists in each of us regardless of gender. Through his image I find the empowerment to live my life as I want to live it and not as how others/society expect us to live it.

Marie-Gabrielle Rotie

The production of *Don Juan. Who? / Don Juan. Kdo?* is available on DVD from www.arts-archives.org/cat10.htm

For further information about the research and production see www.genderforum.org/issues/ and visit: www.athletesoftheheart.org

DON JUAN LEGEND AND TEXTS

Don Juan is a legendary fictional libertine, whose story has been retold by authors of plays, poems, novels, operas and films over five centuries. The name is used figuratively as a synonym for 'womaniser', and thousands of websites will attest to the idea of a Don Juan as a virile seducer. As an existential anti-hero he represents Man for whom conventional morality and religious authority hold no sway, hence his irrepressible need to escape marriage and reproduction. Psycho-analytically he is the *puer aeternus* (eternal boy) who can never let intimacy mature into relationship and who has a compulsion to keep returning to the seduction game (repetition neurosis) where he can replay out his opening moves, always in control. He arguably survives most vigorously in contemporary popular culture as James Bond, a high-tech version of the swashbuckling hero – sexy, adventurous, invincible – *and always on the move*.

In the Don Juan legend, he seduces (or rapes) a young noblewoman and kills her father. Later, he invites this man's posthumous stone statue to dine with him. The statue/ghost-father agrees, then appearing as the harbinger of Don Juan's death. The statue offers to shake Don Juan's hand, and thereupon drags him to Hell. There Don Juan meets The Devil, who tells him that everyone in Hell is cast in a role, and presents him with a Jester's suit, telling him that he would make an excellent fool. Don Juan, insulted, protests that he is unrivalled as a man who has made a thousand sexual conquests. Intrigued by this claim, The Devil tells him that if he can correctly name one conquest, he would not have to wear the suit. Thus begins a parade of women not one of whom Don Juan can name correctly. Finally, one woman stands before him in tears. Struck by her true love, he looks into her eyes, turns to The Devil and takes the suit.

The legend has spawned many versions over the centuries, too numerous to include all here. But to give some idea: most authorities agree that the first recorded tale of Don Juan is the play *The Trickster of Seville and the Stone Guest* by Tirso de Molina (publication date uncertain, 1615–25). Molière's comedy *Dom Juan ou Le Festin de Pierre* was written in 1665, and in 1736 Goldoni wrote *Don Giovanni Tenorio, Ossia il Dissoluto*. Another famous eighteenth-century version is of course Lorenzo da Ponte's libretto for the Mozart opera *Don Giovanni* (1787). In the nineteenth century the Romantic poet Lord Byron's famous epic version of *Don Juan* (1821) is considered his masterpiece, though it remained unfinished at his death. Other significant versions of that century include Pushkin's play *The Stone*

Guest (1830) and Alexandre Dumas's play *Don Juan de Maraña* (1831).

In 1843 the philosopher Søren Kierkegaard discusses Mozart's interpretation of *Don Giovanni* in *Either/Or*, in which he dialectically opposes ethics as boring and dull to the irresponsible bliss of aesthetics. In 1861 another poet takes up the theme: Baudelaire in his *Don Juan aux Enfers*. At the dawn of the twentieth century George Bernard Shaw's play *Man and Superman* (1903) includes a substantial text *Don Juan in Hell* in Act Three. In the same period we have Guillaume Apollinaire's novel *Les Exploits d'un Jeune Don Juan* (1907) and in 1910 Gaston Leroux's novel *Phantom of the Opera*, which includes an opera called *Don Juan Triumphant*.

The period around the Second World War re-examines the figure in relation to war, in Ödön von Horváth's *Don Juan Returns from the War* (1936) and, existentially, in Albert Camus's representation of Don Juan as archetypical absurd man in the essay *The Myth of Sisyphus* (1942). Interestingly, though less well known, in this same period two women approached the theme: Sylvia Townsend Warner in her novel *After the Death of Don Juan* (1938) and Suzanne Lilar in her play *Le Burlador* (1946). Ingmar Bergman's play *Don Juan* in 1955 was followed by his 1960 film *The Devil's Eye*. Other cinematic versions of note include the 1926 silent film *Don Juan* starring John Barrymore, *Adventures of Don Juan* starring Errol Flynn (1949), and in 1934 *The Private Life of Don Juan*, Douglas Fairbanks Senior's last film, which we have quoted in this production. Other films include Jan Svankmajer's animation version *Don Juan* in 1969 and Roger Vadim's gender-reversal *If Don Juan Were a Woman* starring Brigitte Bardot (1973). Contemporary film versions include *Don Juan de Marco* starring Johnny Depp in the title role with Marlon Brando (1995) and Jim Jarmusch's *Broken Flowers* (2005), in which the protagonist, the middle-aged, crumpled, Don Johnson mooches on his couch watching the Douglas Fairbanks movie. Finally in this non-exhaustive list, we might cite among others Peter Handke's 2004 novel *Don Juan* (*As Told by Himself*), Joni Mitchell's song and album *Don Juan's Reckless Daughter* (1977) and most recently, in 2007, Douglas Carlton Abrams's novel *The Lost Diary of Don Juan*. All of which suggests that as an archetype, whether as macho rogue/seducer/careless lover/immoralist /free spirit/existential hero/marriage breaker/sex addict or just the stuff of erotic imagination, Don Juan endures . . .

Anna Furse

This co-production with Athletes of the Heart (UK) and Mladinsko Gledalisce Theatre (Slovenia) premiered at the Mladinsko Theatre, Ljubljana, in July 2007, with performances in Mladinsko in July 2008 and Riverside Studios, London, in November 2008 as part of the FeEast Festival of Eastern European Arts.

Conceived and directed by: Anna Furse
Dramaturg: Željko Hrs
Cast: Damjana Černe, Željko Hrs, Marko Mlačnik, Tanya Myers, Matej Recer, Giovanna Rogante, Marie-Gabrielle Rotie
Text co-written by: Damjana Černe, Anna Furse, Željko Hrs, Tibor Hrs Pandur, Marko Mlačnik, Tanya Myers, Matej Recer, Giovanna Rogante
With contributions from: Maruša Geymayer-Oblak and Ruth Posner
Edited by: Anna Furse and Željko Hrs
Translation to Slovenian: Tibor Hrs Pandur
Translation to Italian: Giovanna Rogante
Scenography: Anna Furse
Realised by: Sandi Mikluž
Costume design: Mateja Benedetti
Composer and sound design: Nick Parkin
Lighting design: Mischa Twitchin
Video: Janez Janša
Language consultant (Slovenian): Mateja Dermelj
Executive producer (for Athletes of the Heart): Mik Flood
Producer (for Athletes of the Heart): Emma Haughton, Artsagenda
Producer (for Mladinsko Theatre): Tina Malič
Stage manager: Mitja Trampuš
Lighting operator: Matjaž Brišar
Sound operator: Marijan Sajovic
Video technician: Dušan Ojdanič
Wardrobe: Nataša Recer, Andreja Kovač, Maja Švagelj, Slavica Janošević
Costume Makers: Jože Koprivec, Marija Boruta
Make-up artist and hair stylist: Barbara Pavlin
Props master: Dare Kragelj
Set construction: Mladinsko Theatre Workshops
Music on the recordings: Matej Recer – Accordion, Marjeta Skoberne – Cello
Composer of 'Mon Dieu': Charles Dumont
Film extracts used: The Private Life of Don Juan, 1934, directed by Alexander Korda; *Crin-Blanc,* 1952, directed by Albert Lamorisse

Production photographs by: Žiga Koritnik and Ludovic des Cognets

Don Juan. Who? / Don Juan. Kdo?

Scenes

NB: In the text that follows, **bold type** indicates what was actually spoken in the original production, in which language (English, Slovene or Italian) and by which performer. Some fragments of text were spoken simultaneously. English readers should only need to read the left-hand column to follow the sense of the text. The photographs and stage directions represent the sequence of action in relation to the text as closely as possible.

1. PROLOGUE: (MYTH) THE WELDER

Deep darkness. Industrial sounds of metal scraping rhythmically, unbearably loud. In the distance upstage, sparks start to fly. We see a Welder working, hunched over, faintly illuminated by this light. A naked Man (Mare) wearing a red crown appears behind this figure, moving like a cave painting on the back wall, furtive, predatory. He creeps up on the Welder, as if stalking his prey, embracing the figure from behind; begins to undress them as they try to keep working. It's a naked Woman (Marie Gabrielle). She downs her tools, reluctantly yields to him. They embrace, naked, lit by a subtle yellow glow.

In the dim light upstage of them we see that they are joined by the cast, wearing evening dress. All face front and walk very slowly downstage, looking at the audience, smiling conspiratorially. They look glamorous, erotic, spent, as if they had been up all night revelling.

They line up downstage, the Welder and her seducer naked, she with a pillow over her body like a fig leaf. They stand for some time, flirting subtly with members of the audience.

2. THE HUMAN SPECIES: DON JUAN AND HIS PREY

Seducer.

Seduced.

TANYA: **For this woman, any intimacy that takes place here** *might* **result in sex.**

For this man, sex *will* result but never become intimacy.

Who is this Man?

ALL: **Don Juan.**

Don Juan Who?

ALL: **The Don Juan in our minds.**

ŽELJKO: **Zapeljivec.**

DAMJANA: **Zapeljana.**

Zanjo vsaka intimnost, ki se zgodi tukaj, *lahko* vodi k seksu.

MATEJ: **Zanj vse vodi k seksu, in v njegovem primeru nikoli v intimnost.**

GIOVANNA: *Chi é questo uomo?*

VSI: **Don Juan.**

GIOVANNA: **Ma Don Giovanni, quale?**

ALL: Don Juan v naši glavi.

Mainline eighteenth-century thought thus came to regard sex as thoroughly natural, indeed as forming the soul of nature itself . . . In real life and in fiction, amorous encounters were cast time and again in the metaphors of a war of the sexes, in which it was the male role to contest, lay siege, overcome and gain a victory.

Roy Porter, *Libertinism and Promiscuity*

TANYA: **Many women have been converted by him, virgins, married women, single women, women who don't want to get involved, women who don't like men at all. Even nuns.**

Because he's a calling, a vocation.

She wants to taste the phenomenon for herself. The man so many books have been written about, poems, operas, movies, websites . . .

Don Juan je spreobrnil veliko žensk, devic, poročenih žensk, samskih žensk, žensk, ki se sploh niso hotele zaplest, ki jim moški sploh niso bili všeč. Celo nekaj nun.

Zato ker je klic, ker je poklican.

DAMJANA: **Ona hoče okusit ta fenomen sama. Moškega, o katerem je nastalo toliko knjig, pesmi oper, filmov in spletnih strani . . .**

During the following the performers clothe the naked Man and Woman in smart suit and black dress respectively as if they were Ken and Barbie dolls, bringing them to life with their costumes. The action is very fluid, choreographed, performed as a shared, collectively familiar task.

The men whistle a military-sounding tune.

3. DRESSING DON JUAN AND HIS PREY FOR SEDUCTION

TANYA: **OK. We need to set the seduction scene. Where does all this happen? Climate: summer? Or winter?**

Let's imagine our Don Juan in the snow. They always put him on some Caribbean island or hot dry lands . . .

ALL: **OK. Winter.**

They can't do this story naked. They have to start dressed and then go naked. And then dressed again!

How does he get himself ready for the task? This naked equestrian pagan?

TANYA: **He showers.**

Does he sing?

He's whistling something.

What about her?

TANYA: **A long hot bath with lemon and olive oils.**

Horse's milk.

It stinks of hot milk and lemon.

She doesn't want to emerge smelling of lemon cheesecake, so she adds some rosewater.

And now we're in a movie we've all seen. Camera catching the soap bubbles on her slightly sweaty cheeks and upper lips.

Dobro. Zdaj moramo postavit prizor zapeljevanja. Kje se dogaja vse to? Letni čas: poletje? Ali zima?

DAMJANA: **Predstavljajmo si Don Juana v snegu. Vedno ga postavijo na kak karibski otok ali v kakšno suho, vročo deželo . . .**

VSI/TUTTI: **Prav, zima. / Bene, inverno.**

ŽELJKO: **In ne moreta bit gola. Začet morata oblečena in se potem sleč in se spet obleč!**

DAMJANA: **Kako se pripravlja na nalogo ta goli pogan?**

Tušira se.

DAMJANA: **Ali poje?**

MATEJ: **Nekaj si žvižga.**

DAMJANA: **Kaj pa ona?!**

Dolga vroča kopel z limoninim in olivnim oljem.

GIOVANNA: **E latte di cavalla.**

MATEJ: **Smrdi po limoni in vročem mleku.**

ŽELJKO: **Noče dišat kot limonina pita, zato doda malo rožne vode.**

MATEJ: **In zdaj smo v filmu, ki smo ga že vsi videli, kamera lovi milne mehurčke in njo, rahlo potnih lic in ustnic.**

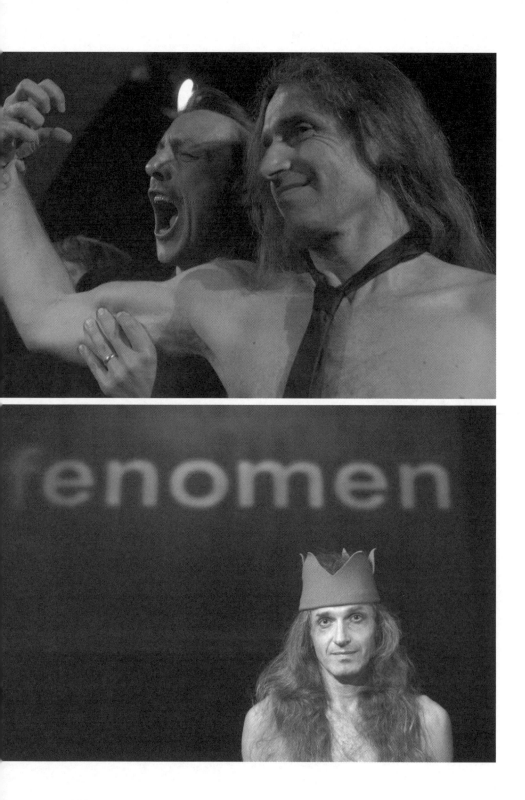

TANYA: **We need to remove this camera! How do we rise above clichés?! How can we do this? How can she do this? Is it possible?**

He likes to watch himself in the steamed-up mirror, likes to write words on the mirror so as to see himself through the lines.

And the mirror's saying to him:

'You-are-the-best-you-are-the-best.'

TANYA: **Sweating,**

very very clean . . .

arsehole clean . . .

balls clean . . .

ALL: **Edible!**

He loves to be clean. It's like a *tabula rasa.* He can think himself into a new conquest with a clean body. His body a blank canvas.

Yes, every time's like the very first time.

Yes, a page of paper needing to be written on.

ALL: **Yes.**

A body to write the smells of this night on to.

TANYA: **Write on my body!**

I am!

There's a kind of special attention he gives to his genitals, touching himself with desire, maybe plucks a hair or two.

To kamero je treba umaknit! Kako naj se dvignemo nad klišeje?! Kako naj to naredimo? Kako naj ona to naredi? Je to sploh mogoče?

ŽELJKO: **Rad se gleda v svojem od pare vlažnem ogledalu. Piše nanj besede, da se lahko vidi v črtah.**

MATEJ: **In ogledalo mu govori:**

MATEJ, ŽELJKO: **'Ti-si-naj-boljši, ti-si-naj-boljši.'**

Ves poten,

MATEJ: **zelo zelo čist . . .**

ŽELJKO: **rit čista . . .**

GIOVANNA: **palle pulite . . .**

VSI/TUTTI: **Užitna! / Mangiabili!**

MATEJ: **Rad je čist. Kot *tabula rasa.* S čistim telesom se zamisli v novo osvojitev. Njegovo telo prazno platno.**

ŽELJKO: **Ja, vsakič je, kot bi bilo prvič.**

MATEJ: **Ja. Kot list papirja, ki ga je treba popisat.**

VSI/TUTTI: **Ja. / Sì.**

DAMJANA: **Telo, da se nanj napiše vonje te noči.**

Piši na moje telo!

MATEJ: **Saj pišem!**

DAMJANA: **Svojim genitalijam posveča posebno pozornost, dotika se jih s poželenjem, mogoče izpuli kocino ali dve.**

The line has split into the women on one side
and the men on the other, clustering around their human subjects.

The women look under her dress.

She isn't actually that interested in his size. She has imagination.

They all do. She's moved by his . . . well, his everything. It's beyond the mechanical.

You know something that occurs to me?

ALL: **What?**

She won't be worrying about the size of her vagina! Odd, no?

TANYA: **Does she shave her pubic hair?**

Yes, but not totally.

ALL: **'Intimfrisur'.**

Is she doing this for him?

TANYA: She's doing this for herself. There's something narcissistic in wishing to please another.

ŽELJKO: **Nje pravzaprav ne zanima njegova veličina. Ona ima domišljijo.**

MATEJ: **Vse jo imajo. Ganjena je zaradi njegovega . . . no, vsega. To je onstran mehaničnega.**

DAMJANA: **Veš, kaj se mi dozdeva?**

VSI/TUTTI: **Kaj? / Che?**

DAMJANA: **Nje ne bo skrbela globina njene vagine, čudno, ne?!**

Si ona brije sramne dlačice?

GIOVANNA: **Sì, ma non del tutto.**

VSI/TUTTI: **'Intimfrisur'.**

MATEJ: **Dela to zaradi njega?**

To počne zaradi sebe. Nekaj narcisističnega je v želji, da bi zadovoljila drugega.

It is possible to construe women's inclusion as willing participants in their own seduction as a sleight-of-hand disguising their exclusion from the language which performs it . . . Stories and novels are bent, like operas, on seduction. They are out to cajole complicity from readers imagined in postures of mutinous independence. So long as the narrative of male seduction ignores the woman as its reader, or at best assumes her to be androgynous, the text will have closed in on itself, protecting its embalmed view of men's and women's libido . . .

Jane Miller, *The Seduction of Women*

In front of the mirror she observes herself from all sides, touches the parts she doesn't like. She hasn't

DAMJANA: **Pred ogledalom se opazuje z vseh strani. Dotika se tistih delov, ki jih ne mara. Ves**

Željko like a conjuror produces a silk scarf from nowhere.

eaten all day to keep her belly tight, now she's starving!

Turquoise scarf?

ALL: **Yes, yes, yes!**

Yes, he has whole collection of them. He chooses them according to his mood. They also come in very useful for mopping up tears, semen, blood, snotty noses from crying.

He can play the silk-scarf erotic thing on her skin with it if she likes.

WOMEN: **Hmmmmm.**

Mess in her head.

Why?

TANYA: **Does she want to go to this place?**

She's confused.

She's on fire. She wants everything.

TANYA: **She's trying on the clichés and they fit.**

She wants her own story.

TANYA: **On the other hand she wants to kiss a frog and change the world.**

Black and white, elegant.

Very elegant, total clichés that work every time.

But no tie.

Well . . .

Maybe something else to untie later.

dan ni zaužila ničesar, da bi bil njen trebuh videt čvrst, in zdaj umira od lakote!

ŽELJKO: **Turkizni šal?**

VSI/TUTTI: **Ja, ja, ja! / Sì, sì, sì!**

MATEJ: **Ja, celo zbirko jih ima. Izbira jih glede na razpoloženje. Poleg tega so zelo uporabni, ko je treba obrisat solze, spermo, kri ali smrkelj iz nosu po dolgi prejokani noči.**

ŽELJKO: **Lahko pa se z njim igra na njeni koži, če si ona to želi.**

ŽENSKE/DONNE: **Hmmmm. Zmeda v njeni glavi. / Hmmmm. Un gran casino in testa.**

MOŠKI: **Zakaj?**

Si sploh želi tja?

GIOVANNA: **È confusa.**

DAMJANA: **Ona gori. Ona hoče vse.**

Pomerja klišeje in prilegajo se.

DAMJANA: **Hoče svojo zgodbo.**

Po drugi strani pa hoče poljubit žabo in spremenit svet.

ŽELJKO: **Črno in belo, prefinjeno.**

MATEJ: **Zelo prefinjeno. Čisti klišeji, ki vsakič vžgejo.**

GIOVANNA: **Niente cravatta.**

MATEJ: **No ja . . .**

ŽELJKO: **Mogoče kaj drugega, kar lahko pozneje odveže.**

All swoon to floor.

He can always use the tie for a little light bondage just for fun.

Yes. OK.

TANYA: **She'd planned on the black dress . . . that falls off her shoulders when she laughs. Yes, black dress on a white soul.**

Jewellery! We forgot his jewellery!

Something very simple.

Natural materials, tooth of grizzly bear, or shark or some mystic symbol,

so he can tell a story later.

Yes, something on his finger he can stroke and talk about after the first fuck always goes down a treat.

He can say:

'Well this ring is . . . blah, blah, blah.'

And she'll be fascinated.

Especially as the ring he's talking about was inside her just minutes ago!

TANYA: **So he chooses his gadgets as storytelling devices?**

Yes.

TANYA: **Talented schmuck.**

Because he knows there'll be questions and he knows that all he'll be wearing when those questions come . . . is his ring.

WOMEN: **I WANT HIM!**

MATEJ: **S kravato jo lahko še vedno zveže, kasneje, tako za hec.**

DAMJANA: **Prav. Naj ti bo.**

V mislih ima črno obleko . . .

Tisto, ki ji spolzi z ramen, ko se smeji. Ja, črna obleka na belo dušo.

ŽELJKO: **Nakit! Pozabili smo njegov nakit!**

DAMJANA: **Nekaj zelo preprostega.**

MATEJ: **Naravni materiali, zob grizlija ali morskega psa ali kak mističen simbol,**

ŽELJKO: **o katerem lahko pripoveduje pozneje.**

MATEJ: **Ja, nekaj za na prst, kar lahko gladi in o čemer lahko govori po prvem fuku, da prebije led.**

ŽELJKO: **Lahko reče:**

MATEJ: **'Oh, ta prstan je . . . bla, bla, bla.'**

ŽELJKO: **In ona bo očarana.**

MATEJ: **Še posebej, ker je bil prstan še pred nekaj trenutki v njej!**

Torej izbira modne dodatke kot pripovedna orodja?

MOŠKI: **Ja.**

Talentiran kurc.

ŽELJKO: **Zato ker ve, da bodo vprašanja, in ker ve, da bo prstan edino, kar bo imel na sebi, ko se bodo začela.**

VSI: **HOČEM GA! / LO VOGLIO!**

The whole company have become aroused.
Tanya decides to cool it all down.

But we haven't even set the scene for the meeting!

She'll pick his dick out of his pants like a small worm tumbling on the edge . . .

This is all in her head still!

In hers and ours. She is us, we are she.

It's a gestalt thing.

ALL: **Yes, our nipples are hard already.**

Yes we're all longing for the moment.

Ooh ahh lalala mmm . . .

When she walks in,

her dress makes that nice shape between her legs.

Describe?

Like a cat rubbing itself between her legs.

I like that image. It kind of works for me.

The legs crossed in front of each other making the fabric fall into the crotch, fabric falling on bones . . .

DAMJANA: **Pa saj nismo niti pripravili prizora za srečanje!**

GIOVANNA: **Gli tira fuori le pantaloni il cazzo, piccolo verme che capitombola dall'orlo dell'abisso.**

DAMJANA: **Vse to je še vedno v njeni glavi!**

TANYA: **Njeni in naši. Ona smo mi, mi smo ona.**

MATEJ: **Taka *gestalt* scena.**

VSI: **Ja, naše bradavičke so že čisto trde.**

Ja, vsi hrepenimo po trenutku.

Ooh ahh lalala mmm . . .

DAMJANA: **Ko vstopi,**

MATEJ: **se njena obleka namesti v tisto prijetno obliko med njenimi nogami.**

ŽELJKO: **Opiši?**

MATEJ: **Kot mačka, ki se drgne med njenimi nogami.**

ŽELJKO: **Všeč mi je ta podoba. Meni špila.**

MATEJ: **Noge, ki stopajo druga pred drugo, tako da se tkanina zliva v njeno mednožje in pada na kosti . . .**

Maybe the best proof that the language is patriarchal is that it oversimplifies feeling. I'd like to have at my disposal complicated hybrid emotions, Germanic train-car constructions like, say 'the happiness that attends disaster'. Or: 'the disappointment of sleeping with one's fantasy'.

Jeffrey Eugenides, *Middlesex*

*The company now in a diagonal, as if a team
of film-makers searching to agree on a film scenario.*

4. LAYING THE SEDUCTION SCENE PLOT

TANYA: **Look, we need to set the scene. Seduction. A dinner. The Man and Woman have met briefly.**

Animal attraction.

He asked her to dinner. Nice restaurant. The table talk and dinner are a cover for the subtext: they'll fuck tonight.

He's a great lover. She'll fall for him.

She'll want him to stay. Get married.

He won't. He goes.

Jumps. Out of the window.

She loves him for the pleasure he gave her, and hates him for quitting.

TANYA: **She thinks a lot about what might have been.**

Houses, babies, holidays, etc.

He's on to the next conquest.

TANYA: **Repetition neurosis.**

TANYA: **She looks out the window. A lot.**

The window he jumped out of.

This is cliché! The bare bones of a plot!

Let's put flesh on this bone.

Moramo postavit prizor. Skušnjava. Večerja. Moški in ženska sta se bežno srečala.

DAMJANA: **Živalska privlačnost.**

MATEJ: **On jo je povabil na večerjo. Prijetna restavracija. Pogovor ob mizi in večerja sta pretveza za podtekst: nocoj bosta fukala.**

ŽELJKO: **On je velik ljubimec. Ona bo padla nanj.**

GIOVANNA: **Lei vorrà che lui rimanga – e poi sposarlo.**

MATEJ: **On pa ne. Odhaja.**

ŽELJKO: **Skoči. Skozi okno.**

DAMJANA: **Ona ga ljubi zaradi užitka, ki ji ga je dal, in ga sovraži, ker je zbežal.**

Veliko razmišlja o tem, kaj bi lahko bilo.

GIOVANNA: **Case, bambini, vaccanze etc.**

DAMJANA: **On je na naslednjem pohodu.**

GIOVANNA: *Repetition neurosis*. DAMJANA: **Nevroza ponavljanja**.

Ona veliko gleda skozi okno.

GIOVANNA: **La finestra di cui è saltato.**

DAMJANA: **To je kliše! Gole kosti zapleta!**

GIOVANNA: **Mettiamo della carne su queste ossa.**

*The men start whistling
the military tune again.*

*The men disperse to
the sides and start a
rhythmic pugnacious
dance like a martial
art with an invisible
opponent. Each man
comes downstage for
his monologue, spoken
direct to audience,
the others sustaining
their rhythmic dance
as backup.*

*He claps his hands,
shooing the women
away.*

*They run to the back
wall, slapping them-
selves against it,
rolling and falling as
if in despair.*

TANYA: **Nuance.**

Finesse.

Contradiction.

TANYA: **Narrative choices.**

Let's see what they do. How they do it. Why. What they think, feel. Let's see why he goes. And why she wants him to stay. What might happen if he does. Why he goes. If he ever comes back. We need to be forensic.

Is there a war on?

TANYA: **There's always a war on.**

No, I mean here.

No. Elsewhere. He returned from it. A changed man. But we'll get to that later.

Odtenke.

DAMJANA: **Finese.**

GIOVANNA: **Contradizioni.**

Pripovedne odločitve.

DAMJANA: **Poglejmo, kaj bosta naredila. Kako se obnašata. Zakaj. Kaj mislita. In čutita. Poglejmo, zakaj bo odšel. In zakaj ona hoče, naj ostane. Kaj se zgodi, če ostane. Zakaj odide. In ali se bo sploh kdaj vrnil. Moramo bit dlakocepski.**

GIOVANNA **C'è la guerra?**

DAMJANA: **Vedno je vojna.**

GIOVANNA: **Ma no, voglio dire, qui.**

DAMJANA: **Ne. Drugje. On se je vrnil iz nje. Kot nekdo drug. Ampak o tem pozneje.**

5. THE DON JUAN IN OUR MINDS

I'm the Don Juan in your mind. I'm a filthy desire you have despite all your politics, all your ideals, all your dreams. I'm the reminder of what we are made of before civilisation, before Christ or Allah. I stink of the sweat of my horse who's always running.

You love me because I can't be trapped by your pathetic desire to cream over the cracks of reality with the froth of the idea that there can ever be a rational emotional relationship. I love you all. Amen.

MARE: **Sem Don Juan v tvoji glavi. Sem umazano poželenje, ki ga imaš vsem svojim prepriča-njem, vsem svojim idealom, vsem svojim sanjam navkljub. Sem opomin na to, iz česa smo zgrajeni, pred civilizacijo, pred Kristusom, pred Alahom. Smrdim po znoju svojega konja, ki vedno teče.**

ŽELJKO: **Ljubiš me, ker me ne moreš ujet s svojim bednim poželenjem in zapolnit špranj resničnosti s peno ideje, da lahko razmerje, ki je hkrati čustveno in razumsko, obstane. Ljubim vas vse. Amen.**

*The women suddenly run towards him
their arms outstretched, maternal, loving.*

*He yells and they run back to the wall, shocked,
their actions intensifying on the wall.*

The women run centre stage, pulling their hair.

I'm the Don Juan in your mind and I just fucked you. Yes, that was me! I thought you got it. I thought you wanted what I wanted. Why do you have to spoil it all?

I'm the Don Juan in your mind and I'm depressed.

WOMEN: **Oh** . . .

I'm so sick of all the lies people tell! I wish I could make you happy, but nobody wants to know. They all want a cat and a casserole.

I'm not really as you imagine me in your pulp fiction clichés. I refuse to be caught, seen, trapped by the eye of consciousness of Man. I insist on remaining, like Schroedinger's cat – a kind of fantastical theorem that you can puzzle over. Whilst I enjoy myself. You wrestle with yourself and I love to watch this struggle between good and evil enacted on your own body as your hands twist and turn and pull neurotically at the fabric of your skirt.

WOMEN: **WILL I LET GO AND FUCK THIS MAN?!**

ITS NO GOOD, YOU FOOL!

I'm in your mind, and I'm count-ing . . .

1, 2, 3, 4. 1, 2, 3, 4. 1, 2, 3, 4.

Your heart is racing.

1, 2, 3, 4. 1, 2, 3, 4. 1, 2, 3, 4.

MATEJ: **Sem Don Juan v tvoji glavi in pravkar sem te pofukal. Ja, to sem bil jaz! Mislil sem, da štekaš, mislil sem, da hočeš, kar hočem jaz. Zakaj vedno vse pokvariš?**

ŽELJKO: **Sem Don Juan v tvoji glavi in ves čas sem potrt.**

ŽENSKE/DONNE: **Oh** . . .

ŽELJKO: **Sit sem laži, ki jih govorijo ljudje. Želim si, da bi te osrečil, ampak to nikogar ne zanima. Vsi hočejo mačko in enolončnico.**

MARE: **Pravzaprav nisem Don Juan iz tvojih cenenih predstav. Upiram se temu, da bi me ujelo, videlo, zasačilo oko človeške zavesti. Vztrajam in ostajam kot Schrödingerjeva mačka – nekakšen fantastičen teorem, s katerim si lahko razbijaš glavo. Medtem ko se uživam. Boriš se sama s sabo in rad gledam ta boj med dobrim in zlom, predpisan tvojemu telesu, ko z rokami nevrotično mečkaš in obračaš in vlečeš tkanino svojega krila.**

ŽENSKE/DONNE: **SI BOM DOVOLILA IN POFUKALA TEGA MOŠKEGA?! / MI LASCERÒ ANDARE E SCOPERÒ QUEST'UOMO?**

MOŠKI: **NIMA SMISLA, TI TRAPA!**

MATEJ: **Jaz sem v tvoji glavi in štejem . . .**

MOŠKI: **1, 2, 3, 4. 1, 2 , 3, 4. 1, 2, 3, 4.**

ŽELJKO: **Tvoje srce drvi.**

MOŠKI: **1, 2, 3, 4. 1, 2 , 3, 4. 1, 2, 3, 4.**

The women are now running round the men trying to catch their attention. The men keep turning away, avoiding their eyes.

The stage is now alive with wild action from each group, the men intensifying their fighting/dancing, the women their falling and swooning on the wall. Damjana stands centre stage.

In Mozart's opera I had 640 Italian women, 231 Germans, 100 French, 91 Turks and 1,003 Spaniards. Click on Amazon.com and you'll find 17,405 hits. Sixty million, three hundred thousand hits when you enter 'Don Juan' on Yahoo. There are 3,220,000 pages if you are looking for dating Don Juan on Yahoo. 'Sex Porn Don Juan' has 1,200,000 pages and if you type 'Sex Don Juan' you'll find 7,780,000 pages.

You disgust me. You disgust me with your ridiculous need to categorise, to produce a taxonomy of desire, your need to be number one. I'm a democrat. All flesh is equal. Stop the heart.

1, 2, 3, 4. 1, 2, 3, 4.

I really don't like it when you ask questions:

When will you come?

TANYA: **When will you go?**

Do you like me?

Do you love me?

TANYA: **How many lovers have you had?**

Do you want sugar in your coffee in the morning?

Etc., etc. Stop asking questions, OK?

I really do have the capacity to love you and leave you.

MARE: **V Mozartovi operi sem imel 640 Italijank, 231 Nemk, 100 Francozinj, 91 Turkinj in 1003 Španke. Vtipkajte Don Juan na Amazon.com, in našli boste 17.405 zadetkov. Šestdeset milijonov tristo tisoč zadetkov, če kliknete na Yahoo. Obstaja 3.220.000 strani, če iščete "dating Don Juan" na Yahooju. "Seks porno Don Juan" ima 1.200.000 strani na Yahooju. Če pa vtipkate "seks Don Juan", boste našli 9.130.000 strani.**

MATEJ: **Gabiš se mi. Gabiš se mi s svojo smešno potrebo po klasifikaciji, izdelavi taksonomije poželenja, s svojo potrebo bit številka ena. Jaz sem demokrat. Vse meso je enakopravno. Ustavi srce.**

MOŠKI: **1, 2, 3, 4. 1, 2 , 3, 4.**

MATEJ: **Resnično sovražim vprašanja:**

DAMJANA: **Kdaj prideš?**

Kdaj greš?

GIOVANNA: **Mi vuoi bene?**

DAMJANA: **Me ljubiš?**

Koliko ljubic si imel?

GIOVANNA: **Prendi lo zucchero nel caffè la mattina?**

MATEJ: **Itd. Itd. Nehaj spraševat, okej?**

ŽELJKO: **Zmožen sem te resnično ljubit in te zapustit.**

She collapses to the floor.

Tanya moves downstage to Matej.

All disperse. Matej moves right down to front row of audience. Checks out the women. Finds one and addresses the text to her.

Melancholic, as if it never happened to her.

> What do you expect of me? Seduction is the habit of the lifetime.
> Tirso de Molina, *The Trickster of Seville and the Stone Guest*

1, 2, 3, 4.

Don Juan is in my mind and I don't judge him, actually. I like him, he's a beautiful man, but I'm trying not to fall . . .

Dio mio, oops!

TANYA: **I have to imagine each man is Don Juan somehow, loving and leaving me, jumping from windows post-coitally forgoing scrambled eggs and coffee, exchanges of address, all that shit. I have to imagine each man is Don Juan unless proved innocent.**

In my mind it's like this: I'm really a very simple guy. I listen to my dick like all men. I'm not evil. I make nice salad. I have good taste in music. I don't have a bank account.

You look great. I like you. So? What's the problem? We'll fuck. You'll fall in love with me. We'll get married. There'll be canapés.

And champagne!

You'll get pregnant. I'll take care of the baby in the middle of the night. So that you can sleep. You'll be more interested in the baby than me. I'll go and fuck a childless foxy woman. You'll never know. You'll never want to know. I'll be Don Juan for ever. And you'll feel as if

MOŠKI: **1, 2, 3, 4.**

DAMJANA: **Don Juan je v moji glavi in pravzaprav ga ne obsojam. Všeč mi je, zelo lep moški je, ampak trudim se, da ne bi padla . . .**

Dio mio, uupsala!

Moram si predstavljat, da je vsak moški na nek način Don Juan, ki me ljubi in zapušča, po koitusu skače skozi okna, se izogiba kavi in zmešanim jajcem, izmenjavi naslovov, vsemu temu sranju. Zame je vsak moški Don Juan, dokler ne dokaže svoje nedolžnosti.

MATEJ: **V moji glavi je tako: V bistvu sem zelo preprost tip. Poslušam svojega tiča kot vsi moški. Nisem hudoben. Delam dobro solato. Imam okus za glasbo. Nimam bančnega računa. Fantastično izgledaš. Všeč si mi. In? V čem je problem? Fukala bova. Ti se boš zaljubila vame. Poročila se bova. Tam bodo kanapeji.**

DAMJANA: **In šampanjec!**

MATEJ: **Zanosila boš. Sredi noči bom pestoval otroka. Tako da boš ti lahko spala. Otrok te bo zanimal bolj kot jaz. Šel bom in pofukal zvito rdečelasko brez otrok. Nikoli ne boš izvedela. Nikoli ne boš hotela vedet. Za vedno bom ostal Don Juan.**

Mare is preening at the side of the stage.
He is doing a ballet barre warm-up.

Mare ignites a cigarette lighter, stares into the flame.
The women move slowly towards him like moths, totally enthralled.
He controls their moves with the flame.

All men are leaning against the sides of the stage, suave. They have now lit flames from lighters. The women are hypnotised.

Damjana runs round the stage frantic-ally, trying to blow them out. Each time she succeeds, the man coolly relights. She eventually collapses exhausted, biting her own arms in rage and frustration.

Tanya interrupts, rushing onstage with a white-clothed table. All give her a wide berth. She screams out.

She establishes the table centre stage, demanding cooperation.
The company gather round as if trying to build their script together again.

you'd conquered me. Tamed me. And this will make you feel proud of yourself.

Počutila se boš, kot da si me osvojila. Ukrotila. In zaradi tega boš ponosna nase.

6. HOW CAN WE HAVE AN AUTHENTIC FEELING IN THIS CULTURE?

Before leaving, the great Don Juan was masturbating.

MATEJ: **Preden je odšel, je veliki Don Juan masturbiral.**

'One has to forgive the tenor for clearing his throat.'

ŽELJKO: **'Tenorju je treba dovolit, da si sčisti grlo.'**

It kind of warms him up like a ballerina with her pliés.

MATEJ: **To ga ogreje kakor plieji balerino.**

It takes the edge off things.

ŽELJKO: **Tako zgladi robove stvari.**

Don Juan is just a dream.

DAMJANA: **Don Juan je le sen.**

No, no, no, he's not a DREAM. HE IS THERE, IN THE RESTAURANT!

MATEJ: **Ne, ne, ne, ni SEN. ON JE TUKAJ, V RESTAVRACIJI!**

Smoking.

ŽELJKO: **Kadi.**

Waiting.

MATEJ: **Čaka.**

A smile curled on his upper lip.

ŽELJKO: **Nasmeh se mu kodra na ustnicah.**

How can I have an authentic feeling? I want an authentic thought, image, feeling, but it's impossible in this culture. I want to feel something new and new and new and . . .

DAMJANA: **Kako naj doživim avtentično čustvo? Hočem pristno misel, podobo, občutek, ampak to v tej kulturi ni mogoče. Hočem občutit nekaj novega in novega in novega in . . .**

7. RESTAURANT SCENE 1: FIRST AND LAST DATE

TANYA: **I need to set the scene!!**

Moram postavit prizor!!

Rain.

GIOVANNA: **Pioggia.**

A restaurant.

ŽELJKO: **Restavracija.**

Marie Gabrielle joins in the action, physicalising her role of seductee without speaking.

Mare joins the action, fixing his eyes on Marie Gabrielle, slowly coming to the table either end of which is a chair without a seat.

Both sit. She is drowning in his eyes. The 'chorus' duck behind the table as if watching the action on a screen, their eyes going from him to her.

Mare/Don Juan and Marie Gabrielle get on to the table, their kissing mutating into wild primitive beasts biting at each other's flesh, hair swinging, violent.

The couple on the table settle back to human and lie on it as if in bed. Someone brings a pillow and lays it under their heads.

Chic.

Chandeliers.

She gets out of the taxi.

TANYA: 'Ahhhhhh! Shit, my mascara!'

She panics.

TANYA: 'My mascara's run in the rain!'

Suddenly she spies him in the chocolate-dark bar nursing a whisky on the rocks, one hand rather near his crotch.

Smoking.

Opium.

Eyes narrow, dusty.

TANYA: Well, she imagines it's opium but really it's just a cigar.

He gets up slowly.

Tells her she's looking good, very good.

They swallow each other's odour. Pretending they're kissing the air.

They both smile.

ALL: Pheromones.

Your eyes are so beautiful.

She looks at him with suspicion.

Here he is:

TANYA: Mr Wrong!

In her mind he's . . .

ALL: Wow!

GIOVANNA: Chic.

DAMJANA: Lestenci.

MATEJ + ŽELJKO: Ona izstopi iz taksija.

'Ahhhhhhh! Šit, moja maskara!'

DAMJANA: zapaničari.

'Moja maskara se je razlila v dež!'

DAMJANA: Nenadoma ga opazi: v čokoladno temnem baru pestuje viski z ledom. Ena roka blizu mednožja.

Kadi.

GIOVANNA: Oppio.

DAMJANA: Oči ozke, prašne.

No, predstavlja si, da je opij, v resnici je samo cigara.

ŽELJKO: On vstane, počasi.

MATEJ: Reče, da izgleda dobro, zelo dobro.

DAMJANA: Požirata vonj drug drugega. Pretvarjata se, da poljubljata zrak.

ŽELJKO: Oba se nasmehneta.

VSI/TUTTI: Feromoni.

MARE: Tvoje oči so brez maskare še lepše.

DAMJANA: Pogleda ga nezaupljivo.

ŽELJKO: Lej ga:

Gospod Napaka!

DAMJANA: V njeni glavi je on . . .

VSI: Vau!

All sing very loud, Matej on accordion. They swirl the bed in a spiral upstage centre. When still again, Mare/Don Juan and Marie Gabrielle/The Seductee are back sitting across from each other at the ends of the table, flirting in gestures. The others watch them closely from the sides, thrilled at how their scenario is going.

Aside to audience.

Action between the two now like a silent movie: a little histrionic from her, he suave and cool, accompanied by the accordion.

The chorus of performers are giddily swooning at the sides of the space.

Well, he's . . .

He's gorgeous!

TANYA: **He wants to know as much as possible about her, so he asks:**

Tell me about yourself so I can talk about me. You're so beautiful it hurts.

TANYA: **Do you tell every woman the same story?**

Oh, no . . .

She stares down at the table.

He says:

Of course not,

but thinks to himself:

'Yes, they're all beautiful, all of them.'

No, no, you are special.

TANYA: **She suddenly feels a pang – like . . . she's fallen into some paperback romance.**

He says:

You seem nervous. Don't be. I've chosen this story just for you.

She says:

TANYA: **I'm not nervous, just a bit confused.**

Why should she trust him?

She begins to get excited by the idea of him.

DAMJANA: **No, on je . . .**

ŽELJKO: **Sijajen!**

O njej hoče izvedet čim več, zato vpraša:

MARE: **Povej mi kaj o sebi, da bom lahko jaz govoril o sebi. Tako si lepa, da boli.**

Poveš vsaki ženski isto zgodbo?

MARE: **O, ne . . .**

DAMJANA: **Ona strmi v vznožje mize.**

ŽELJKO: **On reče:**

MARE: **Seveda ne,**

ŽELJKO: **in si misli:**

MARE: **'Ja, vse so lepe, čisto vse.'**

Ne, ne, ti si nekaj posebnega.

Ona nenadoma začuti ostro bolečino – kot . . . da je pristala v kakšnem cenenem doktor romanu.

MATEJ: **On reče:**

MARE: **Živčna se mi zdiš. Ne bit. To zgodbo sem izbral samo zate.**

DAMJANA: **Ona reče:**

Nisem živčna, samo malce zmedena.

DAMJANA: **Zakaj bi mu zaupala?**

ŽELJKO: **Začne jo vzburjat kot ideja.**

Marie Gabrielle leaps off the table and under it, emerging the other side with the tablecloth in her teeth. Mare comes behind her, she drops the cloth and he has her in his thrall again.

All move suggestively, one leg on the table, in time to the accordion.

I find myself entwined in this scenario.

TANYA: **I'd like to hear some conversation** . . .

Do you like Mozart?

Not the operas.

I'll introduce you.

The waiter comes, interrupts with a:

Grm, grm, madam will have?

TANYA: **Lobster!**

Ahhh!

ALL: **Silence.**

No lobster today.

MARIE: **Shit!**

TANYA: **She says, just like that.**

She bites the menu.

MATEJ: **He says:**

MARE: **Do you like steak tartare?**

I like it raw,

he says.

ALL: **Silence.**

Now he wants to fuck her.

Suddenly she feels his feet touching hers under the table.

He behaves as if nothing were happening, gives a little smile.

TANYA: She's fallen in love!

GIOVANNA: **Mi sento avvinghata in questo scenario.**

Jaz pa bi rada slišala malo dialoga . . .

MARE: **Ti je všeč Mozart?**

DAMJANA: **Samo njegovih oper ne maram.**

MARE: **Te bom že navdušil zanje.**

MATEJ: **Natakar pride, ju prekine:**

ŽELJKO: **Khm, khm, madam si želi?**

Jastoga!

ŽELJKO: **Ahhh!**

VSI/TUTTI: **Tišina. / Silenzio.**

ŽELJKO: **Danes nimamo jastoga.**

Pizda!

reče ona, kar tako.

GIOVANNA: **Addenta il menu.**

On reče:

Ti je všeč tatarski biftek?

MARE: **Rad imam surovo,**

MATEJ: **reče on.**

VSI/TUTTI: **Tišina. / Silenzio.**

MATEJ: **Zdaj bi jo res rad pofukal.**

DAMJANA: **Nenadoma začuti, kako se njegove noge pod mizo dotikajo njenih.**

ŽELJKO: **On se dela, kot da ni nič, in se rahlo nasmehne.**

TANYA: **Zaljubila se je!**

The men and the women split into teams, each team rushing very fast centre stage to compare notes.

The men and women's choruses are now round the table, a fast and choreographed series of actions.

8. WHAT HE IS THINKING / WHAT SHE IS THINKING AND WHAT HE IS PREPARED TO GIVE HER

WOMEN: **He thinks:**

What she wants is a good fuck.

What she wants is my heart, my soul, my delicious mind. She says:

TANYA: **That's fascinating.**

TANYA: **He thinks:**

She wants my babies, my penis and my babies.

She wants to be protected and understood and secure, she wants me to think about her and only her for every second of the day.

What she wants is to know what she wants.

TANYA: **She wants to know her own mind,**

as distinct from my mind.

She wants to ride on a very very big horse without falling off, very fast in the night.

TANYA: **What she wants is unconditional**

– I say unconditional –

love.

She wants to drown in my eyes.

She wants to be my home.

ŽENSKE/DONNE: **On misli: / Lui pensa:**

MATEJ: **Kar ona hoče, je dober fuk.**

ŽELJKO: **Hoče moje srce, mojo dušo, mojo slastno zavest. Ona reče:**

To je očarljivo.

DAMJANA: **On misli:**

ŽELJKO: **Moje otroke hoče, moj penis in moje otroke.**

MATEJ: **Hoče bit varovana in razumljena in varna. Hoče, naj vsako sekundo mislim samo nanjo.**

DAMJANA: **Kar hoče, je vedet, kaj hoče.**

Hoče spoznat svoj um,

ŽELJKO + MATEJ: **tako drugačen od mojega.**

GIOVANNA: **Vuole montare un cavallo grandissimo e senza cadere cavalcare velocissima nella notte. Vuole un amore incondizionale.**

TANYA: Kar ona hoče, je brezpogojna

GIOVANNA: **– incondizionale –**

DAMJANA: **brezpogojna ljubezen.**

ŽELJKO: **Hoče se utopit v mojih očeh.**

MATEJ: **Hoče bit moj dom.**

The men set out their terms. The women in chorus slam their hands on the table in gestures of attention/rejection to each statement.

Matej slowly rises on the table like James Bond, the women's hands reaching to touch him.

He slips away. The women collapse on the table in a heap.

At this the women growl and rush to wings and pull hundreds of pillows, that they chuck at the three men, who have positioned themselves in a chevron, like soldiers giving commands.

TANYA: **She wants to survive.**

I wish I had her moral strength.

TANYA: **She wants to disappear.**

She wants to calm down.

She wants too much! She wants utopia! She wants poetry at breakfast!

She wants beefsteak tartar, the bloody bloody truth on a plate, my heart on a plate!

She wants to rip the meat to pieces, to break my balls!

What you can have is a fuck on the kitchen table, hugs, my sense of humour.

What you can have – no, borrow – is my prick.

You can have my babies, my trying to understand you, my washing up.

You can have the illusion that you're the only woman I ever lust after.

You can have my forgetfulness, my mess, my stubbornness, my apologies, mistakes, multiple orgasms, my appetite.

What you can't have is to enter my cave!

You can't have my soul, my mind, my revolt, my energy, my solitude, my heart –

You can't have that!

Hoče preživet.

MATEJ: **Želim si, da bi imel njeno moralno moč.**

TANYA: **Vuole sparire.**

DAMJANA: **Pomirit se hoče.**

ŽELJKO: **Preveč si želi! Hoče utopijo, za zajtrk hoče poezijo!**

MATEJ: **Tatarski biftek hoče, krvavo krvavo resnico na krožniku, moje srce na krožniku hoče!**

ŽELJKO: **Hoče cefrat meso na drobne koščke! Moja jajca hoče razbit!**

MATEJ: **Kar lahko dobiš, je fuk na kuhinjski mizi, moje objeme, moj smisel za humor.**

ŽELJKO: **Kar lahko vedno dobiš – ne, si sposodiš – je moj kurac.**

MATEJ: **Lahko dobiš moje otroke, moj trud, da bi te razumel, pomivanje posode.**

ŽELJKO: **Lahko dobiš iluzijo, da si edina ženska, po kateri hlepim.**

MATEJ: **Lahko dobiš mojo pozabljivost, moj kaos, mojo trmo, moje napake, opravičila, moj apetit in večkratne orgazme.**

ŽELJKO: **Prostega vstopa v mojo votlino ne moreš dobit!**

Ne moreš imet moje duše, mojega uma, upora in moje energije, samote, mojega srca –

MOŠKI: **Tega ne moreš imet!**

Throughout the following the pillows accumulate like floodwaters up to the men's chins, a mountain of white, while a tango plays. Everything crescendos. The men's words recycle till all pillows have been chucked. The women are burnt out with their effort. They watch the men, who slowly fall like skittles, arms outstretched in surrender, into the pillows.

All slowly recover. Mare stands up, dusts himself down, resumes his dignity and returns to table, where Marie Gabrielle has sat on her chair, waiting.

Matej resumes accordion as before.

You can't have the masterpieces I make, my constant desire, my ejaculation, my secrets!

MATEJ: **Ne moreš imet mojstrovin, ki jih ustvarim, mojega nenehnega poželenja, moje ejakulacije, mojih skrivnosti!**

You can't have my dreams, my fantasies, my gun, my car, my gadgets, my independence, my past!

MARE: **Tega ne moreš imet! Ne moreš imet mojih sanj, mojih fantazij, moje pištole, mojega avtomobila, mojih orodij, moje neodvisnosti, moje preteklosti!**

You really cannot have my past!

MOŠKI: **Moje preteklosti res ne moreš imet!**

My devils, my dreams, my freedom! This is who I am!

ŽELJKO: **Mojih demonov, mojih sanj, moje svobode! To sem jaz!**

What you cannot have is my pain.

MOŠKI: **Moje bolečine ne moreš imet.**

9. RESTAURANT SCENE 2: STEAK TARTARE IS RAW FLESH

He orders:

DAMJANA: **On naroči:**

Waiter! One steak tartare. Two knives!

MARE: **Mojster! En tatarski biftek, dva noža!**

TANYA: **The food tastes weird in their lustful mouths.**

Hrana ima čuden okus v njunih hotnih ustih.

He laughs. He says:

GIOVANNA: **Lui ride e dice:**

What you eat you are.

MARE: **Kar ješ, to si.**

She says:

GIOVANNA: **Lei dice:**

TANYA: **I'm not a piece of meat.**

Jaz nisem kos mesa.

The word phallus comes from Greek. The Latin was *fascinum*, which had the associated meaning of 'magical spirit' and this is the derivation that most dictionaries prudishly give for the modern word 'fascinate'.

Reay Tannahill, *Sex in History*

All climb on the table trying to get a close-up on the couple's action. It is as if they are all in love with the encounter being played out.

They begin to disperse away from table.

She knew she was already lost in the timelessness of his eyes.

What is that she lost?

What colour were they?

I don't remember, black . . .

TANYA: **blue . . .**

green . . .

You remember, brown . . .

TANYA: **Eyes with the sea behind them.**

Big everything.

TANYA: **She's starting to sweat.**

Her hand unwillingly slips under the tablecloth and searches for his knee.

And now, thankfully, we are back in the close-up of erotic promise.

He touches her knee.

TANYA: **She thinks, 'This is mine, my moment.' She thinks: 'Should I just stay passive?'**

He fibrillates.

That's a great verb!

She shudders.

And this gives him confidence.

TANYA: **What does it mean, 'fibrillate'?**

Quiver.

ALL: **Ah!**

GIOVANNA: **Capiva de essere ormai persa dentro suoi occhi senza tempo.**

ŽELJKO: **Kaj je izgubila?**

GIOVANNA: **Di che colore sono?**

DAMJANA: **Ne spomnim se, črne,**

modre,

MATEJ: **zelene . . .**

ŽELJKO: **Saj se spomniš, rjave . . .**

Oči, za njimi morje.

DAMJANA: **Veliko vse.**

Oblije jo pot.

DAMJANA: **Roka ji nehote zdrsne pod prt in išče njegovo koleno.**

MATEJ: **In zdaj smo, hvala pizdi, spet v bližnjem planu erotičnih obljub.**

ŽELJKO: **Dotakne se njenega kolena.**

Ona misli: 'To je moje, moj trenutek.' Pomisli: 'Naj ostanem pasivna?'

ŽELJKO: **On fibrilira.**

MATEJ: **To je odpičen glagol!**

GIOVANNA: **Ha un fremito.**

MATEJ: **Kar ga napolni z drznostjo.**

Kaj pomeni 'fibrilirati'?

ŽELJKO: **Drgetati.**

VSI/TUTTI: **Ah!**

*They're dancing on the table. He produces a turquoise silk scarf identical
to Željko's in the prologue. He plays her skin with the silk.*

*The company enter dancing
a very sexual cha-cha each with an empty-seated chair, that they move
on and through as if another body. Tender and erotic.*

10. WHAT SHE IS MADE OF / WHAT HE IS MADE OF . . .

He says:

Words are sexual organs.

How's your cha cha?

She's made of honey, she's without skeletal structure, so she pours over him. She's made of wanting him to give her bones.

She's made of womb and breast and heart.

ALL: **Yes, her heart.**

TANYA: **She's made of her childhood dreams that pull her on a lead like a dog.**

In the same way his dick does.

She's made of a confusion she calls love.

She's made in China,

India,

Taiwan.

TANYA: **She's made of her freedom, her intellect** . . .

Her hatred, her anger, her pride, her corrosive bitterness, her jealousy.

ALL: **Yes.**

TANYA: **Because she's so made of her hormones, her juices, her headaches, period pains, birth pains.**

MATEJ + ŽELJKO: **On reče:**

Besede so spolni organi.

MARE: **Kako je kaj tvoj čačača?**

DAMJANA: **Ona je iz medu, brez skeletne strukture je, zato se razlije čezenj. Narejena je iz želje, da bi ji on dal kosti.**

GIOVANNA: **È fatta di utero, seni e cuore.**

VSI: **Ja, iz svojega srca.**

Narejena je iz sanj svojega otroštva, ki jo vlečejo na vrvici kot psa.

MATEJ + ŽELJKO: **Prav tako kot njegov tič njega.**

DAMJANA: **Narejena je iz svoje zmede, ki ji reče ljubezen.**

ŽELJKO: **Made in China,**

MATEJ: **in India,**

ŽELJKO: **Taiwan.**

Narejena je iz svobode, iz intelekta . . .

DAMJANA: **Iz sovraštva, svoje jeze, svojega napuha, iz jedke grenkosti in ljubosumja.**

VSI/TUTTI: **Ja. / Sì.**

Zato, ker je tako polna hormonov, svojih sokov, glavobolov, menstrualnih krčev, porodnih krčev.

A looped film from Korda's 1934 The Private Life of Don Juan *plays on the back wall: Don Juan jumping from windows and through glass, building into a frenetic pace. Performers, in histrionic acting style, out front as if watching this movie, break down their own actions as if they were themselves strips of film – reversing, freezing, fast forward, etc.*

They line up their chairs and sit on them gazing out to the audience as if all watching the movie, talking about what they are seeing.

She's made of the contradiction between wanting him to put her on a pedestal and wanting him to push her off it.

TANYA: **She's made of stability – and she hates herself for this, her hunger to collect things:**

Shoes and kitchens and houses.

TANYA: **She's made of wishing she were more mobile.**

She's made of her inability to connect what he wants to what she wants.

She wants to be free and she needs to be loved.

ALL: **Impossible!**

She's made of contradictions, very human contradictions: water, blood, tears, sweat, shit, eggs, underarm hair.

TANYA: **She's made of her vomit, of bread,**

of all the movies she has seen.

Don Juan, my love? Don Juan? Stay . . .

TANYA: **Stay!**

Stay!

I am leaving, *ciao*!

She's made of wetness when she wants to be dry, she's made of really wishing she was in control.

DAMJANA: **Narejena je iz protislovja med željo, da bi jo on postavil na piedestal in da bi jo snel z njega.**

Narejena je iz stabilnosti – in zaradi tega se sovraži, narejena je iz lakote po zbiranju stvari:

GIOVANNA: **Le scarpe, cucine e case.**

Ona je iz želje po večji mobilnosti.

DAMJANA: **Narejena je iz nezmožnosti, da bi povezala tisto, kar hoče on, s tem, kar hoče sama.**

GIOVANNA: **Vuole essere libera e ha bisogno di essere amata.**

VSI: **Nemogoče!**

DAMJANA: **Narejena je iz protislovij, zelo človeških protislovij: vode, krvi, solz, znoja, dreka, jajc, dlak pod pazduhami.**

Narejena je iz svojega bruhanja, iz kruha,

MATEJ + ŽELJKO: **in iz vseh filmov, ki jih je videla.**

GIOVANNA: **Don Giovanni, amore mio? Don Giovanni? Rimani . . .**

Ostani!

DAMJANA: **Ostani!**

MARE: **Odhajam, čao!**

DAMJANA: **Narejena je iz vlažnosti, ko hoče bit suha, narejena je iz resnične želje po nadzoru.**

She's made of feeling that we don't understand her.

Which we probably don't.

He's made of . . .

Erect muscular tissue, ego, cheating, alcohol, fire, tobacco, sparks jumping out of his eyes, quick wings, tight buttocks that press together when he is on alert or fucking. He's made of steel with soft and sweet cream inside.

He's made of hearty laughter –

ALL: **Hahahahahahahahahahaha**

Storytelling –

ALL: **Hooooooho ho ho ho ho**

TANYA: **He's made of our frenzy.**

ALL: **Hahahaha.**

TANYA: **He's made of insecurity.**

Don't get soppy and maternal! He's made of aggression, a map of the world, anger and a hatred of all religions.

He's made of train tickets and saddles, lounges in generic hotels, one station after another. He's made of the hotel bar at two a.m. when he's on his own, lonely, horny. Calling up a prostitute.

But Don Juan gets it for free?! Each woman a different taste in the most delicious and endless

ŽELJKO: **Narejena je iz občutka, da je ne bomo razumeli.**

MATEJ: **In verjetno je ne bomo.**

On je narejen iz . . .

ŽELJKO: **Erektilnega tkiva, ega, prevar, alkohola, ognja, tobaka, isker, ki mu pršijo iz oči, hitrih kril in čvrstih ritnic, ki se stiskajo, ko je na preži ali kadar fuka. Narejen je iz jekla z mehko sladko kremo znotraj.**

MATEJ: **Narejen je iz prešernega smeha,**

VSI/TUTTI: Hahahahahahahahahahaha.

MATEJ: **pripovedovanja zgodb.**

VSI/TUTTI: **Hooooooho ho ho ho ho.**

Narejen je iz naše blaznosti.

VSI/TUTTI: **Hahahaha.**

Narejen je iz negotovosti.

DAMJANA: **Ne bodimo mehkužni in materinski! Narejen je iz agresije, karte sveta, jeze in sovraštva do vseh religij.**

ŽELJKO: **Iz železniških kart in sedel, iz čakalnic povprečnih hotelov, iz enega postanka za drugim. Narejen je iz hotelskega bara ob dveh zjutraj, ko je sam, osamljen, potreben. Pokliče prostitutko.**

MATEJ: **Ampak Don Juan dobi vse zastonj?! Vsaka ženska je drugačen okus v najbolj slastni in**

*Željko is crying. He stands and slowly takes up a gesture of surrender.
He remains still as all move slowly off as they speak. Mare and Marie
Gabrielle embrace at table upstage, others to sides.*

> Don Juan is in perpetual motion. He cannot stop. If anything, masculinity is experienced as a 'lack'. It is something that you have to have which means that you don't 'have' it. And you can 'have' it only by doing it, in the sense that to know that you have to do it, you have to have an outward manifestation of it, an outside guarantee that you have to acquire again and again. In other words, it is only other people [who] can guarantee your masculinity. Or, you need this guarantee and feel you have to have it in order to survive.
>
> Phyllis Chesler, *About Men*

chocolate box sticking his tongue in each flavour, loving them all, unable to choose. No guilt.	neskončni škatli čokolade, jezik potiska v vsako, ljubi vsako in se ne more odločit. Brez krivde.
He's made of vast deserts, literature, poems, plays.	ŽELJKO: **Narejen je iz širnih puščav, literature, pesmi in dram.**
TANYA: **He's made of our need for him.**	ŽENSKE/DONNE: **Narejen je iz naše potrebe po Njem. / È fatto del nostro bisogno per lui.**
He cries when he is alone.	ŽELJKO: **Joče, kadar je sam.**
TANYA: **Yeah? What about?**	ŽENSKE/DONNE: **Aja? Zakaj pa? / Sì? Perché?**
He cries at too much beauty.	ŽELJKO: **Joče zaradi preveč lepote.**

11. RESTAURANT SCENE 3:
THEY BOTH WANT TO BE SURVIVORS

Suddenly . . .	GIOVANNA: **All'improviso . . .**
. . . she takes his hand and pushes it into her panties. She wishes she knew his real name.	DAMJANA: . . . **vzame njegovo roko in si jo potisne v spodnje hlačke. Želi si, da bi poznala njegovo pravo ime.**
TANYA: **He's irresistible as a string symphony. He's wide**	On je neustavljiv kakor simfonija.

Histrionic acting style, as if mimicking the Korda movie.

Tough and contemporary now.

The men's whistling is now on soundtrack, loud and haunting.

awake. **Mysterious and sacred and you feel he'd be able to survive anything if he had to and this is very attractive because it brings out the survivor in a woman.**

ALL: **And vice versa.**

Two survivors.

He says:

'I admire men who've died in battle or who've killed other men, women, kids, because they've looked death in the eye.'

TANYA: **My heart is broken,**

my soul is wounded,

I'm bleeding,

TANYA: **I'm torn apart,**

my life is in shreds.

TANYA: **Love is war.**

Sex is war.

Passion is suffering. It's a Christian idea, com-passion. Feeling for another deeply is to be close to death.

She's rapt.

Široko buden, skrivnosten in svet in čutiš, da bi lahko preživel vse, če bi moral, in to je zelo privlačno, ker v ženski prebudi bojevnika.

VSI/TUTTI: **In obratno. / E *vice versa*.**

GIOVANNA: **Due sopravvissuti.**

MATEJ: **On reče:**

MARE: **Občudujem moške, ki so umrli v boju ali pobijali druge moške, ženske, otroke, ker so zrli smrti v oči.**

Moje srce je zlomljeno,

DAMJANA: **moja duša je ranjena,**

GIOVANNA: **sto sanguinando,**

razdvojena sem,

DAMJANA: **moje življenje je razdejano.**

Ljubezen je vojna.

DAMJANA: **Seks je vojna.**

MARE: **Strast je trpljenje. To je krščanska ideja, sočutje. Globoko sočustvovat z drugimi je bit blizu smrti.**

GIOVANNA: **Lei è rapita.**

I have never known happiness. It was not love for Woman that delivered me into her hands: it was fatigue, exhaustion. When I was a child, and bruised my head against a stone, I ran to the nearest woman and cried away my pain against her apron. When I grew up, and bruised my soul against the brutalities and stupidities with which I had to strive, I did again what I had done as a child.

George Bernard Shaw, *Don Juan in Hell* from *Man and Superman*

The men work an action score over, under and around the table as if it were their battlefield or hideout during the following.

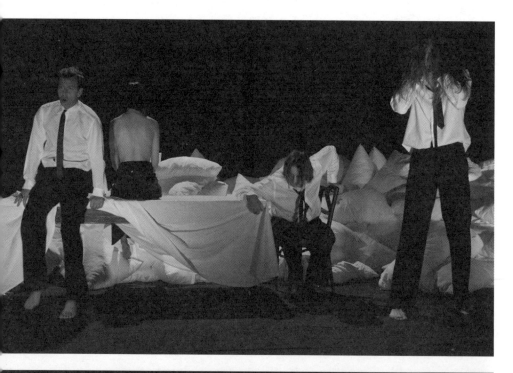

12. WHAT DON JUAN DID IN THE WAR

He tells her what he did in the war.

In the war I lost my appetite. I slept in mud with thousands of other dirty soldiers, lost my hair, lost my friend, lost my mind, lost my memories.

In the war I discovered my beast, I fell in love with a comrade soldier.

I tried to imagine that the bayonet was my dick. They fed me porn movies before the battle. I raped a lot. I broke babies in two. I bit off my friend's penis because if not I would have died.

I wanted to fuck a lot but if men fucked too much on the battlefield they would never kill.

I wanted to win.

I wrote poems. I started to like that smell, mixture of gun oil and dirtiness and sweat of men.

For the very first time I experienced hunger, yes, hunger for food and for flesh.

Someone wrote me a postcard:

TANYA: **'I miss you, darling,'**

and me thinking I can't put a face to the name.

Sometimes I wished I had a real home I could call my own that I

MATEJ: **Zdaj ji pove, kaj je počel med vojno.**

MARE: **Med vojno sem izgubil tek, spal v blatu s tisoči umazanih vojakov, izgubil sem lase, izgubil prijatelja, izgubil svoj um, izgubil spomin.**

ŽELJKO: **Med vojno sem odkril svojo zver, se zaljubil v tovariša vojaka.**

MATEJ: **Med vojno sem si pred-stavljal, da je moj kurac bajonet. Pred bitko so nas pitali s porniči. Posiljeval sem, precej. Sekal dojenčke na dvoje. Odgriznil penis svojemu prijatelju, da sem preživel.**

MARE: **Bil sem zelo potreben, ampak če vojaki preveč fukajo, potem nočejo ubijat.**

MATEJ: **Hotel sem zmago.**

ŽELJKO: **Pisal sem pesmi, vzljubil vonj orožja, olja, umazanije in moškega znoja.**

MARE: **In prvič v življenju sem občutil lakoto. Ja, lakoto po hrani in mesu.**

MATEJ: **Nekdo mi je poslal razglednico:**

'Pogrešam te, dragi,'

MATEJ: **in jaz nisem našel obraza, ki bi se skladal s tem imenom.**

MARE: **Včasih sem si želel, da bi imel dom, ki bi bil samo moj in bi**

The action builds now to a frenetic pace from the men.

might miss, with one woman waiting for me there with my kids.

Everything was so clear in the war. People. Relationships. Life. Death. The word 'fuck' became basic vocabulary. Fuck, fuck, fuck, the lot of you!

I kind of liked the war because it was my kind of place. A place full of men all on the edge of life and death digging themselves into the invisibility of the earth.

I liked to humiliate my prisoners. I liked to make them into animals. I learnt to think of women and men as things. It's the essence of humour, to become just a stupid machine.

Yes. A stupid machine.

Maybe I fuck a lot because I need to forget.

When I returned from the war I felt cleaner.

I felt like a good man. I felt closer to other men.

Some women fought with me (the bitches)!

I didn't listen to voices like this pacifist shit.

I did my duty like any honest man would.

I did what I was told to.

I'm just an ordinary guy, you know, just an ordinary hero who jumps through windows on to my horse and runs away.

ga lahko pogrešal, z eno samo žensko, ki bi me čakala tam, z mojimi otroki.

ŽELJKO: **Med vojno je bilo vse tako jasno. Ljudje. Odnosi. Življenje. Smrt. Beseda 'jebat' je postala naš osnovni besednjak. Jebemo, jebete, jebite se vsi!**

MATEJ: **Na nek način mi je bila vojna všeč, ker je bil to kraj zame. Kraj, poln moških, ki so vsi na robu življenja in smrti, medtem ko se zakopavajo v nevidnost zemlje.**

MARE: **Rad sem poniževal zapornike. Rad sem jih spreminjal v živali. Na ženske in moške sem se naučil gledat kot na stvari. Bistvo humorja je postat stroj.**

MATEJ: **Ja. Glupa mašina.**

MARE: **Mogoče toliko fukam, ker moram pozabit.**

ŽELJKO: **Ko sem se vrnil iz vojne, sem se počutil čisto. Počutil sem se kot dober človek. Počutil sem se bliže drugim moškim.**

MATEJ: **Ženske so se prepirale z mano (prasice)! Nisem poslušal njihovega govorjenja, pacifističnega sranja! Opravil sem svojo dolžnost, kot bi jo vsak pošten moški. Naredil sem, kar mi je bilo ukazano.**

MARE: **Jaz sem čisto navaden tip, veš, samo navaden junak, ki skače skozi okna na svojega konja in odgalopira stran.**

The men have exhausted themselves. An atmosphere of madness and dysfunction prevails as they remain still, broken. Tanya, gentle, hesitant, maternal, comes to them and sits at the table, trying to reach them but they reject her.

The men are outraged at this.

Tanya breaks the melancholic mood, leaps up to summon the company.

> Men go to their caves and women talk.
>
> John Gray, *Men are from Mars, Women are from Venus*

TANYA: **Don Juan my love? Don Juan?**	Don Juan, ljubezen moja? Don Juan?
Aren't you tired of all this? Wouldn't you like to curl up on a sofa like a cat and stay? Stay . . . I'll take care of you. I'll let you display your weapons on the wall. I'll let you tell stories about your war at our dinner parties. I'll let you imagine I'm the soldier friend you loved. I'm the enemy you killed, my friend. I'll let you have your breakdown discreetly. I'll lie next to you and never ask you anything. I'll let you play golf.	Nisi že utrujen od vsega tega? Se ne bi raje kot mačka zvil na moji zofi in ostal? Ostani . . . Poskrbela bom zate. Dovolila ti bom razobesit orožje po stenah, ti dovolila pripovedovat zgodbe o vojni na najinih slavnostnih večerjah. Lahko si boš predstavljal, da sem tvoj tovariš, ki si ga ljubil, da sem sovražnik, ki si ga ubil, tovariš moj. Dovolila ti bom živčni zlom, diskretno. Ležala bom ob tebi in nikoli ne bom spraševala. Lahko boš igral golf.
Golf?!	MOŠKI: **Golf?!**
TANYA & DAMJANA: **Golf . . . is green and slow and bourgeois and you get to hit a very small thing around the place from hole to hole.**	DAMJANA + TANYA: **Golf . . . je zelen in počasen in buržujski in namen je nabijat zelo majhno stvar vse naokrog, iz ene luknje v drugo.**

13. IS DON JUAN OUR ALTER EGO?

TANYA: **OK, I need to get back to the scene . . . more detail . . . Colour?**	Okej, moram nazaj k prizoru . . . Več detajlov . . . Barva?
Magenta, a boudoir colour.	DAMJANA: **Škrlatna, barva budoarja.**
TANYA: **I like that word 'boudoir': a place to sulk and brood in . . .**	Všeč mi je ta beseda, 'boudoir': kraj, kjer lahko ždiš in lenariš . . .

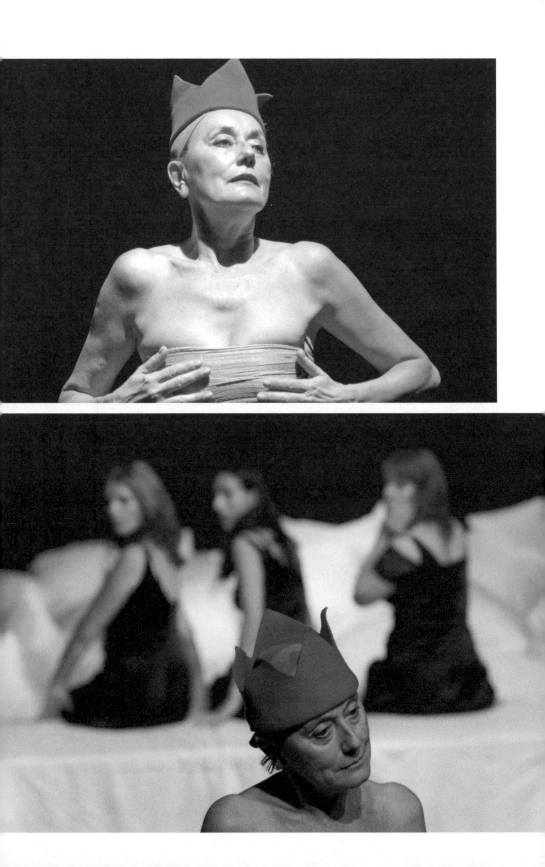

She's delighted at their conversation. She finds words exciting because she thinks in pictures.

TANYA: **She wants to understand men. Get inside their heads.**

By now she is very, very involved, head-over-fucking-heels. And we need to understand the reasons for such behaviour. Don Juan is always jumping out of windows and into windows on upper floors of houses, defying gravity.

TANYA: **He has to come in like an angel, through the window, from the sky, unannounced.**

TANYA & DAMJANA: **A big fucking surprise!**

And we let him into our bedrooms because he's our alter ego?

DAMJANA: **Ona je navdušena nad njunim pogovorom. Besede jo vznemirjajo, ker misli v slikah.**

Rada bi razumela moške, prišla v njihove glave.

DAMJANA: **Zdaj je že zelo vpletena, od glave do jebenih peta. In razumet moramo razloge za takšno obnašanje. Don Juan vedno skače skozi okna ven in skozi okna noter, v višja nadstropja, in se upira težnosti.**

Kot angel mora vstopit skozi okno, z neba, nenapovedan.

TANYA + DAMJANA: **Kot veliko jebeno presenečenje!**

DAMJANA: **In me ga spustimo v svoje spalnice, ker je naš alter ego?**

14. A DRAG KING DON JUAN

GIOVANNA: **I want to be Don Juan, I want to fly into bedroom windows, into silk sheets, into surprised bodies! I want to be a really good lover, the best.**

I do too!

GIOVANNA: **I don't want to feel I have to be bad to be Don Juan. I don't want to kill anybody.**

TANYA: **No, no, no.**

GIOVANNA: **Voglio essere Don Giovanni. Voglio volare dentro finestre di camere da letto, dentro lenzuola di seta, dentro corpi stupefatti. Voglio essere il migliore amante.**

DAMJANA: **Jaz tudi!**

GIOVANNA: **Non voglio dover pensare di dover essere cativo per essere Don Giovanni. Non voglio uccidere nessuno.**

Ne, ne, ne.

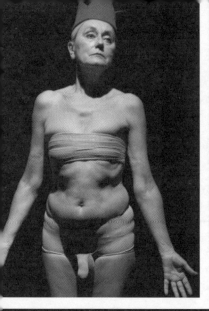

Upstage Giovanna appears, walking very, very slowly towards the audience as if she has a surprise up her sleeve. Downstage, she lets her black dress fall. She is 'naked' as a man, dressed in wrinkled penis, her breasts tied flat.

The company gently lift her up and dress her in full drag during the following. She visibly grows in authority, panache. She speaks as if in a dream, gazing out front, ecstatic.

Giovanna kisses each of the company on the mouth in turn, from which they fall to the ground. The intensity builds. All rise and drift towards the table as if in a trance. Accordion resumes.

GIOVANNA: **I don't want to control anybody.**

I do.

GIOVANNA: **I want this person to love me though.**

That is control!

ALL: **Yes.**

GIOVANNA: **Non voglio controllare nessuno.**

DAMJANA: **Jaz pa.**

GIOVANNA: **Voglio però que questa persona sia innamorata di me.**

MATEJ + ŽELJKO: **Saj to je kontrola!**

VSI: **Ja.**

15. RESTAURANT SCENE 4: DON JUAN HAS NO BED OF HIS OWN

TANYA: **I need to set the scene. Magenta?**

Yes.

TANYA: **And close-ups?**

Yes, it has to be very close to catch the truth behind those

brown,

TANYA: **blue,**

green,

black eyes.

Moram postavit prizor . . . Škrlatno?

VSI/TUTTI: **Ja. / Sì.**

In bližnji plani?

DAMJANA: **Ja, zelo blizu moraš, če hočeš odkrit resnico za temi**

ŽELJKO: **rjavimi,**

modrimi,

MATEJ: **zelenimi,**

DAMJANA: **črnimi očmi.**

Don Juan is forever in search of perfection, in other words something that does not exist in the world. And time and again women want to prove to him, and also to himself, that it is possible for him to find in the world everything he is searching for. The misfortune of these women is that their horizons are worldly – only when they suspect, to their horror, that he is not searching for life but yearning for death, do they recoil from him.

Ödön Von Horváth, Preface to *Don Juan Comes Back from the War*

Marie Gabrielle climbs on to his shoulders. They fall backwards into the pile of pillows and dive through them like dolphins.

Look into his eyes!

'It's a cold night,'

he says, sweating.

'Shall we skip dessert, brandy etc., etc., and just go to bed?'

TANYA: **BED?! Yes, I'd like to come back to your place,**

she says.

He says:

'Unhunh I'm of no fixed abode.

My home is in every body I seduce.'

TANYA: **So he invades other people's spaces, breaks in like a thief!**

But he's also invited to enter.

That's the point. He's invading them with permission.

Yes.

Encouraging the seduced to want to be seduced is the technique, no?

So he's not a thief?

He's a thief.

Why?

Stealing choices.

Because he's not promising eternal life together?

By making it impossible.

TANYA: **No, because he isn't listening.**

ŽELJKO: **Poglej v njegove oči!**

MARE: **Noč je mrzla,**

ŽELJKO: **reče on, ves poten,**

MARE: **Bi preskočila posladek, brendi itd., itd. in šla kar v posteljo?**

V POSTELJO?! Ja, rada bi šla k tebi domov,

DAMJANA: **reče ona.**

ŽELJKO: **On reče:**

MARE: **Jaz nimam stalnega bivališča.**

Moj dom je v vsakem telesu, ki ga zapeljem.

Torej vdira v prostore drugih, vlamlja kakor tat!

ŽELJKO: **Ampak saj ga povabijo, naj vstopi.**

MATEJ: **V tem je finta. Vdira vanje z dovoljenjem.**

ŽELJKO: **Ja.**

MATEJ: **Vzpodbujat zapeljano, naj bo zapeljano, je tehnika, ne?**

ŽELJKO: **Torej ni tat?**

DAMJANA: **Tat je.**

ŽELJKO: **Zakaj?**

DAMJANA: **Krade izbire.**

ŽELJKO: **Ker ne obljublja večnega skupnega življenja?**

DAMJANA: **S tem, da ga onemogoča.**

Ne, zato ker ne posluša.

The women have lined up in a diagonal. The men come behind. Hands all over them throughout the following. But the erotic is ambiguous, as if the women were torn between seduction and revolt.

WOMEN: **The bastard!**

She says.

WOMEN: **And loves him.**

ŽENSKE/DONNE: **Prasec! / Il bastardo!**

MATEJ: **Reče ona.**

ŽENSKE/DONNE: **In ga ljubi. / E lo ama.**

16. WHAT HE WANTS OF HER / WHAT SHE WANTS OF HIM

You enjoy to be enjoyed but then you bloody well go and get emotional. I want you NEVER to fall in love with me, OK? I want you to be emotionally strong! You will not, I repeat, NOT love me!

I want you to dress up in suspender belts, silk stockings, red lipstick, split crotch panties, the lot! I'll tie you up and tattoo my name in your skin with my teeth. All that rubbish really works, gives me a hard-on.

I prefer abstraction, black canvases, doorways, pure thought. Deep thought is very sexy, Rothko is sexy for me! Pure thought distinguishes us even from dolphins! We don't need figurative images to move us! We move from inside.

Excite my intellect! Clean my surfaces! Empty the bins!

Be spontaneous and wicked and very much in demand but choose me!

ŽELJKO: **Uživaš, da te uživam, potem pa postaneš tako prekleto sentimentalna! Hočem, da se NIKOLI ne zaljubiš vame, prav? Hočem, da si čustveno močna, in nikoli, ponavljam, nikoli me NE boš ljubila!**

MATEJ: **Hočem te obleč v pasove s podvezicami, svilene nogavice, rdečo šminko, hlačke, preklane v mednožju, v vse to! Zvezal te bom in vate z zobmi vtetoviral svoje ime. Zaradi vsega tega sranja sem takoj ves trd!**

MARE: **Jaz imam raje abstrakcijo, črna platna, hodnike, čisto misel. Globoke misli so zelo seksi, Rothko je zame seksi! Čista misel nas loči celo od delfinov! Ne potrebujemo figurativnih podob, da bi nas premaknile! Premikamo se od znotraj.**

DAMJANA: **Vzburi moj intelekt! Sčisti moje površine! Odnesi moje smeti!**

GIOVANNA: **Sii spontaneo e astuto e molto molto esigente, ma scegli me!**

*The men
prostrate
themselves in
unison.*

*The men rise,
approach their
women.*

Be really really over the moon when I tell you I'm pregnant. Yes, want my fucking babies!!

TANYA: **I want you to love my being in charge but remain powerful yourself! I want you to lick the lines on my face! I want you to understand the stories behind those lines and tell me my mind blows you away!**

You *will* enjoy my success, my power.

You will say:

'You are the most brilliant and beautiful woman and it is a privilege to be near you.'

TANYA: **Mend all the broken things in my house! I want you to do all this in one night! Make it all come right. Make it all come right.**

Open the window, but don't jump.

Let the moon in.

TANYA: **Rub my butt, be gentle.**

Go naked on the balcony and howl and come back in and jump on me, set your horse free. Tell me you'll end all wars.

TANYA: **Tell me you'll change the world for me. Tell me you under-stand our differences!**

The difference between us is that whenever we come to conflict you think we can work on it, you think we can improve. The difference is you think you can change men, the difference is you really really think we can change!

DAMJANA: **Bodi ves iz sebe, ko ti povem, da sem noseča. Ja, in želi si moje jebene otroke!!**

Ljubi moje vodstvo in hkrati sam ostani močan! Liži gube na mojem obrazu! Hočem, da razumeš vse zgodbe za temi črtami in da mi poveš, da te moj um raznese!

DAMJANA: **Užival *boš* v mojem uspehu, v moji moči. Rekel boš:**

MOŠKI: **Ti si najodličnejša in najlepša ženska in tvoja bližina je privilegij.**

Popravi vse pokvarjene stvari v moji hiši! Hočem, da vse to narediš v eni noči! Naredi, da bo vse dobro. Naredi, da vse pride dobro.

DAMJANA: **Odpri okno, samo ne skoči.**

GIOVANNA: **Fai entrare la luna.**

Drgni mojo rit, bodi nežen.

DAMJANA: **Pojdi gol na balkon in zatuli, pridi nazaj in skoči name, osvobodi svojega konja, reci, reci mi, da boš končal vse vojne.**

Da boš zame spremenil svet! Povej mi, da razumeš razlike med nama!

MATEJ: **Razlika med nama je, da ti misliš, kako lahko vsak konflikt zgladiva, misliš, da lahko posta-neva boljša! Razlika je v tem, ker misliš, da lahko moške spremeniš, razlika je, ker res, res misliš, da se lahko spremenimo!**

OK, I want you to not let me get emotional because I tend to get pleasure and feelings confused.

TANYA: **I want you to leave me my space and totally understand! I want you to disappear without a trace. WITHOUT A TRACE, YOU HEAR?**

GO on your horse! And get the hell out of here!

I want to start the day tomorrow freshly fucked, without a shadow of nostalgia.

TANYA: **Teach me this: make me break the cord of desire, free me! Let me fly away . . .**

I love a demanding opponent.

Strategy, strategy.

I love to know I can get away with everything I do. Telling her I'm busy, but not really being that busy. I love love love when she gets obsessed with why I am too busy.

Breakfast would have been nice but I eat eggs on horseback, I drink coffee on the run.

Don't wait for me!

He sniffs his finger: 'You taste good. I'll text you, I never forget a face.'

TANYA: **Whatever he says is wrong for her.**

DAMJANA: **Ok, ustavi me, če postanem sentimentalna, ker velikokrat zamešam svoje užitke z občutki.**

Hočem, da me zapustiš in popolnoma razumeš. Hočem, da zgineš brez sledu. BREZ SLEDU, SLIŠIŠ?

GIOVANNA: **Vatene col tuo cavallo e vatene fuori di qui all'inferno!**

DAMJANA: **Jutrišnji dan hočem začet sveže pofukana, brez sence nostalgije.**

To me nauči: prisili me, da pretrgam popkovino poželenja, osvobodi me! Naj odletim stran . . .

MARE: **Ljubim zahtevnega nasprotnika.**

ŽELJKO: **Taktika, taktika.**

MATEJ: **Rad vem, da jo lahko odnesem, ne glede na to, kaj naredim. Da ji govorim, kako sem zaposlen, kadar v resnici nisem tako zelo zaposlen. Ljubim ljubim ljubim, kadar jo obsede vprašanje, zakaj sem tako zaposlen.**

ŽELJKO: **Zajtrk bi bil v redu, ampak brez zamere, jajca jem v sedlu, svojo kavo pijem v galopu.**

MOŠKI: **Ne čakaj name!**

MARE: **Povoha svoj prst: 'Dober okus imaš. Mesidž ti bom poslal, obraza nikoli ne pozabim.'**

Karkoli reče, se ji zdi narobe.

Tango creeps in on soundtrack. Women tear their hair.

They jump to pillows, whooping like schoolboys, ragging and wrestling,
ambiguously erotic. Women slowly move to sides of stage.

The men
interrupt
themselves
and come
downstage to
justify them-
selves to
audience.

> Man's love is of man's life a thing apart,
> 'Tis woman's whole existence; man may range
> The court, camp, church, the vessel, and the mart;
> Sword, gown, gain, glory, offer in exchange
> Pride, fame, ambition, to fill up his heart,
> And few there are whom these cannot estrange;
> Men have all these resources, we but one,
> To love again, and be again undone.
>
> Byron, *Don Juan*

Yes, because what he says is not about her.

DAMJANA: **Ja, ker karkoli reče, ne zadeva nje.**

TANYA: **I want and I don't want! I want him here, I want him gone.**

Hočem in nočem! Hočem ga tukaj in hočem, da zgine.

WOMEN: **I HATE THIS FEELING!**

ŽENSKE: **SOVRAŽIM TA OBČUTEK!**

Fuck, stop this shit! Please stop crying! Stop crying!

MARE: **Pizda, nehaj s tem sranjem! Prosim, nehaj se cmerit! Nehaj se cmerit!**

I thought we were eye to eye.

MATEJ: **Mislil sem, da sva si enaka.**

Look, it was GREAT, you were GREAT but there's so much to taste out there. I'm off!

ŽELJKO: **Glej, to je bilo SIJAJNO, ti si bila SIJAJNA, ampak tam zunaj je še toliko različnih okusov. Zdaj pa grem!**

17. DON JUAN'S DISCOURSE ON MARRIAGE

Look, marriage is a farce.

ŽELJKO: **Poglej, poroka je farsa.**

Something I want to break up

MARE: **Nekaj, kar bi rad razdrl.**

Yes, yes, yes. Marriage is for bank accounts, lawyers, heritage,

MATEJ: **Ja, ja, ja. Poroka je za bančne račune, odvetnike, dediščino,**

transgression.

ŽELJKO: **prevare.**

One pillow is thrown.

A very boisterous violent pillow fight builds throughout the following that is played in canon. They tear off their clothes and chuck them on the stage.

I like married women, though, they're gorgeous. Married women like to fuck me and leave quickly (except sometimes when they get carried away by passion).

I love a good marriage! Sometimes I fuck the husband, too.

In the end it is all about nerve endings.

MATEJ: **Ampak meni so všeč poročene ženske, čudovite so. Poročene ženske me rade fukajo in jo hitro pobrišejo (razen ob redkih priložnostih, ko jih zanese strast).**

ŽELJKO: **Rad imam dobro poroko. Včasih nategnem še moža.**

MARE: **Konec koncev se vse vrti okrog živčnih končičev.**

18. THE RAW DEAL: DON JUAN IS BOUND FOR HELL

Look, I'm going to hell. Did you hear what I said? I repeat: I'm going to hell. So come with me if you like but don't then ask for heaven.

She says:

WOMEN: **The bastard!**

TANYA: **And imagines how it might have been if he had stayed and they'd got to know each other very well** . . .

MATEJ: **Poslušaj, jaz grem v pekel. Si slišala, kaj sem rekel, ponavljam, jaz grem v pekel. Zato pridi z mano, če hočeš, ampak ne prosi pozneje za nebesa.**

ŽELJKO: **Ona reče:**

ŽENSKE/DONNE: **Prasec! / Bastardo!**

In si predstavlja, kako bi bilo, če bi ostal in bi se zares spoznala . . .

19. IF DON JUAN HAD STAYED (ONE VERSION)

Go fuck yourself!

It would be more fun than I've had with you!

I gave you everything everything everything and you chucked it away like a piece of shit! You know

DAMJANA: **Pojdi in jebi se!**

ŽELJKO: **Kar bi bilo gotovo bolj zabavno kot s tabo!**

DAMJANA: **Dala sem ti vse, vse, kar ženska lahko da, in ti si vse vrgel stran kot drek! Nič ne veš o**

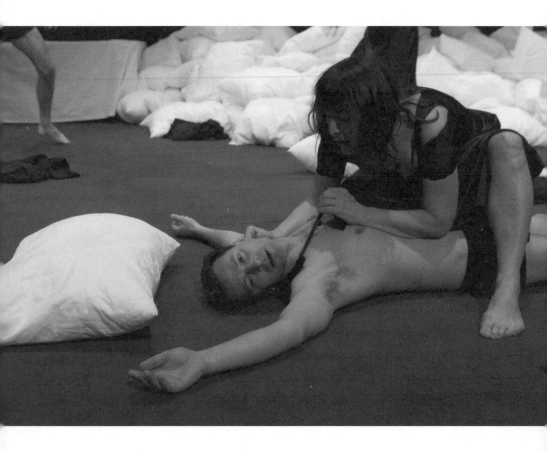

nothing of what women want! You're a cliché! I don't like uncircumcised men!

I don't like uncircumcised women. Your cunt smells of fish.

That's what all men say when they don't know how their sperm smells.

Ah! Somebody calling me on the mobile. Please shut up, I have to talk. Who are you anyway?

No wonder you're lonely! You're infantile, puerile, grow up! I can't bear the thought of you touching me! I like my space when you're gone.

Remind me never to fuck neurotics!

TANYA: **You'll never make it! You'll never make it!**

You're a domineering bitch with far too much testosterone for your own good!

TANYA: **Everywhere you go you leave a trail of mess behind like some dysfunctional garbage truck!**

Women don't know how to fight. Give me a man to fight with!

TANYA: **Fight me! Fight me!**

You know what? You bore me (yawn)!

WOMEN: **Fucking look at me! Fucking look me in the eye!**

I detest the way your mind works! You're an arrogant cow!

tem, kaj ženske hočejo! Ti si navaden kliše! **Ne maram neobrezanih moških!**

ŽELJKO: **Ne maram neobrezanih žensk. Tvoja pizda smrdi po ribah.**

DAMJANA: **To reče vsak moški, ki ne ve, kako smrdi njegova sperma.**

MARE: **Ah, nekdo me kliče na mobi. Prosim, tiho bodi, moram se oglasit! Kdo si že ti?**

GIOVANNA: **Non mi sorprende che tu ti senta solo. Sei infantile e puerile. Cresci! Non sopporto neppure l'idea a che tu mi tocchi. Adoro il mio spazio quando non ci sei.**

MARE: **Opomni me, naj nikoli več ne fukam nevrotikov!**

Nikoli ti ne bo uspelo! Nikoli ti ne bo uspelo!

MATEJ: **Ti si oblastiželjna prasica z veliko več testosterona, kot ga lahko obvladaš!**

Kamorkoli greš, puščaš za sabo sled odpadkov kot kak pokvarjen smetnjak!

MATEJ: **Ženske se ne znajo tepst. Dajte mi moškega za boj!**

Tepi se z mano! Z mano se tepi!

MOŠKI: **Veš kaj? Dolgočasiš me!**

ŽENSKE/DONNE: **Poglej me, jebemti! Jebemti, poglej me v oči! / Guardami, cazzo, guardami negli occhi.**

MARE: **Gabi se mi, kako deluje tvoj um! Ti si ošabna krava!**

The men are now naked/in underpants. They climb the walls at the side of the stage, stuck in a gesture of futile escape.

Atmosphere shifts to remorse. During the following each absent-mindedly puts whatever clothes they find on. They end up cross-dressed but in a chaotic way.

You're derelict. You're worthless and pathetic and I don't love you!

I don't love you!

I hate you!

Fancy a fuck?

You have achieved NOTHING in life except a trail of women mewling in your wake.

Bye bye!

TANYA: **That was ridiculous, I'm so sorry.**

I want to say sorry for what I said about your cunt, I don't know what came over me.

TANYA: **I'm sorry for what I said about your dick. I don't know what came over me.**

I'm sorry for assuming you were such a bastard.

I like your imagination. I'm sorry for saying you're neurotic – I mean, you are – but we all are . . .

I'm sorry I'm jealous.

I'm sorry if I seemed to be saying I might stay longer, if I misled you.

I'm sorry if I became demanding.

I'm sorry I can't ever stay long.

TANYA: **I'm sorry I tried to make you stay and be normal.**

GIOVANNA: **Sei un derelitto. Non vali niente. Sei patetico e io non ti amo.**

MARE: **Jaz pa ne ljubim tebe!**

DAMJANA: **Sovražim te!**

ŽELJKO: **Bi se dala dol?**

DAMJANA: **Ničesar nisi dosegel v življenju, razen sledi strtih žensk, ki se cmerijo v tvojih stopinjah.**

MOŠKI: **Baj baj!**

To je bilo res bedasto, oprosti.

MATEJ: **Rad bi rekel samo, da mi je žal za to, kar sem rekel o tvoji pizdi, ne vem, kaj me je prijelo.**

Žal mi je, da sem rekla tisto o tvojem kurcu, ne vem, kaj me je prijelo.

GIOVANNA: **Scusa per aver pensato che sei un bastardo.**

MARE: **Rad imam tvojo domišljijo. Oprosti, da sem rekel, da si nevrotik – mislim, saj si – ampak saj smo vsi . . .**

DAMJANA: **Oprosti, da sem ljubosumna.**

ŽELJKO: **Oprosti, če je bilo videt, da bom ostal dlje. Oprosti, če sem te zavajal.**

DAMJANA: **Oprosti, če sem postala prezahtevna.**

ŽELJKO: **Oprosti, da nikoli ne morem dolgo ostat.**

Oprosti, če sem te hotela zadržat in te naredit normalnega.

Aside to audience.

To the men.

I'm sorry I can't stay and be normal.

TANYA: **I'm sorry I even mentioned the word normal because I don't even know what it means and I don't think I like the idea.**

I'm sorry I don't do breakfast.

TANYA: **Do you think normal means I eat breakfast?!**

I'm sorry that you've found me less than perfect. I'm just a man.

Don't put me in that cupboard with the other normal jams!

I'm sorry I have to jump out of the window in the night and on to my horse. This is my make-up.

I'm sorry I'm not the zen goddess you thought I was.

I'm sorry I kill.

Sorry for all the wars.

Sorry for all the rapes.

Sorry for every abuse a man has done to a woman.

TANYA: **He's feeling very very guilty and responsible all of a sudden as a man. You can't apologise for all men, for God's sake, that's so grandiose and theatrical!**

Sorry for being grandiose and theatrical.

Sorry for my power to give birth.

MATEJ: **Žal mi je, da ne morem ostat in bit normalen.**

Oprosti, da sem sploh omenila besedo normalno, ker niti ne vem, kaj pomeni, in mislim, da mi ni všeč.

MATEJ: **Žal mi je, da ne zajtrkujem.**

Misliš, da normalno pomeni, da jaz zajtrkujem?!

ŽELJKO: **Oprosti, če se ti zdim manj kot popoln. Samo moški sem.**

DAMJANA: **Ne tlači me v isto omaro z drugimi normalnimi marmeladami!**

MARE: **Oprosti, da moram skočit skozi okno na svojega konja. Takšen pač sem.**

GIOVANNA: **Scusa per non essere quella monaca zen che credevo di essere.**

ŽELJKO: **Oprosti, da ubijam.**

MARE: **Oprosti za vse vojne.**

MATEJ: **Žal mi je za vsa posilstva.**

ŽELJKO: **Za vsako nasilje, ki ga je moški kdaj zagrešil nad žensko.**

Nenadoma se kot moški počuti zelo krivega in odgovornega. Ne moreš se opravičevat v imenu vseh moških, zaboga, to je tako grandiozno in teatralno!

MATEJ: **Oprosti, da sem grandiozen in teatralen.**

DAMJANA: **Oprosti, da lahko rojevam.**

I hate your power, but it's politically impossible to say this and I'd never get you into bed if I told you the truth.

ŽELJKO: **Sovražim tvojo moč, ampak glede tega je nemogoče bit politično korekten in nikoli te ne bi spravil v posteljo, če bi ti povedal resnico.**

Sorry for feeding my intellect at your expense.

MARE: **Oprosti, da hranim svoj intelekt na tvoj račun.**

Sorry I'm now trying to get you to stay. It's a reflex.

DAMJANA: **Oprosti, če te spet prepričujem, da bi ostal. To je refleks.**

Sorry I don't do love. I love the seduction game so much.

ŽELJKO: **Oprosti, nisem za ljubezen, preveč ljubim igro zapeljevanja.**

I do love, you don't do love, who wins here?

DAMJANA: **Jaz sem za ljubezen, ti si proti, kdo bo zmagal?**

Sorry my dick's in charge.

MATEJ: **Oprosti, moj kurac je tukaj car.**

TANYA: **I understand. Sorry I say I understand when really I'm just suffering.**

Razumem. Oprosti, če rečem, da razumem, ko pa v resnici samo trpim.

Sorry about breakfast. Sorry I let the eggs go to waste.

ŽELJKO: **Oprosti glede zajtrka. Oprosti, da so šla jajca v nič.**

TANYA: **Sorry I want babies.**

Oprosti, da hočem dojenčke.

I'm sorried out.

MARE: **Čisto sem se izprosil.**

Eggs are a metaphor.

DAMJANA: **Jajca so metafora.**

If *Don Giovanni* can be said to be about anything, it is, among other things, about the dangers of over-reaching. Faust loses his soul by impudently using it to purchase omniscience. Don Giovanni spends his soul trying to assert sexual omnipotence. Both characters come to grief by failing to recognise that human powers are bounded and that the identifiability of an individual personality is annihilated by the attempt to include everything.

Jonathan Miller, Introduction to *The Don Giovanni Book*

Matej quietly breaks away and comes to speak directly to the audience. He is dressed in his underpants and jacket, a woman's dress tied like a bandana round his head.

20. DON JUAN'S COMPULSION TO QUIT: A SEPARATION SCENE

I love a demanding opponent.

I love saying sorry from time to time.

The spice of guilt, shame, doubt, in the soup of total abandon.

What I love is life meaning nothing very much and she touching my heart . . . Just a beat . . . That feels good. Dangerous.

I love to show her there are no rules.

There is no god.

I love digging in her with words first.

I love her searching for words.

I love that the words are on the tip of my tongue,

and that I use these words.

What I love is that I can put the words into her mouth like wine.

What I love is that I might just might one day fall in love.

And eat my heart out.

I might just might fall in love and . . . and want to stay for breakfast.

I am an elastic band.

I love my horse waiting for me outside.

I love my cave.

I love my penis.

MATEJ: **Ljubim zahtevnega nasprotnika.**

Rad se opravičim, kdaj pa kdaj.

Ljubim priokus krivde, sramu in dvoma v čorbi popolnega opustošenja.

Ljubim to, da življenje ne pomeni veliko, in njo, ko se dotakne mojega srca . . . Samo utrip . . . To je dober občutek. Nevaren.

Rad ji pokažem, da ni pravil.

Da ni boga.

Rad rijem po njej, najprej z besedami.

Ljubim jo, ko išče besede.

Rad imam besede na koncu svojega jezika, ko jih uporabim.

Ljubim to, da jih lahko polagam v njena usta kot vino.

Ljubim to, da se bom mogoče, mogoče nekoč res zaljubil.

In se požrl.

Mogoče se bom res zaljubil in . . . in hotel ostat na zajtrku.

Elastična gumica sem.

Ljubim svojega konja, ki me čaka zunaj.

Ljubim svojo jamo.

Ljubim svoj penis.

He turns to the women who have been watching him from the sides.
He jumps on to the table.

He looks over the edge as if it were a very high ledge and he suffered from vertigo.

He jumps spreadeagled into the heap of pillows below.

The three women are now in their men's clothes.
They gather centre stage.

I love my freedom.

What I love is knowing that we could be together for ever . . .

What I love is saying goodbye.

Any minute now I'll jump out of your window and never see you again, gotta go to hell.

TANYA: **Yes, go to hell.**

Sorry, but I don't believe in hell.

TANYA: **Neither do I. Have a good trip. Wrap up warm.**

He says: 'Sorry, but wrapping up warm on a journey to hell is bad mothering.'

TANYA: **She gives him a thermos of ice-cold water.**

Erm, it's a bit high this window.

TANYA: **Your horse is getting impatient.**

Sorry, but the scene's taking longer.

TANYA: **Please, jump, I'm exhausted.**

Sorry, but there's one last thing.

WOMEN: **Go, go, go!**

You seem in such a hurry to get rid of me.

He jumps.

She sits.

The horse canters off, paddada-padadda, into the distance the horse is pounding . . .

Ljubim svojo svobodo.

Rad vem, da bi lahko ostala skupaj za vedno . . .

Najraje pa rečem zbogom.

Vsak hip bom skočil skozi okno in videla se ne bova nikoli več. Treba je v pekel.

Ja, pejt v pekel.

MATEJ: **Oprosti, ampak jaz ne verjamem v pekel.**

Jaz tudi ne. Lepo potuj. Toplo se obleci.

MATEJ: **Oprosti, ampak topla obleka za v pekel ni najboljši nasvet.**

Podari mu termovko ledene vode.

MATEJ: **Hm, to okno je malo visoko.**

Tvoj konj postaja nemiren.

MATEJ: **Oprosti, ampak ta prizor traja dlje.**

Prosim, skoči, izmučena sem.

MATEJ: **Oprosti, ampak še nekaj je.**

ŽENSKE/DONNE: **Pojdi, pojdi, pojdi! / Vai, vai, vai!**

MATEJ: **Izgleda, da se me hočeš na hitro znebit.**

ŽELJKO: **On skoči.**

GIOVANNA: **Lei si siede.**

MARE: **Konj odpeketa, pekete-pekete v daljavo, konj peketa . . .**

Damjana lights his lighter, the flame burns.

Željko in Damjana's dress now, snuffs it out.

The three women compare notes, returning to the 'Seduction Scene' table and the debris of pillows.

She really laughs because inside her he remains.

DAMJANA: **Ona se odkrito zasmeji, ker znotraj nje ostaja on.**

He'll be back.

Vrnil se bo.

Darkness. The End.

ŽELJKO: **Tema. The End.**

21. COULD SHE HAVE MADE HIM STAY?

So, the scene was like this: He jumped in the window. They fleshed it out. She panicked.

DAMJANA: **Torej, prizor je bil tak: Skozi okno je skočil noter. Zgrizla sta se. Ona je zagnala u paniko.**

What was she panicking for?

GIOVANNA: **Perché questo panico?**

She panicked at the idea of him jumping away.

DAMJANA: **Zakaj panika? Ustrašila se je, da bi pobegnil stran.**

TANYA: **What could I have done to make him stay? Shut the window and lock it, put the key in my cunt. Sit legs apart on the steps of the doorway, fill his nose with my smell.**

Kaj bi lahko naredila, da bi ostal? Zapri okno in ga zakleni, ključ skrij v svojo pičko. Z razprtimi nogami se usedi na stopnice pred vežo, naj mu moj vonj napolni nosnice.

Tell him you'll never never never fall in love with him, it's just the sex you like, you don't need him.

DAMJANA: **Reče naj mu, da se ne bo nikoli zaljubila vanj, da jo zanima samo seks, njega sploh ne potrebuje.**

Cook him spaghetti, do a striptease on the table, laugh very loudly at his jokes, listen with your whole life. Aghhhhhh.

GIOVANNA: **Cucinagli gli spagetti, fa uno spogliarello sul tavolo, ridi a crepapelle alle sue barzellette, ascolta con tutta te stessa. Aghhhhhh.**

Tell him you'll always be there when he needs but without any strings or pressure.

DAMJANA: **Reče naj mu, da bo vedno tam, ko jo bo potreboval, ampak brez vsakih obveznosti ali kakršnegakoli pritiska.**

> Never mind the disagreeable things that may happen. Let us think of the pleasant ones.
>
> Molière, *Don Juan or The Statue at the Feast*

The men are now throwing the pillows at the women from upstage, gradually drowning them out throughout the following:

Marie Gabrielle enters downstage right with a chair. She performs a wildly despairing and angry dance with the chair, and pillow, recalling gestures from previously, leaping, falling, swinging her hair.

NO PRESSURE OK?

BUT DON'T DON'T DON'T BEG!

Be everything that you can ingeniously think he'll want and then contradict yourself and be the opposite, 'cause he'll want that as well.

NOBENEGA PRITISKA, PRAV?

GIOVANNA: **MA NON NON NON NON NON MAI MENDICARE!**

DAMJANA: **Naj bo vse, kar si lahko predstavlja, da si on želi, in si potem nasprotuje in naj bo to nasprotje, ker si bo želel tudi to.**

22. SHE AND HE AFTER HE QUIT

TANYA: **We need to get back to the seduction scene though.**

This has been imagined. It's a future that never happened.

TANYA: **So he fucked off? Where's she then?**

Did she pay the bill!?

Of course.

TANYA: **How did she get home?**

Desperate now! She got devoured with feelings, passion.

TANYA: **Smelling him on her still – she brushes her hair, moisturises, sits on the toilet, tidies the kitchen, puts a few things away, vomits. Vomits again.**

He's meanwhile ten miles away already, his horse steaming, feeling very very positive. He's laughing because he had a wonderful time and his willy's all spent and she was good in bed, very good. He might check her up

Moramo se vrnit k prizoru zapeljevanja.

DAMJANA: **Vse to je bilo izmišljeno. Bila je prihodnost, ki se ni zgodila.**

Torej je spizdil? Kje je potem ona?

GIOVANNA: **Ha pagato il conto?**

DAMJANA: **Seveda.**

Kako je prišla domov?

DAMJANA: **Zdaj je obupana! Pogoltnila so jo čustva. Globoka penetracija v njeno dušo.**

Še vedno ga voha na sebi. Počeše si lase, se navlaži, sedi na stranišču, čisti kuhinjo, pospravi nekaj stvari, bruha. Še enkrat bruha.

DAMJANA: **On je medtem že deset kilometrov stran. Izpod konja se praši, počuti se zelo zelo pozitivno. Smeji se, ker se je odlično zabaval, in njegov lulček je ves znucan in ona je bila dobra v postelji, zelo dobra. Mogoče jo bo obiskal naslednjič, ko bo spet**

The trio collapse in a heap into the mountain of pillows centre stage. Marie Gabrielle exits. Stillness, and a video of a white horse galloping. One by one the women rise from the pillows and mutter the following in their own language, acting out being Dolores, a kind of bridled beast/woman, one woman's voice taking the audible lead.

next time he's in town. She smelt nice and was intelligent, which helped. He quoted Shakespeare as he left:

MATEJ: **'For ever and for ever farewell, if we do meet again, we'll smile indeed; If not, 'tis true indeed this parting was well made.'**

TANYA: **It broke her heart. He had no fucking idea!**

She shuts the window, sits on her bed . . .

. . . picks up her pillow,

TANYA: **looks at the phone for messages, just in case, jumps each time it rings. She drinks a bottle of gin,**

takes the pillow and beats it, kisses it and straightens it out.

TANYA: **I'm angry!!**

Puts the pillow between her legs.

Cut to Don Juan riding away. On the hot dusty road.

No, no, no. We said it would be a cold climate, remember?

OK. Icy road. Horse is slipping around.

v mestu, lepo je dišala in pametna je bila, kar je pomagalo. Citiral ji je Shakespeara, medtem ko je odhajal:

'Zbogom, na vek in vek! Če srečava se, res, se bova nasmejala. Če ne, je prav, da vzela sva slovo.'

In strlo ji je srce. Niti sanjalo se mu ni!

DAMJANA: **Ona zapre okno, sede na posteljo . . .**

GIOVANNA: **. . . prende il cuscino,**

za vsak primer preveri, če je na telefonu kako sporočilo, poskoči vsakič, ko zazvoni. Ona spije steklenico džina,

GIOVANNA: **prende il cuscino e lo piglia a pugni, lo bacia e lo riassetta.**

Jezna sem!!

GIOVANNA: **Se lo mette fra le gambe.**

DAMJANA: **Rez na Don Juana, ki jezdi stran. Po vroči zaprašeni cesti.**

GIOVANNA: **No, no, no. Habbiamo detto che sabbe stato un clima freddo, ricordi?**

DAMJANA: **Dobro. Zaledenela cesta. Konju drsi.**

To be faithful to one woman means neglecting the others. My feelings are so wide-ranging and extensive, I'd have all the women share them. But they, alas, can't grasp this fine conception; my generous nature they call deception.

Mozart, *Don Giovanni* (libretto by Lorenzo da Ponte)

23. DOLORES, DON JUAN'S FAITHFUL STEED: A PERSPECTIVE

TANYA: I'm his escape, his freedom. He always returns to me. It's hard carrying Don Juan on your back and waiting for him while he fucks around. I take him away from the bourgeois hell of rattling sabres and weeping women, faster and faster and faster. My back is hot and exudes oily sweat. I can smell the sperm still on him. I'm excited by his need to get away, my lips are drooling. We're partners in combat, his bridle and bit in my mouth pulling at my smile. He likes to get his oats I like to get mine. I eat out of his hand . . .

Neeeeeehahahahhahahahh . . .

HE LOVES ME BEST,

HE LOVES LOVES LOVES ME!

I know his secrets, and keep them, I know his demons and dark thoughts, I know his moods. He whispers: 'Now, Dolores, dance for us, take me far away from her. I never ever want to see her again.'

Patapatapatapapatapa . . .

I love him, I carry secrets, burdens, a man, through water, snow, across borders, through deserts, past checkpoints, over mountains. I'm an erotic experience in itself.

DAMJANA: Sem njegov pobeg, njegova svoboda. K meni se vedno vrača. Težko je na svojem hrbtu prenašat Don Juana in ga čakat, medtem ko se kurba naokrog. Odnesem ga iz buržuj-skega pekla rožljanja sabelj in ihtečih žensk, hitreje in hitreje in hitreje. Moj hrbet je vroč in izloča oljnat pot. Voham spermo, še vedno na njem.

Vznemirja me njegova potreba po begu, z mojih ustnic se cedi. Partnerja v boju sva, njegova uzda v mojih ustih me sili v nasmeh. On ima rad svoj oves in jaz svojega. Jem mu iz rok . . .

Neeeeeehahahahhahahhah . . .

MENE IMA NAJRAJE,

LJUBI ME LJUBI LJUBI ME!

Poznam njegove skrivnosti in jih hranim, poznam njegove demone in temne misli, njegova razpolo-ženja poznam. On šepeta: Dolores, zapleši, daj, za naju, odnesi me daleč stran od nje. Nikoli več je nočem videt.

Patapatapatapapatapa . . .

Ljubim ga, nosim skrivnosti, bremena moškega, čez vode, sneg, čez meje, čez puščave, mimo mejnikov, čez gorovja. Jaz sem erotično doživetje samo po sebi.

He loves me. We're a team, a *pas de deux*.

I love his jumping out of windows on to my back. THUMP as his butt hits my spine. Go go go go go go go, girl! I want sparks to fly from my hooves. I want to give Don Juan the world!

Reader: I carried him . . .

Ljubi me. Midva sva tim, *pas de deux*.

Ljubim to, kako skozi okna skače na moj hrbet. TUMP, ko njegova rit pristane na moji hrbtenici. Gremo, gremo, gremo, gremo, punca! Hočem, da iskre letijo izpod mojih podkev. Hočem mu podarit svet!

Ja, bralec: Nosila sem ga . . .

GIOVANNA: Io sono il suo rifugio, la sua libertà. Lui torna sempre da me. È dura portare sulla schiena Don Giovanni, aspettarlo mentre se ne va a scopare in giro. Veloce, sempre più veloce lo trascino via dall'inferno borghese di spade (clinghine) e donne in lacrime. Il mio dorso è caldo e trasuda da olii dolciastri. Posso sentire l'odore dello sprema che gli è rimasto adosso. Mi eccita il suo bisogno di andare, mi fa sbavare. Siamo compagni di battaglia con le briglie e il morso. Mi rtira afino al sorriso. A lui piacciono le sue gran aglie e a me piacciono le mie. Mangio dalla sua mano.

Neeeeeehahahahhahah . . .

Sono quella che lui ama di più.

MI AMA MI AMA MI AMA PIÙ DI TUTTE

Conosco i suoi segreti e li tengo per me. Conosco i suoi demoni e i supi stati d'animo.

Mi sussurra: Dolores, danza per noi, portami via da lei, non la voglio rivedere mai più.

Patapatapatapapatapa . . .

Darkness except for the horse video. A slow, strange apparition in white far upstage appears, gliding under the horse footage. Blue light glows on her face from the laptop she's carrying: Marie Gabrielle, now a very ancient woman, trembling as a butoh dancer in the dark empty space. The following recorded text is spoken in a whisper.

Lo amo. Ne trasporto i segreti e i legami, un uomo, attraverso l'acqua, la neve, attraverso fronttere, deserti, dogane, montagne. Io sono un esperienza erotica di per se stessa.

Mi ama. Diamo un duetto. Un pas de deux.

Mi piace quando salta dalle finestre sulla mia groppa – THUMP, e il suo didietro mi colpisce spina dorsale. Vai, vai, vai, vai ragazza! Voglio farle volare scintille dai miei zoccoli io a don Giovanni voglio dare il mondo.

Lettore: Io lo ho trasportato.

The rebel character of the hero made him a pattern of Romanticism: a loner, a kind of suicide, a saint of love and personal quest for knowledge, whose final incarnation perhaps was Genet, seen through the eyes of Sartre . . . But one has to take care with this type of lure: a fantasy of control will always seduce the disenfranchised. (Unemployed teenagers wear combat fatigues and gigantic boots; prostitutes solicit business by boasting of their dominatrix methods.) This is perhaps the final twist in the seductions of Don Juan, that the victims are flattered into believing themselves in charge.

Marina Warner, *Valmont – or The Marquis Unmasked*

---

24. FRIENDS REUNITED.COM:
THE SEDUCTEE AS AN OLD WOMAN / DON JUAN AS AN OLD MAN

Some many years later a woman wonders if he's still alive. She goes on the internet. She finds thousands of Don Juans. She tracks him down on FriendsReunited.com.

DAMJANA: **Mnogo let pozneje se ženska sprašuje, ali je še živ. Priklopi se na internet in najde na tisoče Don Juanov. Končno ga najde na FriendsReunited.com.**

Suddenly the
mobile phone
rings.

Each man
leaning in the
shadows at
the sides of
the space,
dimly lit by his
mobile phone.

Suspicious.

Don Juan was here. Bruised this orifice inside and out, this heart, this shattered mind. Yes, he fucked us all up.

TANYA: **Hello?**

Hello, this is Juan here, remember me? We had a lovely night together.

TANYA: **Yeeees?**

Steak tartare, rain, etc., and I rode off on my horse . . .

Yes?

. . . into the dawn.

Yes?

Well . . . I never told you how much I am deeply grateful for all the muck and gems we made together. I never told you that I'm frightened of you.

I'm TIRED of sex, in fact I'm a catastrophe. I'd really like to disappear.

She says:

TANYA: **I'm too tired to go on with this story, it's exhausting. We fetishise our emotions.**

Yes, illusions of escape . . .

. . . Yes, oh, oh, oh and danger . . .

ALL: **Yes** . . .

TANYA: **I repeat, we fetishise sensations and emotions. They're cultural – ideas about ideas, fantasies about fantasies.**

Don Juan je bil tu. Ranil je to odprtino znotraj in zunaj, to srce, ta raztreščeni um. Ja, vse nas je zajebal.

Prosim?

MATEJ: **Halo, Juan tukaj, se me še spomniš? Prijetno noč sva preživela skupaj.**

Jaaaa?

ŽELJKO: **Tatarski biftek, dež, maskara itd. in odjezdil sem na svojem konju . . .**

DAMJANA: **Ja?**

ŽELJKO: **. . . proti zori.**

GIOVANNA: **Sì?**

MATEJ: **No . . . nikoli ti nisem povedal, kako zelo hvaležen sem ti za ves gnoj in vse dragulje, ki sva jih naredila skupaj. Nikoli ti nisem povedal, da se te bojim.**

ŽELJKO: **Izmučen sem od seksa, v bistvu sem katastrofa. Želim si, da bi izginil.**

GIOVANNA: **Lei dice:**

Preveč sem utrujena, da bi nadaljevala to zgodbo, prenaporno je, fetišiziramo svoja čustva.

MATEJ: **Ja, iluzije pobegov . . .**

DAMJANA: **. . . ja, oh, oh, oh in nevarnost . . .**

VSI/TUTTI: **Ja . . . / Sì . . .**

Ponavljam, malikujemo svoje vtise in čustva, kulturno so pogojena kot vse drugo, ideje o idejah, fantazije o fantazijah.

Mare appears, naked, in his now battered red crown, as in the prologue, moving limply against the back wall.

Mare lights a small sparkler. He comes to Marie Gabrielle, who is now downstage staring into her computer screen, her lips trembling, her eyes barely open.

Somebody else's hot wax, somebody else's silks, somebody else's basques.

ALL: **Yes . . .**

When desire connects . . .

ALL: **Yes . . .**

transcending logic . . .

ALL: **Yes . . .**

daily life is illuminated . . .

ALL: **Yes . . .**

TANYA: **With sex we make it all disappear. It's the great illusion.**

The door opens. He walks in.

I'm an idea, an erotic idea, a construct, paradise, hell. I'm a wish fulfilment.

TANYA: **He takes my hand,**

lifts me up,

TANYA: **takes me to the window where my old mind has been.**

He throws me out

and I'm flying.

TANYA: **Flying.**

Flying.

Flying.

DAMJANA: **Vroč vosek nekoga drugega, nekoga drugega svila, nekoga drugega korzeti . . .**

VSI/TUTTI: **Ja . . . / Sì . . .**

DAMJANA: **Ko nas poželenje poveže . . .**

VSI/TUTTI: **Ja . . . / Sì . . .**

DAMJANA: **transcendira logiko . . .**

VSI/TUTTI: **Ja . . . / Sì . . .**

DAMJANA: **razsvetli vsakdan . . .**

VSI/TUTTI: **Ja . . . / Sì . . .**

S seksom dosežemo, da vse izgine. To je velika iluzija.

GIOVANNA: **La porta si apre. Lui entra.**

MARE: **Jaz sem ideja, erotična ideja, konstrukt, raj, pekel. Pravzaprav sem izpolnitev želje.**

Prime me za roko,

DAMJANA: **me dvigne,**

nese do okna, kjer je bdela moja stara duša.

DAMJANA: **Zaluča me ven**

GIOVANNA: **e sto volando.**

Letim.

GIOVANA: **Volando.**

DAMJANA: **Letim.**

Under the picture of the breaker of the rules of marriage, as the thief of wives, seducer of virgins, shame of families and insult for men and fathers – appears another person: human character led against his own will by obscure craziness of sex. Under the image of epicurean is a pervert. He deliberately breaks the law, at the same time driven by kind of fallacy nature far away from any nature . . . Leave the questioning was he homosexual, narcissistic or impotent to psychoanalysts.

Michel Foucault, *The History of Sexuality*

Miss America

written and performed by
Peggy Shaw and Lois Weaver

Peggy in New York had a dream that she was the first
81-year-old woman to win the Miss America pageant.
Lois in London watched news coverage of Hurricane
Katrina and realised what it meant to miss America.
In response, they created this exploration of what is lost
in a society that hopelessly clings to winning.

Miss America was first presented at La Mama Experimental Theatre Club, New York, in June 2008.

Written and performed by Peggy Shaw and Lois Weaver
Developed in collaboration with Stormy Brandenberger
Choreography by Stormy Brandenberger
Sound design and original music by Vivian Stoll
New media consultant Campbell X
Creative midwife Judith Katz
Photography Lori E. Seid

The UK stage premiere of *Miss America* was presented at the People's Palace, Mile End Road, London, and ran from 21 March to 23 March 2009.

During its US run, the *New York Times* described Weaver as 'a playful pixie of performance art' who 'conveys a delightful sense of mischief', and proclaimed that the show was 'a freewheeling attack on American foreign policy, beauty pageants, evening news programmes and machismo posturing, generously seasoned with free verse and gay humour'.

Peggy Shaw was awarded a NYSCA Individual Artist Grant for writing *Miss America* and a MAP Fund grant for producing it at La Mama.

Most photos throughout the text were taken during performances by Lois Weaver. However some are selected performance documentation by Lori E. Seid.

Miss America

Lois is sitting in the last row on the left side of the house dressed in a fur coat and tiara with a large camera round her neck.

The stage is bare except for a pile of large appliances assembled in a runway formation just left of centre stage and an old portable projection screen and industrial fan on a stand upstage right. Peggy is dressed in a black suit that is much too small for her and is sitting on a chair in the extreme upstage left corner, facing stage right.

Lois moves towards the stage by climbing over the backs of chairs. She stops and takes photos of individual audience members as she speaks these lines

Lois You never told me . . .

that it hurts every time you get up from a chair.

You never told me . . .

that your mother's smoke
kept you from seeing the kindness in her eyes.

You never told me . . .
that you don't really love anyone.

You never told me . . .
that the cherries in your neighbour's backyard were sour
and that your thoughts were poison

You never told me . . .
you want to be buried in the ground,
that you want to deteriorate not pollute.

You never told me . . .
that a maraschino cherry never deteriorates.

You never told me . . .
that every time you try to do something important,
you get lost on YouTube.

You never told me what happened last night.

You never told me . . .
that you don't like the guy upstairs.

You never told me . . .
that you have a good time at the beach but don't like to swim.

You never told me . . . you once rented a car and never picked it up.

You never told me . . .
that your sense of justice came from a father who worked too hard.

You never told me . . . that you feel despair as you age,
that you think this age is full of despair,
that you think despair is a dark canyon where the downdraught
pushes your own voice back down your own throat.

You never told me . . .
that you have lost the belief that things happen for a reason.

You never told me . . .
that all countries have a hard edge of steel at their hearts,
that a soft heart has no place in this world.

You never told me . . .
that you could not make a list
of things you care about because you can't remember.

You never told me . . .
that you want to stand on this rubbish heap and stamp your feet until
something changes.

You never told me . . .
that the flood came once when you didn't notice
so that when it returned, the ground was already full of water and refuse.

You never told me . . .
that refuse and refuse are spelled the same.

You never told me . . .
that when you are in the audience you think you are alone.

You never told me . . . that after thirty years,
she would still sit in the dark and wait for me to finish.

Lois sits in the front row of the audience. The lights go out.

Music up. It is a recording of Patty Smith singing 'You Light Up My Life'. A spotlight comes up on a doll-sized red chair. Peggy moves into the spot. We see only her feet and then her hands as she attempts to sit in the tiny chair.

This is choreographed to the music. Lights and music go out just as Peggy gets to a sitting position that would ultimately crush the chair.

Note: Peggy spent hours on YouTube researching beauty pageants and talent shows. She found footage of Patty Smith struggling through a version of 'You Light Up My Life' on the 1980s TV programme, Kids are People Too. She became obsessed with this awkward juxtaposition of vulnerability and success. It resonated with Peggy's improbable dream and her impossible task of squeezing a tall, 65-year-old, butch body into the role of a beauty contestant for the Miss America Pageant.

Lights up in a circle spot just right of centre stage. Peggy is lying face down in the circle as if she has fallen and one of her shoes has come off. This is a recurring image referred to as the 'accident pose'.

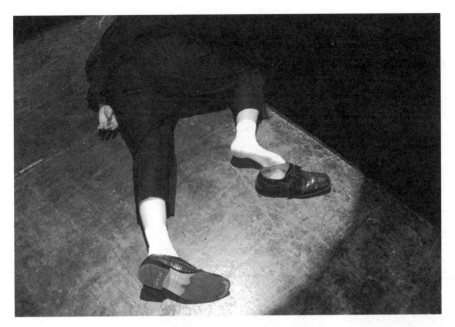

Lois takes a photo of this from her seat in the audience.

Peggy Why are you here again?

Lois I came for the picture.

Peggy But why do you come back over and over?

Lois There is something in the repetition, something about going over and over things until you understand

Peggy . . . or forget.

Lois What?

Peggy I don't know . . . I think it was a picnic or a parade, a stampede or a contest, a littered beach or a landfill.

Lois It was a storm.

Peggy Have you ever noticed that when someone is hit by something one or both of their shoes comes off? I wonder why this happens, I wonder if someone takes them off, or if the force of the impact removes them.

Lois Is that a tragedy or a shame?

Peggy I don't know. I'm sure this has happened before, but it feels like the first time.

Lois . . . a gift or an hand-out, a surprise or a catastrophe, a lake or a flood?

Peggy I don't understand what's happening,

why my shoes are off,
why the water won't stop.

Why it stays on the pavement so long becoming fields, becoming lakes, with no objects in sight, with no here to there.

Peggy exits.

Lois walks on stage and stands in the circle of light.

Note: We looked for ways to hold the conversation, to build dialogue between the photographer and the subject; the media and the event, the judge and the contestant, between the hopeful and the hopeless. While Peggy mined her actual dream for broken and buried fragments of the American dream, Lois searched for ways to embody a critical response. She turned to the photographer, Diane Arbus; to Weegee, an American photo journalist famous for capturing human catastrophe; and to Anderson Cooper, the CNN reporter who lost the ability to maintain objectivity in the face of the New Orleans disaster.

Lois I am there before it happens,
I'm the Ouija-board reporter, storm-chaser, rain-spotter, photojournalist,
inside pitchman, master of ceremonies.
I am on the cusp of a hurricane, upwind of a wildfire,
at the scene of a car crash.
I am the person in the car behind the one dangling from the bridge.
I am on the crossroads of a deserted downtown, preserved
at the bottom of the man-made lake, just ahead
of the monoculture and inside the parasite.
I am your co-dependent Cassandra of a falling empire
and I am on the scene.

*Lois moves upstage and sets up the old projection screen next to the floor
fan. There is video footage of a hurricane wind with particular focus on huge
palm trees bending in the wind. The fan comes on and Lois takes a hand-
held microphone out of her pocket and speaks against the wind of the fan.
There is the sound of a raging storm in the background*

Can you hear me? Come in, Come in . . . Come in . . .

This is a giant of a storm, ladies and gentlemen,
and I'm standing on edge, standing at *the* edge

of a computer-generated, pollution-incinerated, post-temperate,
flooded coastline, anti-ice age, snow globe, storm of the century
and we are all very happy.
Very, very happy.
And ready.
Windows are already boarded up,
garbage is piling up, people lining up,
and behind me you can see beautiful women stepping out of limousines.
Their pedicured toes and carefully selected mules are plunging into the
sludge. They don't seem to notice.
They pick up their gowns and make their way into the coliseum.
In front of me, ancient braless women are still carrying signs.
They're walking barefoot through the rising water.
They have been camping out here in this city of culture and commerce,
built on the edge of an ocean and left open,
and receptive to anything the tide might bring.
'Bring it on,' they keep chanting.
Bring on the violent tide set in motion by the beauty of a competition
that's crashing the shores of a beautiful Atlantis.

*There is a giant crash of thunder and the sound of giant steps getting louder
as if moving closer. Peggy steps on to the runway.*

This is it. She's making landfall
and she's a whopper, ladies and gentlemen.
She's the type every American girl might well emulate
and she's whistling a tune that bears a startling resemblance
to *Dixie* and *America the Beautiful.*
She is . . .
oh my god . . .
so . . .
beautiful
and
happy.
She's . . . what can I say? She's . . . courtly, regal, imperial, august,
majestic . . . You know something there just isn't any better way to say
it than . . . Would you like to be queen for a day?

*Lois sings 'A Pretty Girl is Like a Melody', the theme tune of the Miss
America Pageant, as Peggy walks down the runway in a dance of awkward
gestures. She reaches the end as the song finishes.*

Peggy Whenever I pick up the
phone, I sigh . . .
So I pick it up slowly
and hope the sigh is out
before my mouth
reaches the phone.
It's just cause I don't
bleed any more.
That's why I have to sigh.
Today I answered with a sigh
and they told me
I had been elected Miss America.

Lois You never told me that.

Peggy I dreamt I was Miss America.
I was 86 years old in a bikini
with the words 'Miss America'
written across my chest.

The lights were hot on me.
They were low and coming down
toward me
in what you could call a shaft.
With backlight shining
through me like an x-ray.
I had so much going on inside
it appeared that I was distracted
but I was very focused.

Note: In Split Britches' work, there are always several levels of performance happening at once. Lois is performing Lois, as well as the audience interlocutor, photographer, news reporter and contest host. Peggy performs Peggy and shifts between the gentleman, the freak, the giant and the Miss America contestant. Together we perform the conflict of these multiple relationships while negotiating the complicated landscape of our own thirty-year work/life partnership.

Peggy You could see that I had long legs,
and you could see how great they looked.
I had shiny hair and a waist.
My lips were slightly parted
and red with lipstick.
I was aware of you watching my lips.
When I opened my mouth,
there were films of moisture parting my lips
like Marilyn Monroe's drool
dripping from her mouth to the counter in *Bus Stop*.

It was a miracle.
I was special.
I wasn't what you would call young.
I was sexy.
I was holding my arms in the air
receiving thunderous applause from the audience
who were soooooo happy for me.
I was happy,
they were happy,
all my runners-up were happy.

Lois Happy. We are all very, very happy.
Now everyone on the count of 3, look happy. Ready? 1 2 3 happy.

Great and *taking another section of the audience* again, 1 2 3 happy. And
again 1 2 3 . . . happy.

Lois (*moving to stand in front of Peggy and looking up at her*) You never told me that you wanted to be Miss America, that you wanted to be in the contest. You never told me that you wanted to dance for America and that you figured your best shot in the talent competition would be to do a striptease. You never told me that you decided you would strip for Miss America. That you wanted to take your clothes off in the rain and throw your hands up and say whoooooeeee. You never told me . . .

Peggy They told me I could buy a rug, or a lawn, or a swimming pool to celebrate. They told me there was a cash prize. I got it for being the most beautiful girl in America. (*Lois turns to audience with a disbelieving look.*) It was my body and my answer to the question.

Lois Polls have shown that one-fifth of Americans can't locate the US on a world map. Why do you think this is?

Peggy 'I personally believe that US Americans are unable to do so because . . . uh some . . . uh people out there in our nation don't have maps and I believe our education, like such as South African and uh the Iraq and everywhere like such as and I believe that they should . . . and our education over here in the US should help the US or should help South Africa and should help the Iraq and the Asian countries so we will be . . . so we will build up our future so our children will be able to be . . . '

Lois Happy, Happy, Happy, Happy, Happy, Happy, Happy, Happy, Happy, Happy, Happy, Happy, Happy, Happy, Happy, Happy Happy, Happy . . .

Continuing this rant until the words transform to . . .

Help me, Help me, Help me, Help me, Help me, Help me, Help me, Help me, Help me, Help me, Help me, Help me, Help me, Help me, Help me! . . .

Recovering. That was probably your worst performance yet . . . It wasn't nearly as good as last week but we're going to give you another chance. So, *little* lady, let me ask you this . . . what does America mean to you?

Peggy Good evening, ladies and gentlemen.
What is America?

Music in. It is a 1960s jazz instrumental. Lois and Peggy do a jazz dance to this text inspired by the' What is Jazz?' routine by Sid Caesar and Imogene Coco.

Peggy America is the feeling and the emotional upheaval such as the cataclysmic purple mountain majesty of the inner dynamic of reverberating vibrations,
from sea to shining sea ...

Good evening, ladies and gentlemen.
What is America?

I personally believe that America is the sound you can see in
the dawn's early light.
America is the wild waves breaking against the shores
from California to the New York islands.
America is a swinging spacious sky
America is a fruit and a plain and a purple bird such as
flying against the amorphous Gulf Stream water, white with foam.

Good evening, ladies and gentlemen,
What is America?
America is a woman whose land that I love ...

Then I told them a little something about myself
and my time in America
I told them
I always fantasised about tiny people when I was young
Not even doll size,
but tiny doll-size people ...

I was always the boy of course
And there was a girl
naked in the house.
Breasts,
I was aware of her breasts.
Her breasts were beautiful
I loved each breast
differently.
I was aware of my forehead.
I became aware of it
against her
breasts . . .

Lois stops dancing and stares at Peggy.
Music stops.

Peggy Good evening, ladies and gentlemen.
What is America?
I don't know.

Lois Everything is *known* now. Tourette's, Asperger's, hamburgers, high
jinks, jacks, data banks, failed banks. All available at the Gap and
downloadable on the internet.

Peggy I *almost* know many things.
I almost know that 'My country 'tis of thee!'

Lois takes microphone out of her coat pocket and continues in reporter
persona

Lois Can you see any damage from where you are standing?
This is a level-five hurricane force with an expected storm surge.
Evacuation procedures in effect and I'm standing by when and if we regain
radio contact. Standing by . . . standing . . .

Music up. It is a slightly altered instrumental version of 'Stand by Me' that
ends with the recording of Rev. Jeremiah Wright's church choir singing the
same song.

I'm standing . . .
standing on ceremony,
standing on hollow ground
standing up for your rights
standing in the shadow of love

standing
stand
united we stand
hot dog stand
Izbecistand
headstand
mic stand
stand

stand-off
stand firm
stand and deliver
stand-pede
stand down
stand around
stand here
stand there

stand by your man
I can't stand the rain
stand on your own two feet

Let me give you a footnote . . .

Note: Lois now quotes from a sermon given by Rev. Jeremiah
Wright just after the 9/11 terrorist attacks. He was quoting
Edward Peck, former US Ambassador to Iraq and deputy
director of President Reagan's terrorism task force who, by
referencing Malcolm X's 1963 'Chickens Come Home to Roost'
speech, was stating that America's foreign policy had put the
nation in peril. These remarks by Rev. Wright, Barack Obama's
former minister, were used as 'proof' of Obama's anti-Americanism
during the 2008 US presidential campaign.

. . . So we don't lose sight of the big picture
Turn to you neighbour and say, 'Footnote'

America's chickens, are coming home to roost.
We took this country by terror away from the Sioux, the Apache,
the Comanche, the Arapaho, the Navajo. Terrorism.
We took Africans away from their country to build our way of ease
and kept them enslaved and living in fear. Terrorism.
We bombed Grenada and killed innocent civilians, babies,
non-military personnel.
We bombed the black civilian community of Panama with stealth bombers
and killed unarmed teenagers and toddlers, pregnant mothers and
hard-working fathers.
We bombed Qaddafi's home, and killed his child. Blessed are they who
bash your children's head against the rock.
We bombed Iraq. We killed unarmed civilians trying to make a living. We
bombed a plant in Sudan to pay back for the attack on our embassy, killed
hundreds of hard-working people, mothers and fathers who left home to go
to work that day not knowing that they'd never get back home. Kids playing
in the playground, mothers picking up children after school. Civilians, not
soldiers, people just trying to make it day by day.
We bombed Hiroshima. We bombed Nagasaki, and we nuked far more than
the thousands in New York and the Pentagon and we never batted an eye.
America's chickens have come home to roost.
End of footnote. Now turn to your neighbour and say, 'End of footnote.'

Music out

Peggy They told me if I was going to be Miss America, it would be wrong to say anything bad about the country.

Lois That wasn't wrong. It was right. Rev. Jeremiah Wright.

Peggy That's not funny

Lois You want funny? I'll show you funny . . . (*Referring to Peggy who is standing on the edge of the runway.*) Here she is ladies and gentlemen, somewhere between the age of eighteen and twenty-two, weighing 121 pounds and . . . exactly how tall are you?

Peggy Realistically I am 8 feet 9 inches.

Lois Aren't you supposed to be 5 feet 2 inches?

Peggy I don't think I am much over seven feet, although I was told eight and a half. I forget what the hell they said I was . . . What did they say I was?

Lois You are an attraction.

Peggy I am an attraction.

Lois Not attractive, but an attraction.

Peggy Anywhere I go, I attract attention.

Lois (*crossing to Peggy and looking up*) It's your height.

Peggy I always feel watched, even when I am alone. Like they can even see me not checking my breasts for lumps in the shower like I am supposed to.

Lois (*speaking to audience*) You never told me that when you look at her hand, her neck and her haircut . . . that it's hard to imagine that she gave birth to a child.

Peggy I decided to be Miss America to keep people's minds off what I really am.

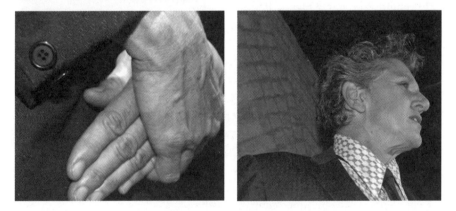

Lois Step right up, step right up. Have your photo taken with Miss America. (*Taking two people from the audience.*) Come stand up here. You can be the mother. You are looking up at your child and you have a wet belly from washing too many dishes. You can be the father. You stand next to the mother with your hands in your pockets and you just look away. Now let's set the scene. It's a living room. There is a box of tissues on the couch. The clock in the back says ten past eleven. There is a picture on the wall. I think it is Jerusalem. There is a TV and a crack in the ceiling. I think it is a leak. OK, ready?

Note: References to the life, philosophy and artistic practice of Diane Arbus occur throughout the piece. This moment is inspired by the photograph 'Jewish Giant at Home with His Parents in the Bronx, NY, 1970'. The preceding scene includes some biographical details of the real-life subject of the photo, Eddie Carmel, who was once billed as the 'Tallest Man on Earth' by the Ringling Brothers Circus. The photo, which shows an 8'9" Carmel towering over his average-sized parents, was part of an exhibit at New York's Museum of Modern Art and was featured in magazines all over the US.

Lois (*sitting in the audience*) I am going to hold on to that photo. It might be worth millions some day.

Peggy (*making her way slowly back to where she was sitting at the beginning*) I dreamt . . . I was a plastic bag in a tree.
Lasting for years till I shredded and turned grey
and never untied myself.
Rough and almost natural, almost within reach out the window.
There is something about a plastic bag
caught in a tree that is beautiful.
You notice it. You want to do something about it, but you know
you have to leave it there for years until it wears itself out.
It never goes away. None of them have ever gone away.
I know this, especially at night,
I can hear them out my window.
Like weather. Keeping me company in the dark.

Blackout.

Lois You never told me you were afraid of the dark. (*Taking picture of audience.*) OK, everyone, show me fear . . .

Ready? Fear on a count of three. 1, 2, 3 . . .

Lois And now show me shock on a count of three. 1, 2, 3 . . .

Peggy Oh my God.

Lois OK now, God on a count of three. 1, 2, 3 . . .

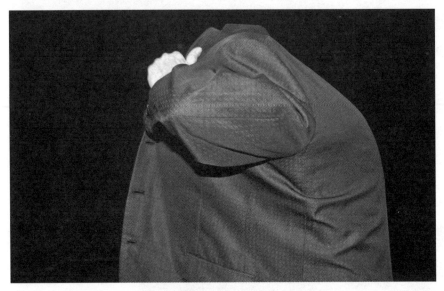

Peggy I am honoured to accept the title of Miss America. I would like to thank everyone who voted for me. This makes me very happy.

Lois OK. Happy on a count of three. 1 . . . 2 . . . 3 . . .

Peggy It is almost like how could this be? Not only am I tall, but my hands are very big, my face is very big, my feet are very large, my Adam's apple . . . A lot of people are curious about my genitals, but my genitals, ladies and gentlemen, are normal.

Lois OK now, normal on a count of three. 1, 2, 3 . . .

Peggy I have a lot of work to do as Miss America.
I hope this is not the year I will get a headache like Bob did
and have a stroke and my brain will be robbed of oxygen and I'll lose my social skills and in order to do a show someone will have to write the whole script and tape it to the back wall of the theatre like they did for Joe Chaikin so I won't have to learn it.

Peggy Why are you here again?

Lois (*walking back to sit in Peggy's chair upstage left*) I worry that there are some things you wouldn't see if you didn't photograph them.

Peggy sits up in the spotlight. Behind her on the screen is video footage of flooding in New Orleans during Hurricane Katrina.

Peggy I worry a lot that I will drown in the dark.
I picture the very black flood, miles and miles of darkness down under me.
My feet dangling like a tiny insect from the surface.
Searchlights far away on the surface of the water
are looking for me but not finding me.
Panic coming up my throat, gulping water and choking,
knowing I am a goner.
Knowing that I will fall slowly down, down, miles and miles
till I hit the dark bottom as fish food.
That's why I don't go on cruises.
You know with drowning people,
they just miss you by a moment and you're gone.
Or they rescue you just in time and you're saved.
Or you could lose your crown.
Or you could lose your wig like Jayne Mansfield did
and the world will think you lost your head.

And that is the end of that.

There is a massive explosion of lightning with loud cracks of thunder and a recording of the biggest storm so far. Lois flings herself across the stage in a burlesque of fake 'storm acting'. At a certain point she gets the microphone from her coat pocket and breathlessly delivers these lines.

Lois The bridge is broken, the streets are flooded, the lines are down, the power is out. We won't have Christmas lights or New Year's fireworks. We won't even have candles. We'll live in the grey mud of what-is-the-point?

Lighting and sound effect out. Lois drops the acting and walks down stage centre.

What *is* the point of doing a show when we are living on a landfill where every plastic bag ever made still exists?

Lois goes offstage and gets a bucket to catch an imaginary drip from the ceiling, then addresses Peggy lying on the floor.

I have been waiting in the rain and the wind in the storm . . .
for forty-three minutes.
Put on your shoes get your coat get your hat and come home.
Put on your shoes get your coat get your hat and come home.
Put on your shoes get your coat get your hat and come home.

Lois walks upstage and sits on Peggy's upstage-left chair. Peggy sits up and puts on her shoe as the sound of the storm transforms into a rhythmic trickle of drips. She does a lip-synched Gene Kelly-style tap dance to the rhythm of the drips. At the end of her big finish Lois pulls Peggy aside.

Lois I need to talk to you.

Peggy Me?

Lois Yeah.

Peggy You know . . . you . . .

Lois What?

Peggy You just show up . . .

Lois Yeah?

Peggy If you want to talk to me, say to me, 'I'd like to sit down with you and talk. When can we do that?' But you just show up and that's wrong. You know, I am not dressed . . . I was not expecting you.

Lois What?

Peggy You're intruding on my privacy.

Lois If we continue to avoid talking about the relationship all we'll have left is the weather and YouTube.

Peggy Why are we here again?

Lois There is something in the repetition, something about going over and over something until you understand it.

Peggy Oh, I know why are we here again. It's that old talking about our relationship. That is an old act.

Lois Old act?

Peggy Old act.

Lois (*moving to face Peggy*) I never told you that I always wanted to be Miss America, or rather I wanted to be in the contest, and when I was nine I thought my best chance in the talent competition was to do a striptease. So I spent hours in the bathroom mirror working on my routine. I wanted to strip for Miss America. But I never made it to the Miss America contest although I do sometimes *miss* America. I've put pictures on the backs of milk cartons, signs on the lampposts around the city, and even now the city is littered with these signs. I miss it. I miss the USA in your Chevrolet. I miss the old act, the old neighbourhood, the Second Avenue Deli. I miss the Orchidia. I miss you sometimes. I miss the old . . . 1, 2, 3.

Peggy relinquishes and steps forward into a centre spot to do the 'old act', an adaptation of a Mike Nicols and Elaine May routine from the 1960s on the subject of adultery.

Note: In previous performance pieces we usually manage to include at least one reference or tribute to a 1950s or 1960s comedy duo such as Mike Nicols and Elaine May, or Sid Caesar and Imogen Coco. We study the way they manage the 'live' of live television, their absolute faith in humour, the structure of their timing, the way they manage the gender and power dynamics of personal and professional partnerships. We study them and we copy them and, even though we resist, we end up 'performing' them.

Peggy Hold it hold it
I don't want to do the old act.

Peggy stops the act and takes her rant into the audience. Lois gets on the runway and performs a striptease while singing the jingle from a Dinah Shore Chevrolet commercial from the 1950s. The following lines are delivered simultaneously.

Peggy I don't have time for this.
I have a lot of work to do as Miss America.
I have to travel twenty thousand miles a month,
I have to change my location every twenty-four to forty-eight hours.

Lois *See the USA in your Chevrolet*
America is asking you to call
Drive your Chevrolet through the USA
America is the greatest land of all.

Peggy I am America, I am the storm, I am the future.
I have to make a change.
I can, I know I can I know. Yes, I can.
I am a dangerous and hungry Miss America
with an appetite to be somebody
and a great hunger to be a star.

She continues ad-libbing about being famous, with references to local mainstream theatres and current symbols of fame and success.

Lois *On a highway or a road along a levee...*
Performance is sweeter, nothing can beat her,
Life is completer in a Chevy.
So make a date today to see the USA
And see it in your Chevrolet.
Mwah

Peggy (*looking at Lois who has now stripped down to an American flag bikini*) I don't want to be a runner-up or a vice-president.
I want to be America's next top something.

Lois (*stopping the act and looking at Peggy*) What is wrong with just being Miss America?

Peggy I don't want people to come just to see my body.
I don't want to be known just for my beauty.
Just another pretty face.
I want to be known for creating something new.
(*Getting increasingly worked up.*)
I gotta dance. I gotta make ... new steps.
That's it I want make new steps. New steps.
New STEPS that come up to here!!
(*She mimes a staircase running up her body.*)
And people will say 'What's that? What's she doing?'

Lois (*giving up on her striptease and sitting on the edge of the refrigerator*) What *is* she doing?

Peggy And I might not even use my feet ...
I don't just dance with my feet, I dance from here,
I dance from here – (*Pointing to her heart.*)
I got ten toes on my heart.

Lois Did you know that hearts don't grow with the body?
That's why giants die, their hearts aren't big enough to pump the blood to places that far away. Like a giraffe, giraffes have high blood pressure because they have to pump blood up a such a long neck.

Peggy I *think* I know what you mean.

Lois (*walking over to Peggy, engaging in an unconscious partnering dance*)
Maybe you need a partner, a running mate . . .
somebody to show off your great dancing talent.

Peggy (*finishing the dance*) I don't think so. I think I want to dance alone.
I gotta go solo. It's got to be me, myself, alone.
You know what I mean? I need to create a new step.

*Peggy steps away from Lois and tries out ridiculous, frantic, full-body
movements until she finally realises they are not working.*

Peggy (*defeated*) That was the worst one yet.

Lois Do you know that more people voted for American *Pop Idol* than
voted in the 2008 election, and they had to pay for the call?

Peggy I'm a complete failure. I am quitting.

*She starts to walk out, trips, thinks it might be a good idea for a step, walks
back and repeats it.*

Did you see that? This might be it.
Could we have some music?

*Music in. It is a version of a song from a Sid Caesar movie. Peggy sings and
dances to it.*

Peggy *First you walk across the floor*
And then you do that step
(*She grabbs Lois and forces her to join in.*) Come with me . . .
Then you walk across some more
And then you do that step

Then you take your partner's hand
And then you do that step

Then you listen to the band
And then take that step . . .

*She trips and falls into the accident pose, shoes off, face down in the
spotlight. Music out. Lights change.*

Lois This is a catastrophe.
Catastrophe, a word stolen from people who have had too much stolen
from them already. Catastrophe, like the apostrophe hanging in the air
containing acres of paper and bone ground to dust.

Lois picks up microphone and walks back to the screen. She stands in front of video footage of Dinah Shore's iconic 1950s Chevrolet commercial, 'See the USA in Your Chevrolet'.

Come in, come in. Is anyone there?
I am standing neck deep in dirty water.
I can't see below the surface.
Things brush past me,
a torn oven mitt, a shoe dislodged from an owner.
This is more than a flooded basement, ladies and gentlemen,
and we've lost the chance to go for higher ground.
There's only one small spot left here on the tip of landfill,
the touchdown, the fire line, the fault line, the fabric
store of patchwork melting
pot-luck suppers across this great and worn
out sourced country
fried
sink hole
lot of shaking going on
and unless they finally give us the final word
on who wants to be a millionaire
and why not lose weight for fame

or fall down for glory
or ask the 64,000-dollar question
whose answer could be a case of life or death
or Budweiser just in time for the game. Off. No play. Rained out,
upstaged, care free, care less, care much more about the skins of animals
and the flight of bees
whose plight is still to be determined to win
no matter what the consequences.
And truth ladies and gentlemen, truth has nothing to do with it.
And love? Love?
What's love got to do with the border
line personality
whose pickin's are slim in the first place
with no way to get there without the airfare
and what if plane shadows were footprints
that might put corn out of business
as usual when the suspects
are few and far between those of us who know for a fact
that this digital noise is a false wind that blows our mind
and restricts the frequency of free speech
and free will and free lunches
for those who try but can no longer STAND
in line for the cash back on a dream house.

She drops the microphone and talks directly into the fan, which distorts her voice.

I'm talking fast to keep from drowning.
Talking to keep the mud from sucking me down.
Talking so you won't notice how scared I am.

Peggy (*standing up and speaking directly to audience*) What did Miss America say when they asked her how she felt about waterboarding? I don't like sports.

Lois That's not funny.

Peggy You have no sense of humour.

Lois (*walking down and standing beside Peggy*)
I lost my sense of humour in the flood.
It shorted out.

When the water rose and came in the outlet
and blew out my 1950s TV
and took with it all the sitcoms ever made.
When I tried to remember all that had gone and gone before
I couldn't because my external memory
had melted in the fire that electrified the water . . .

Lois starts to lose it and Peggy puts her arm around her and speaks on her behalf.

Peggy Ladies and gentlemen, I am afraid we are having a hard time making a comedy out of America.

Lois (*looking at Peggy*) You want funny? OK, I'll show you funny.

Now that's funny.

Peggy That's not funny.

Lois OK then, I'll show you funny.

She places Peggy where she had placed the bucket earlier and a steady drip starts to hit Peggy on the head.

Now that's funny.

Peggy (*standing under a steady stream of cold water*) What if I am the most beautiful woman in America?

What if I do represent the real America? What if I marry your daughter?

*Peggy moves
to far upstage spot,
Lois moves next
to the drip.*

Lois What if we
didn't do enough,
we didn't rescue,
we didn't rally,
we didn't prevent?
What if we weren't
as big
as we thought
we were,
what if we sat still,
we didn't say,
we were silent,
witnesses?
What if we
couldn't forgive?

Music in. It combines the rhythm of the dripping water, tap-dancing sequence and fragments of Patsy's Kline's recording of 'She's Got You'.

Lois joins Peggy in upstage spot.

Lois I am sorry I took your picture.

Peggy Just don't let it happen again.

Peggy exits.

Lois (*to audience*) One of the risks of appearing in public is the likelihood of being photographed.

Lois exits. Photos that she took during the show, including those of the audience, are projected on the back wall as the music continues.

48 Minutes
for
Palestine

created by
Mojisola Adebayo and Ashtar Theatre

with original music by
Rami Washara

48 Minutes for Palestine premiered at Ashtar Theatre in Ramallah on 4 May 2010.

The work was created by:

Mojisola Adebayo	*Concept, direction, design and 'script'/transcription of action*
Edward Muallem	*Deviser, performer and lighting designer*
Riham Issac	*Deviser and performer*
Rami Washara	*Composer and musician*
Mohammad Eid	*Deviser and assistant director*
Rasha Jahshan	*Deviser*
Mohammad Ali	*Technician and operator*

Ashtar Theatre are:

Iman Auon	*Artistic director*
Fida Jiryis	*Executive director*
Edward Muallem	*General manager*
Abdallah Mesleh	*Accountant*
Rabie Abu Dayeh	*Administrative assistant*

With many thanks to Iman Auon for her artistic support and all the Ashtar team, everyone at British Council Palestine, Qattan Foundation, SIDA, Anna Furse and Goldsmiths, University of London, Rebecca Watts, and all those who attended the open dress rehearsal and offered advice and support, and all the teachers mentioned who influenced the development of this work.

For permission to perform this work, or further information on the company, please contact: Ashtar Theatre, PO Box 17170, East Jerusalem 91171

tel: +972-2-2980037, 2964348/9   *fax:* + 972-2-2960326
email: info@ashtar-theatre.org

Notes
Mojisola Adebayo

I am a British citizen, which is one of the reasons I wanted to make this work. I will talk about this more later. I am also a theatre-maker. I have been working on various theatre projects in the Occupied Palestinian Territories (Palestine) since 1999. Much of my work over that period has been with Ashtar Theatre.

Ashtar was established in Jerusalem in 1991 by Iman Auon and Edward Muallem with the aim of running training courses and creating experimental theatre. Their stated mission is to:

> [make] theatre a fundamental need within the Palestinian society, through stimulating cultural awareness, awakening perceptions towards aesthetics and arousing artistic sensibility and taste. It also seeks to build and strengthen cultural bridges with the theatre world through creative works and ideas. Ashtar is actively engaged in researching and experimenting with various artistic elements, tools and techniques. It aims at creating a theatre that has the scent of musk, the colour of amber and the taste of figs. A theatre that is capable of penetrating all walls including that of the audience's unconscious. www.ashtartheatre.com

Ashtar first invited me to work with them in 2000 when they were experimenting with Forum Theatre, the interactive theatrical debating technique from Augusto Boal's *Theatre of the Oppressed*. I ran training courses for Ashtar and co-devised and directed two Forum plays in their *Abu Shakers Affairs* series. The first play explored the position of women in Palestinian society and the second highlighted the exploitation of young people during the *intifada* (uprising against Israeli occupation). I have always been impressed that despite living under such extremely oppressive conditions, Ashtar remained focused on making theatre that engaged the audience in debating problems within their own Palestinian society, rather than making Israel and the occupation their direct focus. The work we made together toured Palestine and the Middle East and was, by all accounts, very successful in entertaining and engaging audiences in debate.

However, I was frustrated – not with the work I was undertaking in Palestine, which always went very well. The root of my frustration was in the conversations I had with people when I came back home to Britain. People would ask, 'Where have you been, Moj?' I would say, 'Palestine.'

They'd say 'Pakistan?' 'No, Palestine.' 'Oh, you mean Israel?' I would say, 'Not exactly, I mean the Occupied Palestinian Territories.' 'Where's that?'

I once had an argument with an uncle who insisted I had actually been to Lebanon. I would try to explain that the Palestinians are living 'under occupation', which is why you won't find it on a map. Despite the fact that the experience of occupation is horrific, I could see in people's faces that the word did not resonate with them, on an emotional level. A toilet is occupied, so what? Theatre is your occupation, what's the problem? I would say one of the issues is that the Israeli government is allowing settlements to be built on Palestinian people's land. *Settlement*. A settlement sounds like a safe, warm place – a place where people who have travelled make a simple home which does not disrupt anyone. We are all expected to 'settle down' one day, aren't we? English is my language and I love it, but I find the English language can be rather deceptive, especially when it comes to describing oppressive regimes and colonial projects, in which it has an investment.

I have since come to feel that one of the reasons the situation in Palestine has been allowed to continue for as long as it has is because of both the power and also the impotence of spoken language. The word *holocaust* makes people shudder at the horror of the genocide committed against the Jewish people. As soon as most people associate the State of Israel with the holocaust, their attention is turned away from the plight of the Palestinians. The Palestinians – who are mainly Arabs but who are also themselves Jews, Armenians, Greeks, Africans – had nothing to do with the Jewish holocaust, yet they suffer as a direct consequence of the racism enacted in Europe over centuries, culminating in that terrible holocaust. The Afrikaans word *apartheid* conjures up images of an ugly and nasty system of racism perpetrated by white minority rulers against the majority black population in South Africa. Words to describe the condition of the Palestinian people lack the potency of the words 'holocaust' and 'apartheid'. Yet, for the past sixty years, the Palestinian people have experienced massacres, whole villages have been wiped out, there have been bombings, land clearances, evictions, enforced ghettos behind walls topped with razor wire, armed checkpoints, confinement, arrest without trial, race-based pass laws, widespread torture and breaches of all aspects of their human rights including freedom of movement, free-dom of speech, freedom of education – and, crucially today, access to water without which no human being can survive; all on the basis of ethnicity. Palestinian people know the meaning of the words *holocaust* and *apartheid*.

Having witnessed with my own eyes the widespread abuses of human rights while working in Palestine, I was not only frustrated that to many of my fellow British citizens the word 'occupation' does not resonate on an emotional level; I was also shocked that most people do not know that Britain is at the root of the conflict. The British government ruled the land of Palestine under a (so-called) mandate. *Mandate*: yet another manipulation of meaning in the English language. The word implies consent, a vote even. The Palestinian people were, of course, never consulted about whether they would like the British to govern them. During the British mandate in Palestine, our Foreign Office effectively handed over the land of Palestine and legitimated what was to become the Jewish State – Israel – through the Balfour Declaration to the Zionist Federation written in 1917. That infamous document was to be a death sentence for Palestine, a *sentence* written by a British hand. The problem of Palestine is a British problem. That is a fact every Palestinian I have met knows only too well. Yet most British people have no idea how implicated we are in the Middle East crisis. We are simply uneducated about it. The last ten years of working in Palestine has been a tough education for me. As a British citizen, I feel some responsibility. As a theatre artist I have a need to express this artistically.

Another factor that turns many people away from wanting to understand what is going on is that the problem is considered complex – too complicated to engage with, so people turn away. But the central problem in Palestine is the illegal occupation of Palestinian land by the State of Israel, a state based on race/religion. This is not complex at all. It is very simple; terrifyingly simple, so simple that even the United Nations agrees.

Some, in an attempt to understand this 'confusing' situation, are reduced to describing it as a conflict between two equal powers, Jews and Arabs, which is far from the truth. People say to me, 'Oh yes, they are always fighting, it will never end . . .' But there is no equality of power between Jews and Arabs in Israel/Palestine any more than there is equality of power between men and women in this world – whether economically, educationally, in employment, housing, weapons, politics, the media – you name it. This is not a battle between equal powers. Palestinians, like women, are the ones who are disempowered in the grand scenario. Perhaps the only power the Palestinians have is the power of culture. Indeed the Palestinian cultural scene is vibrant and very much alive. Ashtar Theatre is just one example of many.

Of course this belief in a conflict between two equal groups is also racialised. Most people I talk to in Britain, if you dig away at the surface, have a notion that the Israelis are somehow European (they take part in the *Eurovision* song contest after all!) and the Palestinians are the dark ones. Israel is an Asian country, though it is rarely referred to as such. I recall taking my partner to Jerusalem and her not quite believing at first that those black soldiers are in fact Jewish Israelis and that white, blond street seller is a Palestinian Arab! I remember talking with Catholic pilgrims from Spain who had been to church and were shocked to find the mass was in Arabic. Of course, why wouldn't a Catholic mass be in Arabic, since most Christians in Palestine are Arabs? It is my belief that racism against the perceived dark-skinned people and Islamophobia towards those who are all assumed to be Muslims, add to the reasons why we do not do enough to defend the Palestinians.

Then of course there is European guilt over centuries of racism against the Jewish people, coupled with the fear that one might be considered anti-Semitic if one questions the Israeli occupation. Therein lies another linguistic trick: the Palestinian people are Semitic too. To equate an illegal military occupation with being Jewish is an insult to the thousands of Jews who stand in opposition to it. It was not for this that six million innocents were murdered in Europe during the Second World War, it was not for this that so many fought, died and survived. For more on the occupation from a Jewish perspective see <www.jewsagainsttheoccupation.org> and <Jews for Justice for the Palestinians: www.jfjfp.com>.

So, in order to challenge language, to implicate and express myself as a British citizen, to diffuse the notion of complexity, to dispel the myth of a conflict between two races of equal power, to equate this inequality with gender relations, I decided I wanted to create a very *simple* play, a play without any words, performed by two actors, one man and one woman, who look as though they could be relatives. I wanted to make a piece of theatre, which would provide audiences in Britain and beyond with a visual image of occupation, through two characters with whom they could emotionally connect, in a story that would resonate, universally.

Picture this, or perhaps better still, imagine yourself in this situation. You are a woman. You live, happily, alone, in your home. You spend your days tending your garden, growing fruit and writing poetry. One day, a man walks into your home. He is carrying a suitcase. He looks dishevelled and close to death. He behaves as if he has arrived home. But you have no idea who he is. He hands you a document you do not understand. He starts to unpack his suitcase. You try various strategies to get him out, but he resists. A conflict unfolds. Eventually you are pushed out of your home. You end up carrying the suitcase. You are dishevelled and close to death.

Years ago, I had been inspired by the idea of a play without words through exploring Samuel Beckett's *Act without Words 1* and *2*, in workshops with Phillip Zarrilli. It was during my training with Professor Zarrilli that I came up with the scenario you have just read. This would later form the basis of *48 Minutes for Palestine*.

Following some discussion, Ashtar Theatre decided that they would like to work together with me on creating the play. The British Council agreed to support my trip and Ashtar secured funds from SIDA, A.M. Qattan Foundation and others. We set about our work, at Ashtar Theatre, Ramallah on the West Bank in January 2009. We decided Edward Muallem would play the man, and Riham Issac the woman. The devising process was supported by Rasha Jahshan and Mohammad Eid, who joined in warm-ups, games, exercises and improvisation tasks.

As director, I felt that we needed to have a shared preparation for performance that would inform the style of our work and provide us with a shared approach. The devising process was also bound to be quite painful. The actors live under occupation every day and every day they were going to come in and devise a play about it. I felt we needed a shared daily practice that would enable us to quieten our minds and strengthen our bodies – a method that would enable us to stay focused and work in harmony together, no matter if bombs fell down outside, no matter the daily drudgery of getting through checkpoints at gunpoint, no matter what depressing news of increased restrictions had been heard on television the night before. Occupation is exhausting for both body and mind, and we needed a preparation that would get us through. So, I chose to use Mind–Body (M–B).

M–B is a technique I learnt from choreographer Cindy Cummings while working at the Abbey Theatre in Ireland. M–B is informed by Butoh performance, from Japan. Like Butoh, the M–B walk is extremely slow; it has a low centre of gravity, with bended knees, rolling through the feet, external gaze, internal focus and connected breath. It is important that there is no extraneous movement, just a simple walk. Movements are layered on to this basic walk, one by one: walking with turning heads, walking with rolling shoulders, walking with reaching arms, etc. The actors travel across the space in pairs, in perfect synchronicity with each other, and music can be incorporated to support timing.

I also chose this as our basic daily preparation because I wanted us to have a shared reference point for our style of work and to enable the actors to develop their physical presence on stage. We could not rely on words to connect with the audience; the actors would need to have that special something else that would draw people in and hold them. My work with Phillip Zarrilli and later with choreographer Emilyn Claid was based on the notion that an actor's presence can be developed by connecting the mind, an aligned body, stillness in the eyes, external and internal focus, breath and movement, with a stripping away of all unnecessary action and *attitude*.

Following our M–B warm up, we would play games of power and taking space. Through our work in Theatre of the Oppressed, Ashtar was already familiar with many of these games and I knew they enjoyed playing them. Because of that familiarity we could start to push the games beyond what we knew and allow ourselves to be surprised into improvisation. I have always felt that so many theatre games are microcosms of plays. We tried to find the drama embedded inside the games. This choice was also based on the fact that many Palestinian people (Ashtar members included) describe the workings of the occupation as a kind of game, a power game, of space taking. Playing games gave us rich material for exploring the strategies that both characters would use in the home. We laughed a lot in the process, which was really liberating and healing for all of us. Laughter was an important element in dealing with such a serious subject. These theatre games also do not require speech in order to be effective; games communicate dramatically very clearly without words. Through playing and watching games, we gained the confidence to do away with spoken language. The play came from playing.

We also knew early on that both actors would need to be very clear on the style of acting we were working in. This was going to be a play, a play without words, not a mime show, not physical theatre, not stylized acting, not a dance but a play in action. We agreed everything had to be real. Every gesture, every look, every move had to be real. My direction was that the acting needed to be almost filmic; a film where the actor draws the audience in through what is going on internally. This internal connection is read in the eyes, the breath, the gestures, the moves, but everything must come from deep inside.

In order for the work to be real, the actors needed to know and believe their own characters. We had to be detailed. The play was not going to work if the characters were just symbolic figures or political metaphors. So the actors did a lot of research. We used imaginative meditations on the characters and drawings – all tasks that did not require words. Though we did feel the need to name the characters, just for ourselves. The woman became Samar and the man, Issac.

One challenge we had to overcome was to understand and relate to Issac, the occupier. Edward had to get inside the head, inside the shoes of a man occupying someone's home. This was especially painful for Edward as he has had his own home occupied by a group of abusive soldiers, and was forced to live with his family in one room as the occupiers took over the house. Yet now he had to put himself in the occupier's position: he had to understand Issac as a human being. He had to know why Issac walks in dishevelled and close to death. He had to connect with and feel the stories in the children's clothes in the suitcase. Issac could not just be a one-dimensional, evil abuser. For the play to work one must understand Issac. So I suggested that Edward visit Yad Vashem, the holocaust memorial in Jerusalem, with Mohammad, our co-deviser and later assistant director and I. Going to Yad Vashem was a difficult decision to take for many reasons. It is never easy to put yourself in the shoes of someone who is hurting you and to try to understand what they have been through. But this is what we did. What was very moving was that many of the scenes from photographs in the holocaust memorial resonated on a very personal level with Edward and Mohammad. There were photos of ghettos, walls, camps, maps, indiscriminate shooting and mass graves. All sights we recognised from the West Bank and Gaza. Yet there were also images of the gas chambers . . . Out of the silence, Mohammad asked, 'Do you think this is what they will do to us?'

The trip to Yad Vashem deepened Edward's understanding of his role and made for a useful reference point when at times the acting slipped into archetypes of 'baddie' and 'goodie'. The improvisations between Riham and Edward continued to work well, but we soon felt we needed to establish a sense of place and space. We had been working three-dimensionally to increase our sense of reality, using a few household objects from Samar's home and garden. But we needed clearly to establish the home and its boundaries. However, our budget was extremely limited. We had almost no money to work with. We also knew that we wanted a 'set' which we could easily tour anywhere in the world. I looked around Ramallah and asked myself what I could see. I saw rocks, lots of rocks and oranges, and very little water. As we had been working in the round, I came in one day and made a circle of oranges and rocks. We all felt it was very simple but very beautiful. It seemed to convey the Palestinian landscape, dry and harsh yet warm and rich. The oranges also had the effect of little bulbs of light and added a subtle glow to the stage. Water and water scarcity became a central motif in the play.

The next element we wanted to work with was music. We felt that music would help the audience to deal with the fact there were no words, even though they were watching a realistic play. Music would also enable the actors to have a shared sense of time. The music in the M–B warm-ups played an important part in connecting the actors rhythmically and the rhythms for this show are crucial.

Composer and musician Rami Washara joined us for rehearsals and improvised with instruments from the Middle East. As with the acting and the set, everything had to be real. So the instruments were mainly string and he avoided using synthetic sounds. Rami's music was designed to support the action and not dictate it. There was a fine balance between music and action. It was important to us that the action spoke and the music supported that. Otherwise we were in danger of creating a wordless opera.

After three weeks of devising, we had an open rehearsal with audience feedback. The main point we took from this was that the characters had to be more real – not metaphors, not archetypes. We could not represent the establishment of the State of Israel and the occupation of Palestine in a play. We could only show what happens to a woman in her home when a man whom she does not know decides to move in. For logistical reasons we had to take a break from the project for a while and then we returned for one week more of rehearsals. It was actually very useful to have some distance and time to reflect. Often devising processes are very intense and it is sometimes useful to let the work marinate for a while. When we gathered again for the final week, we worked intensively on character and made some adjustments to the play in response to the audience feedback. The show then premiered on 4 May 2010 at Ashtar Theatre in Ramallah. *48 Minutes for Palestine* has since toured Spain, Brazil and Palestine and is going on to tour the Middle East, South Africa, Europe and North America. It was during the tour that I began transcribing the action/writing the 'script' below.

What is powerful about this play is that people from different places in the world understand it in different ways. As it is free from speech, it is accessible to people from all cultures, is accessible to deaf audiences, and has been audio-described for people who are blind. The performances are followed by lively debates. For some it is about a woman experiencing domestic violence, for others it is about divorce, homelessness, being a refugee, apartheid, genocide, war . . . It is called *48 Minutes for Palestine* in memory of the *nakba*, the disaster which befell the Palestinian people through the formation of the State of Israel in 1948. The 48 minutes or so that the play takes to perform is dedicated to them. Yet it can be performed and understood by any one of you, even if you have never heard of Israel-Palestine. Yet we also hope the play will increase debate and get people engaged with the subject of occupation.

If you want to perform the piece and/or music, do contact Ashtar Theatre for permission. If you do perform it, the stage directions outlined below are guidelines. It is not a holy text. Not every single breath and precise action is given in detail, but it will give you a sense of how the piece works; and our audiences tell us it does work. It is worth noting that there is much more comic potential and humour in the play than you might read at first on the page. Of course, like any play, it will change if you perform it and it is still in development for us too. Treat the 'script' like a map: if you want to take a different route, do. It is a map but it is not the destination, the journey can only be undertaken by you.

Here are a few notes we found helpful in rehearsals and performances:

▸ Be in the present.

▸ Connect your breath with your eyes, body, mind, emotion, action . . .

▸ In rehearsal, approach the movement as task.

▸ Let all unnecessary action and attitude fall away. Let go of all you don't need.

▸ If you over-express with your face, you leave the audience unsatisfied, expecting and wanting words.

▸ Release the tension in your face and let the action speak for itself.

▸ As in acting for film, draw the audience in rather than pushing meaning out.

▸ The emotion must be truthful: no short cuts, no tricks, no lies.

▸ Know your character, be detailed.

▸ It is called a play for a reason. Play, play games, keep the dynamic of those games in the play.

▸ Hold it within.

▸ The 'script' has and can be used as audio-description material for audience members who are blind or visually impaired. The play is for everyone.

Photos from 2011 production by Taryn Burger.

For an up-to-date version of the script, contact Ashtar Theatre.

CAST

Samar
female

Issac
male

*Issac begins the play looking thin and dishevelled and close to death.
He wears a dark, dirty, broken-down dated suit which is far too big
for him now, a dirty white shirt and scuffed black leather shoes.*

*Samar begins the play looking young and healthy. She wears a long skirt
and top of natural earthy colours. She is barefoot.*

*Whatever the cultural background of the players, it is important
that the two could be related – their skin tone and features are similar.*

48 MINUTES FOR PALESTINE

SPACE

It is possible for the play to be performed in the round, with the audience at two ends or end-on. For the purposes of this script the action will be described as if the play was performed end-on, therefore upstage, downstage, stage left and stage right will be used to describe positioning.

Laid out upon the black ground is a perfect circle of rocks, approximately 5.5 metres in diameter, with approximately 30 centimetres between each rock. At the upstage-right diagonal the circle of rocks is interrupted by a large basket containing oranges, a fruit knife with a wooden handle and a beautiful old porcelain plate. On the diagonal opposite the basket, downstage left, the circle is interrupted by a mound of rocks out of which shoots up a single sunflower, about the same height as the knee of the female player. The rocks are covered with small fragments of orange peel. Hidden in the rocks are pieces of white chalk. Next to the stage-left of the rock mound, inside the circle, there is an old chipped and slightly rusty white aluminium bowl. Inside the bowl is a similar mug. Next to the bowl is yellow coloured cloth and a large glass jug half full of clean water.

Inside the centre of the circle, exactly centre stage, is a rug, no longer than the body of the female player, made of natural fibres with similar colours to her costume. At the same end of the rug as the basket, stage left, there is a soft pillow inside a white embroidered cotton pillowcase. Under the pillow is a hand-made leatherbound notebook and an aged ink pen. Inside the circle, stage right and on the same line as the mound of rocks, there is a fine old wooden chair. On the seat of the chair is a beautifully embroidered cushion of natural dyes. On the downstage back of the chair hangs a large key, strung on to a piece of black elastic. On the opposite diagonal to the chair, stage left, inside the circle, on the same line as the basket of oranges, sits a wooden crate. On top of the wooden crate is an old chess board, which folds in half and will open to reveal inside a wooden backgammon board, with black and white wooden backgammon pieces.

MUSIC

Numbers of the pieces, by the composer Rami Washara, are indicated in the script, and are provided following the script.

LIGHTING

if available, can be used in the storytelling to great effect. For purposes of simplicity the design we used is not described here.

ACTION

The action below was transcribed after the play was devised and performed. The action is still alive and would be best interpreted as a living thing.

Music 1   Samar's line

➤ *Samar holds her skirt gathered full of oranges. Beginning at the basket, with one foot inside the circle and one foot outside, Samar takes oranges from her skirt and places them, one by one, between the rocks. Rock, place orange, step forward, rock, place orange, step forward, rock, place orange, step forward ... As she does this, the audience enter.*

➤ *Rock, place orange, step forward ... until the circle is complete.*

➤ *Samar topples the remaining oranges from her skirt into the basket.*

➤ *Samar stands.*

➤ *Samar stretches.*

➤ *Samar smiles.*

➤ *Samar decides.*

➤ *She goes to the rug, takes the notebook and pen from under her pillow and writes contemplations on a good morning. She shifts position every now and then, on to her belly, her back, her side ...*

➤ *When the audience is settled, Samar places her notebook under the pillow.*

➤ *She gets up and steps with a spring in her step, to the basket. Her internal music is lighter and higher in tone than the music we hear.*

➤ *She takes her plate and knife from the basket. She examines several oranges and then picks one for herself. The first of the season.*

➤ *She goes to sit on the rug, on her knees, facing downstage. She places the plate on her lap. She takes the orange and throws it in the air, catches it, passes it from one hand to another and back again. Then she peels the orange in one series of motions, careful not to break the curling, falling, orange peel dropping into her plate. She carefully cuts her orange. She places a piece into her mouth, chews it, tastes it, swallows, takes a pip from her mouth and places it on the plate, smiling and nodding all the while.*

➤ *Samar stands and walks, with the tiniest skip, back to the basket. She returns the remainder of the orange and takes the used plate and knife across the circle towards the water jug.*

> Samar bends down and picks up the long curl of orange peel and holds it in the air. She admires the peel and then has an idea. She curls the orange peel delicately around the stem of the sunflower.

> Samar picks up the plate with knife inside, takes the water jug, and pours a tiny amount of water into the plate. She checks how much she has taken from the jug. The muscles in her eyebrows pull together a little into a small frown.

> Samar places the jug of water back down on the ground by the rocks. She carefully swirls the water around the plate, three times. She pours the remaining water in the plate over the knife and over the root of the plant. She slides her forefinger and thumb down each side of the flat of the blade and flicks the excess water on to the sunflower.

> Now she bends over the sunflower, closes her eyes and smells it with a deep intake of breath and a motion that brings her back up to standing.

> Samar looks at her plate, places it face down on the mound of rocks. She buries the knife in the mound of rocks, handle up.

> She grabs the cloth at the side of the rocks and swiftly crosses to the chair. She goes to clean it, then stops. She notices her key.

> Music fades.

> Samar lifts the key from the chair slowly and places it about her neck. It hangs at her breastbone. She touches the key to her body.

> Then Samar wipes the chair industriously, lovingly, starting at the top, down the sides. She kneels as she works.

> As Samar is cleaning the chair, Issac silently approaches, backwards, extremely slowly, from upstage centre.

> Issac wears a suit that is now too big for him. He carries a heavy suitcase in his left hand and his body is bent from the weight and the exhaustion of a long, hard journey.

> Samar does not see Issac. She pauses cleaning as she notices the embroidered cushion. She exhales. Drops her head and upper body on to the cushion, smiling. She takes her upstage hand and caresses her own hair, as if it were someone else doing the action.

> She sits up, looks at the chair and wags her finger, smiling. She stands and picks up the pillow and beats the dust out of it, holding the cloth in the other hand.

> Samar looks at the chair, then goes to cross to the water as Issac steps over the line of rocks and oranges and turns into the circle.

Music 2   Issac's entrance

> Samar sees Issac. She inhales sharply, jumps slightly and steps back, only just remaining inside the circle, slightly off balance.

> Issac sees Samar. He takes a slight step back while holding her gaze. He then steps, very slowly, into the circle. Still holding her gaze, he places the case down, beside him, stage left, then slowly walks to his right.

➤ *Samar, looking back at him, walks slowly to her right.*

➤ *Issac stops at the basket of oranges.*

➤ *Samar stops at the rocks and water.*

➤ *Issac's focus slowly wanders down to the jug.*

➤ *Samar looks at the water jug. She drops the cloth on the floor. She looks at Issac.*

➤ *Samar decides.*

➤ *She picks up the jug and the mug. She pauses. She turns towards Issac. She walks around the circle upstage left. She pauses before the wooden crate.*

➤ *Samar looks at Issac.*

➤ *Issac looks at Samar.*

➤ *Hesitantly, carefully, she pours a little water into the mug.*

➤ *Issac steps forward, reaching slightly. Samar walks a little towards him.*

➤ *Issac takes the mug of water and with his feet close together, slightly bent forward, he drinks the water, quickly, leaning back until every drop is gone.*

➤ *Samar watches Issac drink.*

> *Issac looks at Samar, hands her the mug. His eyes turn to the jug of water. He takes the jug from Samar's hands, she resists slightly but loses her grip. Issac drinks a greater quantity from the jug.*

> *Samar watches briefly then pulls the jug away from him.*

> *She looks at the remaining water, frowning. She inhales and walks swiftly back towards the mound of rocks, placing the water back down. Issac watches Samar.*

> *She turns round. Hesitantly she goes back towards Issac, pausing before the crate.*

> *Issac reaches inside his jacket.*

Foreign Office,

November 2nd, 1917.

Dear Lord Rothschild,

    I have much pleasure in conveying to you, on behalf of His Majesty's Government, the following declaration of sympathy with Jewish Zionist aspirations which has been submitted to, and approved by, the Cabinet

    "His Majesty's Government view with favour the establishment in Palestine of a national home for the Jewish people, and will use their best endeavours to facilitate the achievement of this object, it being clearly understood that nothing shall be done which may prejudice the civil and religious rights of existing non-Jewish communities in Palestine, or the rights and political status enjoyed by Jews in any other country"

    I should be grateful if you would bring this declaration to the knowledge of the Zionist Federation.

Music 3   The letter

> Samar backs away slightly. Issac takes out a rolled document. He gestures towards Samar with it. Samar steps forward and takes it.

> Samar turns aside to read the letter silently as Issac bends to pick up his suitcase and walks stage left. Samar turns to see him move and then turns back to read. Samar breathes deeper than before. She looks at Issac. He is looking around the circle. Samar continues to read quickly.

> Samar rolls up the letter swiftly. Issac stands behind his suitcase on the opposite side of the circle, looking at her.

> Silence.

> Samar walks directly across the circle to Issac. She hands him the document, sharply. He takes it from her, slowly, and places it back in his inside pocket.

> Issac pauses slightly, then notices Samar's key. He handles it, but Samar grabs it away and places it under her top.

> Samar notices the case. She picks it up, turns and places it outside the circle, where Issac first entered.

> Issac follows her, steps outside the circle, picks up the case and walks past Samar with a slight look, he brings the case back into the circle and places it back in exactly the same spot.

> Samar picks up the case again, looks at Issac and puts it back outside the circle.

> Issac picks up the case, this time not looking at Samar, and places it back inside the circle.

> Samar picks up the case, more quickly this time. She looks at him and places it back outside, landing the case harder now.

> Issac goes and picks up the case. This time Samar stands inside the circle with her arms and legs outstretched, blocking his way back in.

> Issac pauses briefly, then lifts the case to push Samar out of the way.

> Samar blocks the case and Issac behind it with her hands, body and strength.

➤ *Issac pushes Samar until she is almost out of the opposite end of the circle. Samar pushes back hard. They struggle with all their strength. The rug is disrupted. Samar turns and pushes with her back. They make a complete circle in the struggle. Samar turns and uses her head against the case, Issac does the same. They turn another circle, pushing harder still, until Samar turns to her side and Issac pushes Samar off balance with the case, knocking her to the ground. Samar lands in a heap on the floor inside the circle, landing badly on her hand. She winces.*

➤ *Issac looks slightly at Samar as she curls up from the ground. Still with the case in his arms, he walks back to the position stage right and places the case back down. He stands again behind the case as Samar recovers, tending to her injury.*

➤ *Issac reaches back inside his pocket. Samar turns on the floor to look at him. Issac takes out the document again. He shakes it in the air, gesturing to her, and places it back in his pocket.*

➤ *Issac looks at Samar. He takes off his jacket. She watches him from the floor, cradling her hand.*

➤ *Issac looks around, goes to hang his jacket on the chair.*

➤ *Samar breathes in sharply and comes to her knees.*

- *Issac pauses slightly, looks at Samar, continues to hang his jacket on the chair.*

- *Issac looks at Samar, then goes back to stand behind his case, in the same position as when he first put down the case. She watches him.*

- *Issac pauses slightly at his case and looks at it.*

Music 4 and 5   The suitcase

- *Issac bends down and touches the case. He places his ear to the case, as if to listen to it. He comes up and looks at it, intently. He brings the case down so it is flat on the ground. He flicks the right catch open, and then the left. He lifts the lid of the case, very slowly and gently. Samar watches intently.*

- *Issac takes a black waistcoat from the case. He stands and puts it on. He pulls it into shape, dressing himself correctly.*

- *Slowly he bends down and pulls a crumpled lady's dress from the case. The dress is long and dark with pretty red flowers on it. Issac holds the dress up and then folds it over his left shoulder and holds it close to him, as if embracing a loved one. He sways gently with the dress while walking it a couple of steps upstage. He places the dress down on the floor, by the edge of the circle.*

> Issac returns to the case. He reaches down and takes out a child's sky-blue woollen cardigan. It is dirty and has holes in it. He places it further upstage in the circle, on the edge of the basket.

> Issac returns to the case. He takes out a pair of red baby's boots. He places the boots at the point in the circle where he first entered, upstage centre, facing inwards.

> Issac returns to the case. He picks out a family photograph, crumpled and burnt at the edges. He holds up the photograph to Samar as he walks past the dress, cardigan and boots to the wooden crate. He leans the photo up against the backgammon board.

Music 6   Rearranging the space (*rhythmic percussion*)

> Issac returns more briskly to the case now.

> Samar gets up to look more closely at the photo.

> As she is looking at the photo, Issac takes out an old carved wooden toy car from the case and 'drives' the car quickly along the ground, from the case round the circle, downstage right towards the mound of rocks, where he parks it.

> Samar turns to see Issac parking the toy car.

> Samar quickly crosses the circle from the crate to the rocks. She picks up the car and marches to Issac's case and throws it back into the case as Issac takes out his mug and fork inside and places it next to the basket. A beat. They look at each other, then cross each other at a pace. Issac walks towards the case as Samar walks to the basket. She picks up his mug and fork and puts it back in the case as he picks out a book. He walks towards the wooden crate, removes the backgammon board, slamming it on the floor, places his book on the crate and moves the crate slightly downstage in the circle. Samar immediately picks up the book as Issac crosses her briskly, going back to the case to pick out the mug again, placing it back next to the basket as she throws the book back into the suitcase. They cross each other again as she again takes the mug and fork from next to the basket to put it back in the case. Issac takes yet another book from the case and places it on the wooden crate. He now moves the wooden crate upstage centre as Samar throws the mug back in the

suitcase and slams it. Issac, meanwhile, steps up on to the wooden crate, takes matches from his waistcoat pocket and a sparkler from the other pocket and lights it. The music becomes faster and more celebratory.

➤ Samar watches Issac from behind the suitcase as he dances in sharp jerky rhythmical movements on the wooden crate with his lit firework. He writes of his arrival in the air with his sparkler as he dances on the crate.

➤ Out of breath, Samar watches Issac. She steps back slightly as he dances.

➤ The sparkler fades out with the music.

➤ Issac stops dancing and writing in the air. He breathes heavily from the activity.

➤ Samar looks at Issac.

➤ She walks around the circle and collects the lady's dress, the child's cardigan, the baby's boots and Issac's family photograph from behind Issac, who watches her. She continues walking briskly around the circle and then turns halfway to face Issac, showing him the bundle of clothes and photo in her outstretched arms. He looks at her. He steps down from the wooden crate and moves towards his things. Samar moves backwards as Issac moves forwards, around the circle. As his pace quickens she changes direction and runs past the chair, the case, the basket, around the circle back to the basket, where he changes direction. She too changes direction and then runs away from Issac in a circle three times as he chases her. She then runs down the centre of the stage, jumping over the wooden crate and throwing the bundle of clothes outside the circle, centre, where Issac first entered. He slows down slightly to go outside the circle towards his possessions as Samar continues to walk quickly around the circle on her own, breathing heavily.

➤ Samar looks and walks around the space, changing direction. Issac, outside, slowly puts on his jacket and gathers the clothes from the ground.

➤ Samar sees the disrupted rug. She straightens the rug briskly. She kicks the case. She paces. She sees the cloth she dropped. She picks it up and begins frantically to scrub the chair with it. She moves away, changing direction, looking around her home. She sees the crate. She begins to clean that also. She paces. She sees the basket. She wipes the basket. She paces. She goes to her mug. She picks it up and wipes it, hard.

➤ Issac slowly turns around, facing the circle.

Music 7   Issac's return

> Samar continues wiping the mug, looking downstage, breathing heavily. She places the mug back down. She turns and picks up the backgammon board. She wipes it hard and fast while pacing the circle. She puts it on the wooden crate and kneels in front of it, facing directly downstage. She looks at the game. Throws the cloth towards the mound of rocks and opens the board.

> Issac stands, very still, outside the circle, but right behind her.

> Samar opens the board and starts frantically to line the backgammon pieces up into position on the board. He watches her. She takes the dice and shakes them quickly in her hand for a long while her eyes fix on Issac's suitcase.

> Issac slowly steps into the circle, holding his things, watching Samar.

> Music fades out.

> Issac puts the clothes back in the case. Samar watches him. He takes off his jacket, folds it carefully and puts it in the case. He closes the suitcase and stands, looking at Samar. She is still. He then walks across, and kneels in front of her at the crate and board, with his back facing downstage.

> She picks up the crate and board, stands up and places it downstage centre, this time facing in the direction of the chair, stage right. Issac is still kneeling in the same position. She shakes the dice, throws them on the board and begins to play backgammon with herself.

> Issac meanwhile gets up and stands by his suitcase, watching Samar. She continues to play, trying not to look at him.

> Issac opens his case. He takes out a small black velvet pouch. Remaining by the suitcase he shakes the pouch in the air. It makes a sound.

> Samar looks at him but continues playing, slamming the backgammon pieces down on the board.

> Issac walks round the case and chair and stands in front of Samar and the board. She continues to play , throwing the dice, moving her own and the opponent's pieces.

➤ *Issac bends down. He takes one of her pieces, slips it swiftly into his pocket. He places two white chess pieces on his side of the backgammon board and three black pieces on her side of the board.*

➤ *She picks up the dice. She throws them on the board. Then she picks up his chess pieces and on her knees shoves them back into his velvet pouch.*

➤ *Issac looks at the board. Bends down, picks up the two dice, shakes them and then throws them on the floor. Samar sees the dice. She looks back at him sharply and then goes to collect the dice.*

➤ *Meanwhile Issac kneels down by the board, picks it up, and tosses the backgammon pieces up in the air in Samar's direction so that they land on the ground. Samar turns around suddenly. He turns the board over, chess side up, placing it back down on the wooden crate.*

➤ *Samar steps back, watching him, breathing and looking around the ground. She goes to pick up the backgammon pieces as Issac empties his pouch of chess pieces on to the board and begins to set them up.*

➤ *Issac places the chess pieces firmly in place. Samar watches. She then takes her backgammon pieces and begins to throw them at the chess pieces one by one, knocking them over. Issac does not look at her. He continues placing his chess pieces as Samar knocks all over with her* backgammon pieces. She kneels and picks up the chessboard and reverses it back over to the backgammon side. He looks at her.

➤ Samar goes to place her backgammon pieces back, but Issac takes the board and closes it. Samar opens the board again sharply. Issac closes it more sharply still. Samar opens the board. Issac closes the board. Samar opens the board. Issac closes the board. Samar opens the board and turns it round so it is open in the opposite direction. Issac closes the board. Samar turns the board again and opens it. Issac closes it. Samar opens it. They open and close the board several times, extremely quickly but neatly, until Samar finally places both hands on the open board, and up on her knees presses her weight into it. They glare into each other's eyes.

➤ A beat.

➤ Then they simultaneously scuttle around the ground, quickly picking up their respective pieces, scattered all over the circle. Issac places his chess pieces back in his pouch. Samar collects her pieces in her hands and puts them back on the board. Both standing, Issac slowly throws another chess piece into the board. Samar looks at the piece, looks at Issac, takes the piece and stands opposite Issac looking at him. She coolly throws the piece in the air towards him. He catches it, uncomfortably. She goes to move away but stops as Issac reaches in his pocket and reveals one of her backgammon pieces. He waves it in the air, as he did before with the document. Issac walks behind the chair and places her backgammon piece inside his suitcase.

➤ Issac then takes a book from his suitcase as Samar collects the last of her backgammon pieces from the floor and puts them back on the board.

➤ Issac goes and lies on the rug, leaning on his elbow and his side, facing downstage. He reads his book. Samar notices him but continues to clear away the backgammon board. She places the board and crate back in place, glaring at Issac as she passes him. She places the crate down, turns round.

➤ Samar looks at Issac, then from behind him grabs and closes his book. Issac stands up quickly and goes towards her. She throws the book on to the suitcase and takes up a place on her rug.

➤ Samar kneels by her pillow, takes her notebook and pen from under her pillow as Issac goes over to the suitcase. They look at each other briefly.

*Samar finds a blank page and begins to write. Issac watches her from a
distance and tries to read her words.*

Music 8   Writing

➤   *Samar holds her book close to her upper body. Intermittently she looks at
Issac, writes, looks at his suitcase, writes, looks around the space, writes,
looks at Issac and writes … documenting everything that has happened.*

➤   *Issac crosses behind her, still watching. He bends over her shoulder and
looks at the writing. He cannot read it. Issac then kneels very closely next
to Samar, on her left. She looks at him. He smiles a wide smile showing all
his teeth. She looks sharply back at her book. He continues to look very*

*closely over her shoulder. She continues writing, but shoves him away with
her hip. He moves slightly but continues to look. She shoves him again, this
time moving herself further along the rug at the same time. She shoves
again and again until she is at the opposite end of the rug. She sits on the
rug, to the side now, with her back facing stage left and legs outstretched,
taking up as much of the rug as possible. She reaches for the pillow and
places it on her lap, using it as a surface from which to write. Issac gets up
and faces her from the other end of the rug.*

➤   *Samar writes very quickly and intently now, still taking in the objects in
the space. Issac watches her. Samar continues to write until she feels a*

pain in her writing hand from where she fell earlier. She stops for a brief moment to flex her injured hand at which point Issac swiftly grabs the book and rips out a page. She stands quickly as he throws the book back down on the rug.

➤ *Samar goes to pick up her notebook as Issac folds the ripped paper twice and places it in his book (on top of the case), using it as a bookmark.*

➤ *Meanwhile Samar stands, upstage left, and writes on a fresh page.*

➤ *Issac takes his book and goes to stand behind the chair, diagonal to Samar, watching her.*

➤ *Then Issac picks up the cushion and throws it on the floor in front of the chair, at which point Samar drops her book on the floor and goes to grab the cushion just before he can place his feet on it. She backs off away with the cushion, now holding it close to her body, with her head down. Meanwhile Issac sits on the chair and begins to read.*

➤ *Samar strokes the embroidery, presses her nose into the cushion, sways and thinks. She looks at Issac. He looks at her. He turns his chair, clockwise, facing downstage. He returns to reading his book.*

➤ *Suddenly Samar throws the cushion hard at Issac. It bounces off his head and lands on the floor. Shocked, Issac looks over his shoulder towards her. Then, half smiling, he shakes his head and continues reading.*

➤ *Samar goes over to Issac and tries to pull the chair, from the left. Issac continues to read, expressionless. She scrambles up and attempts to lift the chair from behind. He is unmoved. She goes to his other side, places her foot on his leg, grabbing the back of the chair and attempting to throw him off that way. He is still. Samar then buries her face in Issac's book and makes inaudible sounds. Issac lifts the book, throwing Samar's head off the page. She goes to his back and rhythmically slaps his bald head (or forehead). He casually sweeps his hand across his head as if brushing away drops of rain. Samar grabs Issac's shoulders and begins to press. Issac's eyebrows raise. He lifts his head up from reading the book and gently smiles.*

Music 9   Massage

➤ *Samar massages Issac, very hard. She works from his shoulders and neck all the way down his spine. As she works down his vertebrae, he bends forward. She arrives at his tail bone, digging in. Issac is totally bent over with his weight on his toes and slightly lifted off the chair with his head and body hanging over. Suddenly Samar shoves his bottom, throwing him off balance, thus finally getting him off her chair. Issac falls forward, only just avoiding falling to the ground.*

➤ *Samar quickly picks up the chair and sprints away, placing it upstage left of the orange basket. He recovers, turning to watch her.*

➤ *Samar grabs the embroidered pillow and her notebook and stands by the chair, breathing, as Issac walks around the rug to face her.*

➤ *Issac looks at the rug; then, calmly, he goes to it, places his book downstage of it, takes off his shoes and socks, folds his socks, places them carefully inside his shoes and puts them neatly at the end of the rug, facing downstage. Samar watches him do all this, then takes a silk eye-mask on elastic from his right pocket, places it over his eyes, leans back and lies on the rug, with his head on the pillow, perfectly relaxed.*

➤ *Silence.*

➤ *Samar slumps on to the chair, watching Issac.*

➤ *Head down, she opens her notebook and begins to read her words. She slowly looks up at Issac.*

Music 10   Thinking

➤ *Samar places the book on her lap. She brings her hands together, leans forward and looks at Issac, breathing.*

➤ *Issac is perfectly still.*

➤ *Still looking at Issac, Samar slowly gets up. She places her book on the chair and walks around him in a clockwise circle, slowly placing each foot carefully on the ground, heel to toe.*

➤ *Issac does not stir.*

➤ *Samar pauses briefly by the mound of rocks. She looks to the knife. She looks back at Issac, she looks back at the knife, she breathes in, breathes*

out and smiles slightly, looking away from the knife. She looks at Issac's
suitcase.

➤ *On tiptoes now, Samar moves quickly, towards his suitcase.*

➤ *There is silence.*

➤ *She bends down and, still looking at Issac, she gently opens the case. She*
  searches, finds his jacket, searches his pockets and hears the jangle of
  keys.

➤ *Issac moves at the sound.*

➤ *Samar notices Issac's slight response. She then deliberately turns the keys*
  in her hand, making a sound again. Issac moves. Samar then jangles the
  keys in different places in the circle. Issac moves towards the sound, still
  blindfold. Samar becomes more playful, jangling the keys at different
  heights, quietly, more loudly, throwing them on the ground then running
  to pick them up before Issac can get to them. She builds in pace until she is
  running all over the circle with Issac following the sounds, sightless. Finally
  she throws the keys right outside the circle, on to the floor downstage left.

➤ *Issac pulls off his blindfold and glares at Samar, who is behind the*
  suitcase. Issac puts the eye-mask back in his pocket, sees the keys and,
  picking his book up on the way, steps outside the circle and gathers his

keys. Samar immediately follows him and when he is outside the circle she blocks his return.

➤ *Issac steps left, Samar blocks him, steps right, Samar blocks him, looks down and suddenly sees the handle of the knife, sticking out of the mound of rocks. Issac grabs the knife.*

➤ *He holds the knife to Samar's throat and walks her backwards. When they are at the centre of the circle, he stops.*

Music 11 Sharp sound

➤ *Issac runs the blade of the knife along Samar's body, down her chest, round her breast, along her right thigh, round her hip, round her bottom, up her back, across her shoulders and across her neck.*

➤ *Samar's body tenses at his movements. Her breathing is high in her chest.*

➤ *Issac comes away, stands in front and to the side of her at some distance. He holds out the knife, and gestures with it, as he has done before with the document and the backgammon piece. He backs off, and bends down to put the knife and book in the suitcase.*

➤ *Suddenly Samar runs to the mound of rocks, picks one up and goes to throw it at him.*

➤ *Issac jumps with fright, breathing in sharply, protecting his body.*

➤ *Samar looks at Issac, realising his fear. She goes to throw the rock again but this time lets it drop on the floor behind her. Issac jumps again, protecting himself behind the suitcase. Samar goes towards him but backs off smiling. She picks the rock up from the ground and laughs. Again she makes to throw the rock at him but instead throws it in the air above her, just moving out of the way before it hits her, releasing a mock cry of fear. She laughs harshly.*

➤ *When she is briefly out of his way, Issac grabs his shoes, placing his hands inside them, like gloves. Samar continues to throw the rock in the air and jump out of the way, fake-screaming. Laughing, she starts towards Issac and backs away. Issac protects himself with his shoes. Laughing, Samar throws the rock at Issac. He bats the rock away with his shoes. She moves him around the circle in different directions through throwing the rock. She is light on her feet, leaping from place to place. He walks in short jaunty steps.*

➤ *Issac decides.*

➤ *He places the shoes in one hand then takes a piece of chalk from the mound of rocks, throws the rug out of the way and draws a line between them on the floor, upstage to downstage centre. Samar watches him draw the line, still holding the rock in her hand.*

➤ *Issac places his shoes next to the basket and then stands on the stage-right side of the line, with his toes at the chalk mark. He holds his hands behind his back and bounces slightly on his heels, looking at Samar with his chin inclined upwards.*

➤ *Samar stands directly opposite Issac, on the other side of the line. Then she takes the rock and gestures with it in the air, close to Issac's face. Issac copies her gesture with the chalk in his hand. Samar takes the chalk from Issac's hand and surveys the line. Samar then uses the whole length of the line as a base line from which she draws out a large game of hopscotch.*

➤ *Hopscotch ('eks' in Arabic): a pyramid shape drawn on the ground made of three large squares at the bottom, then two squares on top of them, then one square.*

➤ *Samar draws the hopscotch pattern, occasionally looking up at Issac who stares at her and the pattern on the ground.*

➤ *Samar throws the chalk on the rock mound. She walks briskly over to the base line and spontaneously gestures with the rock, under arm, towards*

Issac's groin, making a sound with her lips. Issac instinctively bends to protect his crotch and back away from her.

➤ Samar stands dynamically, facing the base line of the hopscotch game. Without looking, she coolly kicks the lid of Issac's suitcase shut behind her.

Music 12 'Eks' (*percussive rhythms*)

➤ Samar tosses the rock, landing it on the top square.

➤ She looks back at Issac who looks at her and the game.

➤ Samar jumps energetically and skilfully on the squares, feet together, feet apart, crossing her feet, turning around and so on until she lands on the square with the rock. Samar picks up the rock, swirls around and chooses another square to throw it to. Again she jumps many squares, on one leg, two legs etc., making her way to the square with the rock.

➤ Issac watches.

➤ Samar continues playing until she (unintentionally) throws the rock just outside the square.

➤ Very quickly, Issac picks up a piece of chalk from the rock mound and draws a square around Samar's rock. He then picks it up.

- ➤ *Issac looks at Samar.*

- ➤ *Samar looks at Issac.*

- ➤ *Samar jumps a series of squares, sophisticatedly, dynamically, playfully, until she successfully arrives at the square Issac has just drawn.*

- ➤ *Issac throws the rock to a different place in the circle, not connected to the hopscotch squares. They look at each other. Issac briskly draws a square around where the rock has landed.*

- ➤ *Samar jumps from square to square, more artfully and rhythmically now, jumping back and forth, to the side, on one foot etc., until she reaches the new square.*

- ➤ *Meanwhile, Issac quickly throws the rock in another place, at a greater distance still, and draws another square around it. Samar jumps to it again.*

- ➤ *Issac draws many squares at increasing pace and distance from the hopscotch game. Each time, no matter the challenge, Samar is able to get to the squares. Issac then throws the rock the furthest distance yet, and for the first time, outside the circle, far downstage left. Issac draws a square around the rock again and picks it up.*

- ➤ *Samar jumps a complicated sequence of squares and then takes a huge jump, outside the circle, landing successfully on the square with a vocalised exhalation, gesturing with both arms in the air, in celebration.*

- ➤ *Issac quickly grabs the cloth and rubs out all of the squares inside the circle.*

- ➤ *Samar stamps her feet, faster and harder until she is jumping up and down in her square, her facial muscles tense.*

- ➤ *When Issac has rubbed out all of the squares he goes to the edge of the circle and smiles at Samar with arms outstretched. He begins to walk backwards.*

- ➤ *Samar is breathing heavily from the jumping.*

- ➤ *Issac goes to the chair, looking at Samar. He picks up her book, throws it on the ground towards the rocks, and sits on the chair with his feet together.*

- *She watches him.*
- *Issac leans over to the basket next to him. He selects an orange. He bites into the orange and begins to peel it.*
- *She watches him.*
- *Issac takes the bits of peel and throws them on the ground all over the circle. He bites into the orange.*
- *She watches him.*
- *Issac chews the orange and with raised eyebrows looks at Samar, cocks his head, then looks at the basket. He places the remainder of the orange in the basket, then picks up a fresh orange and offers it to her in a gesture.*

Music 13 *Juggling.*

- *Issac rolls the orange on the ground, towards Samar.*
- *Samar then marches directly towards Issac, who stops her by throwing an orange at her.*
- *Samar catches the orange.*
- *Samar marches towards Issac again.*
- *He throws another orange.*
- *Samar catches it and heads for him again.*
- *He throws a third orange.*
- *With three oranges in her two hands, Samar walks slowly now towards Issac.*
- *Issac's hand hovers over the basket of oranges, ready to throw another if necessary.*
- *Samar pauses in front of the crate, looking sideways at Issac.*
- *Samar looks at the oranges in her hands, turns away from Issac and begins to juggle brilliantly with the oranges, turning a full circle while doing so.*
- *Issac removes his hand from the orange basket.*

- ➤ *When she arrives back round to face Issac, she deliberately drops an orange on the floor. Samar stops, drops her head down looking at the fallen orange. With her two hands upwards, she sarcastically shrugs her shoulders.*

- ➤ *Samar looks at Issac, then gestures towards him with the orange in her right hand.*

- ➤ *Issac closes his body in.*

- ➤ *Samar then gestures towards herself with the orange in her left hand. She repeats the action. She gestures towards Issac with the orange in her right hand a third time and then uses the orange in her right hand to hit the orange in her left hand, three times.*

- ➤ *Samar decides.*

- ➤ *She walks down stage right in the circle and takes a place, feet apart, facing inside the circle.*

- ➤ *Samar gestures again towards Issac with the orange in her right hand. She throws that orange into the air, then swiftly throws the orange in her left hand across to her right hand and back again to her left hand, by the time the orange in the air lands back down into her empty hand. She repeats this juggle, twice.*

- ➤ *Samar takes a mocking bow, towards Issac.*

- ➤ *Samar crosses diagonally back towards the crate. She gestures to Issac with her right hand. She then juggles with the two oranges with her right hand only. One orange follows the other, follows the other ... She repeats the motion three times.*

- ➤ *Then Samar looks towards Issac, who is still watching her from the chair.*

- ➤ *Samar lifts the orange in her right hand into the air. She holds it in her left hand below. She then puppeteers the orange in her left from the orange in her right hand, using an imagined piece of string. At the same time, Samar moves her body, puppet-like, towards Issac, swaying her head from one side to the other, lifting one leg at a time in a heightened motion, as she gets closer and closer.*

- ➤ *Issac makes a grab for the oranges but Samar quickly moves them out of the way.*

- ➤ *Samar offers both the oranges to Issac.*

- ➤ *Issac grabs for the oranges again, but Samar is too fast.*

- ➤ *With her back to Issac, she turns round slowly, and looks at the oranges in her hands.*

- ➤ *She thinks.*

- ➤ *Samar walks forwards, looking at the oranges.*

- ➤ *She looks up.*

- ➤ *Samar decides.*

- ➤ *Issac watches her from behind.*

Music 14   Seduction

> *From downstage centre Samar rolls the oranges in her hands and then bends over. She places the oranges under her top and on to her breasts.*

> *Samar looks at her now larger breasts.*

> *She looks straight ahead without expression and raises her arms with palms up.*

> *Samar turns around slowly. Looking at Issac, she walks the circle, past the rocks, towards the crate and towards Issac again and takes him by the hands. Issac smiles.*

> *Hands in his hands, Samar pulls Issac off her chair. Issac smiles. Samar looks to her chair, and turns Issac round, slowly at first, moving with the music, and then faster and faster until she is spinning him. On each turn she looks at her chair. She spins him so fast he flies out of the circle, downstage left, towards where she jumped before. Issac stands breathing in a broken pattern.*

> *Samar takes the oranges from her breasts and throws them both at him violently. She grabs the third orange on the ground and slams her arm on to the inside of her elbow, bringing the under arm up (a 'fuck you' gesture), simultaneously casting the orange at Issac with a long punctuating exhalation as the music ends suddenly.*

> *Samar backs off and stands in front of her chair, holding it. She turns her face towards Issac.*

> *Issac stares at Samar. He walks determinedly back in to the circle straight to her.*

Music 15   The kiss

> *Issac moves very close to Samar. He grabs the key hanging round her neck. Samar takes a sharp breath in, pulling away from Issac. He continues to pull her, by the key round her neck, back into the centre of the circle. Samar focuses on the key. She grabs it, but Issac continues to pull. Issac then puts his head under the elastic on to which the key is strung. He shoves his knee between Samar's legs, grabs her from the back, still pulling tightly. She struggles away, still holding the key. He slowly leans in, she*

struggles and with his full force he kisses her on the lips. Samar gets out of the clinch by pulling the elastic up over her head and letting go of the key. She collapses on to the ground. Issac looks at her, looks at the key that is now in his hand and kisses it gently.

➤ *Samar is crumpled, shaking on the ground.*

➤ *Issac sits on the chair and places the key round his neck.*

Music 16   After the kiss

➤ *Samar scrambles, on her knees, over to the bowl. She pours water into the bowl and looks into the water for a brief moment. She then cups the water and scrubs her face, neck, hands and body, with violent vigour.*

➤ *Issac picks the remainder of his orange from the basket and eats it.*

➤ *Samar is more and more vigorous. The scrubbing becomes scratching – her body, thighs, feet …*

➤ *Issac watches Samar as he swallows the last of the orange.*

➤ *Issac decides.*

➤ *He gets up, crosses the circle, lifts his trousers slightly and steps into Samar's water bowl in his bare feet .*

> *Samar stops.*

> *Issac stands in the bowl and walks a small circle, splashing the water.*

> *Samar watches Issac's feet.*

> *Issac steps out of the bowl, shaking the water off his feet, and dries them on the rug, then continues back to the chair.*

> *Samar looks at the water bowl.*

> *Issac sits looking at Samar.*

> *Silence.*

> *Samar suddenly picks up the water bowl and standing, throws the remainder of the dirty water at Issac, splashing him in the face as he attempts to get out of the way.*

> *Issac glares at Samar.*

> *Samar looks at the empty bowl from downstage right.*

> *Issac crosses the circle towards the rocks as Samar backs away, shielding her body with the bowl.*

> *Issac looks at the water jug, grabs it, drinks from it. Samar looks up at Issac with widened eyes.*

> *Looking at Samar, Issac pours the water over his head as he walks round the circle clockwise.*

> *Samar, with short breath, runs towards Issac, holding the bowl under his head to try to catch the cascading water. She follows him desperately as he turns circles, shakes his head, dances, all the while pouring the water over himself without looking at Samar. Samar tries to catch every drop of water in the bowl. By the time Issac has walked one full circle the water jug is empty.*

> *Arrving back at the rocks, Issac pulls the sunflower out of the ground and places the stem, lengthways, into his mouth. He smiles at Samar with the stem between his teeth. Samar looks at Issac. He walks away.*

> *Samar looks at the mound of rocks.*

> *Issac places the empty jug down on the ground, mid-downstage right, puts the sunflower in the jug and looks at it. He begins to rearrange the objects, establishing a new space.*

Music 17   Issac makes an office

➤ *Samar sees water on the ground downstage. She puts the bowl down by the rocks and picks up her cloth. She tries to wipe up all the water over the ground downstage with her cloth. She desperately wrings the cloth out back into the bowl, trying to collect as much of the now sparse water as she can. Her focus is on the task. She does not look at Issac. Neither does he look at her.*

➤ *Meanwhile, Issac gets Samar's rug and lays it out, centre stage, diagonally. He gets the wooden crate with the backgammon board on top. He places the crate and board on the downstage edge of the rug. He looks around. He picks up Samar's chair. He places it on the rug, facing the crate. He adjusts the cushion. He looks around. He picks up Samar's pillow and puts it on the back of the chair. Issac then goes to his suitcase. He opens it and takes out an old typewriter and a candle. He places the typewriter on the ground, picks up the suitcase and puts it between the chair and the crate. Issac then places the typewriter on top of the suitcase, at the stage-left end and puts the candle at the other end, using the suitcase as a table. Issac then takes the jug with sunflower and puts it at the other end of the 'table', next to the candle. Issac looks around. He sees the bowl. While Samar is mopping up water, he lifts the bowl, tips out the water Samar has gathered and shakes it on the ground. Samar looks at Issac. Her mouth falls open.*

➤ *Issac goes to the rock mound and walks swiftly around the inside of the circle, throwing the oranges into the bowl, one by one.*

➤ *Samar is still at first, looking at the ground, then she slowly crawls to the rocks and begins to smash them against one another.*

➤ *When Issac gets to the basket, he empties the oranges into it. He continues round the circle, filling the bowl with oranges until they are all collected.*

➤ *Issac places the bowl full of oranges on the downstage-right end of the rug. Issac looks at the bowl of oranges.*

➤ *Samar is still smashing rocks. Her injured hand hurts.*

➤ *Issac walks around the back of his newly arranged area, down to the mound of rocks, and picks up Samar's cup. He goes and sits on the chair, holding his cup in his right hand close to his face, looking at Samar.*

- ➤ *Samar spreads the mound of rocks. She looks for water beneath it.*
- ➤ *Samar finds no water under the rocks.*
- ➤ *Samar sees her book. She sits on the now flat area of rocks and starts to re-read what she wrote before. She reads quickly, her head almost buried in the book.*
- ➤ *Issac watches Samar read, cocking his head to one side.*
- ➤ *Samar takes out her pen and writes very quickly, her hand and mind in pain. She grimaces, rocking herself backwards and forwards as she continues to write.*
- ➤ *Issac watches.*
- ➤ *Time passes.*
- ➤ *Issac looks at his typewriter, then up at Samar.*
- ➤ *He places the mug down on the 'table'.*
- ➤ *Issac breathes in.*
- ➤ *Issac decides.*
- ➤ *He walks swiftly over to Samar and grabs her pen and then her book.*
- ➤ *Samar stands, by the rocks, watching Issac, breathing heavily.*
- ➤ *Issac puts Samar's pen in the mug, rips several pages out of her book and throws it on the ground. He places several sheets on to the 'table', then sits and rolls a piece of Samar's paper into his typewriter.*
- ➤ *Issac types on Samar's words.*
- ➤ *Samar grabs the paper from the typewriter, screws it into a ball and throws it at Issac's head.*
- ➤ *Issac looks at Samar. He takes another piece of paper and rolls it into the typewriter.*
- ➤ *Issac types.*
- ➤ *Samar grabs the paper, screws it up and throws it at him again.*
- ➤ *Issac takes another piece of paper.*
- ➤ *Samar turns around and takes chalk from the rocks.*

- ➤ *Issac watches her.*

- ➤ *Samar goes to the ground downstage of Issac's 'area' and writes, with difficulty, 'Help' in Arabic, on the floor, diagonally downstage right.*

Music 18   The wall

- ➤ *Issac stands, picks up the bowl of oranges and slams it down on top of Samar's writing.*

- ➤ *Samar looks at Issac. Samar goes to the downstage-left diagonal and continues to write.*

- ➤ *Issac picks up the backgammon board and slams it down on the writing.*

- ➤ *Samar goes towards the rocks instead.*

- ➤ *She draws the jug of water. She goes to another place downstage and draws a game of noughts and crosses, breaking all the rules of the game as she strikes through it with the chalk. She goes to the edge of the circle and draws the oranges, where they once were. She continues to draw all that was there before as Issac works behind her.*

- ➤ *Issac is making a wall: he places the wooden crate next to the backgammon board, the jug and flower next to the bowl, the candle in the middle of the suitcase, the chair (with cushions) on its side next to the suitcase, and throws the rug over the chair. Finally Issac takes matches from his pocket and lights the candle.*

➤ *Samar looks at her drawing and writing. She has covered the ground: there is nowhere left to mark.*

➤ *Issac stands behind the suitcase. He looks at Samar.*

➤ *Samar looks at Issac.*

➤ *There is silence.*

➤ *Issac smiles and then reaches his hand across the 'wall' to shake hands.*

➤ *Samar looks at Issac's hand.*

➤ *Samar spits on the candle.*

➤ *Issac drops his hand.*

➤ *Issac looks at Samar.*

➤ *Issac takes the matches again and relights the candle. He places the matches back in his pocket and, not looking at Samar, he folds his hands on to his stomach, closes his eyes, turns round, and with his back to Samar and the 'wall', he starts to sway.*

➤ *Samar pauses.*

➤ *Samar kicks the suitcase hard, hitting Issac in the back of the knees, bringing him to the ground. He turns round, wide-eyed.*

➤ *They look at each other and at the case.*

➤ *Issac makes a long deep exhalation. Slowly, he pulls the case towards him, looks up at Samar and opens it. Issac lays the case on its side, takes out his jacket and puts it on. He then goes over to the bowl of oranges and takes three of them. He throws the oranges into his suitcase, closes it, picks it up and stands, looking at Samar.*

➤ *Issac slowly crosses through the gap in the wall and walks towards Samar. He walks behind her and uses the case to push her through the gap in the 'wall'. She resists with less strength than before. He walks her upstage to the point in the circle where he first entered and shoves her out.*

Music 19   Samar returns

➤ *Samar stands with her head down and her back facing the circle. Issac dumps his case outside, by Samar's feet.*

➤ *Issac turns round and strides into the circle. He looks about the space.*

➤ *Issac decides.*

➤ *He takes the rug and places it, square on, centre stage.*

➤ *Samar slowly turns round and watches Issac rearranging what was her home.*

➤ *With energy and matching breath, Issac takes the crate, typewriter and book and places them mid-stage right. He places the cushions at the upstage-left corner of the rug. He places the chair centre stage, facing downstage. He places the basket of oranges on the left side of the chair. He places the backgammon board, standing upright, upstage of the cushions. He places the bowl of oranges on the other side of the chair. He places the jug and flower on the left side of the crate and picks up Samar's book. Issac smiles.*

➤ *Issac sits on the chair, opens the book and looks at the writing.*

Music 20   The end

➤ *Issac carefully rips the page from Samar's book.*

➤ *Samar slowly lifts the suitcase in her right hand and walks the exterior of the circle, stage-left side. She looks inside the circle as she walks.*

➤ *Issac folds the paper carefully and makes an aeroplane.*

➤ *Samar walks until she arrives at the flattened rocks. She steps on to the rocks and stands looking out at the audience.*

➤ *Issac flies his paper aeroplane up and out in the direction of the audience.*

➤ *Samar looks at us.*

The Music

Rami Washara

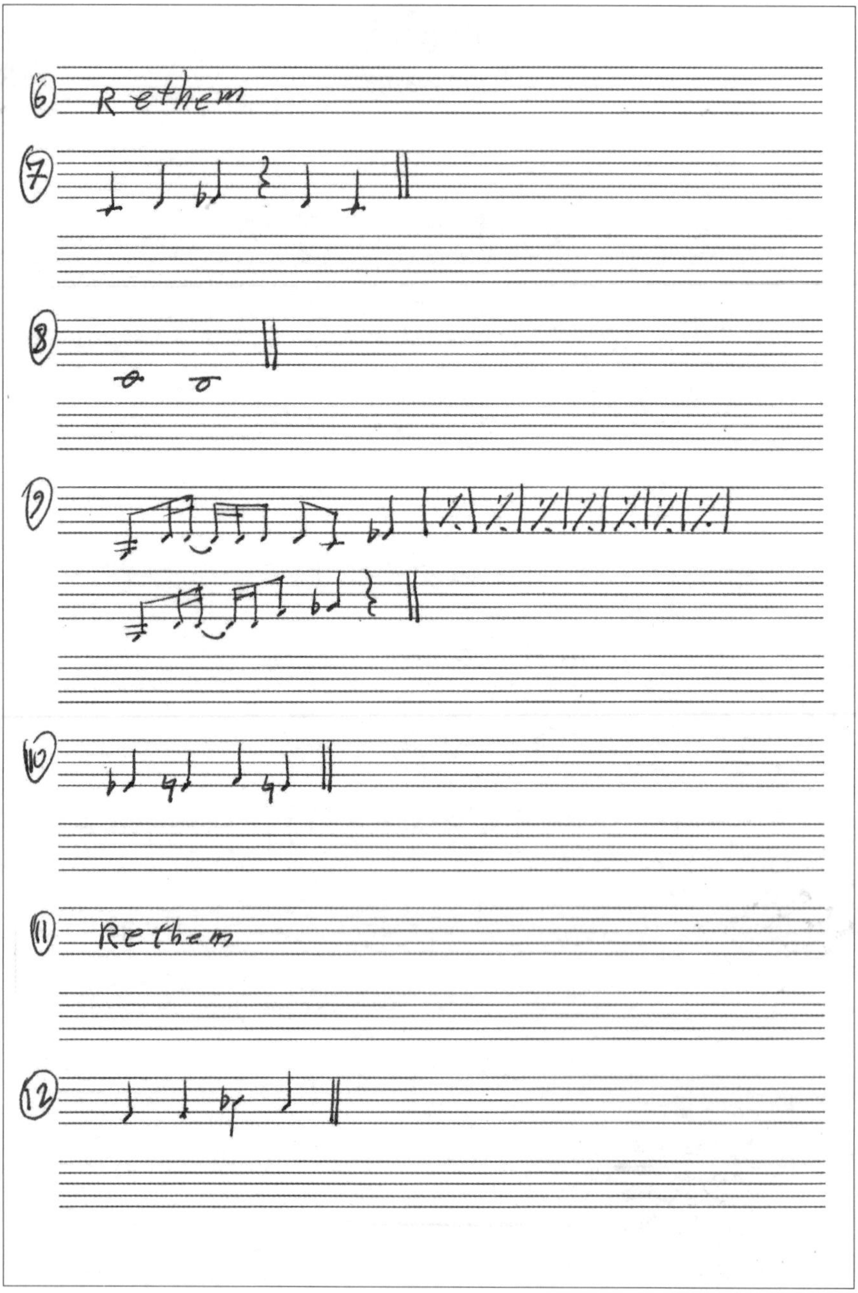
6
Rethem
7
8
9
10
11
Rethem
12

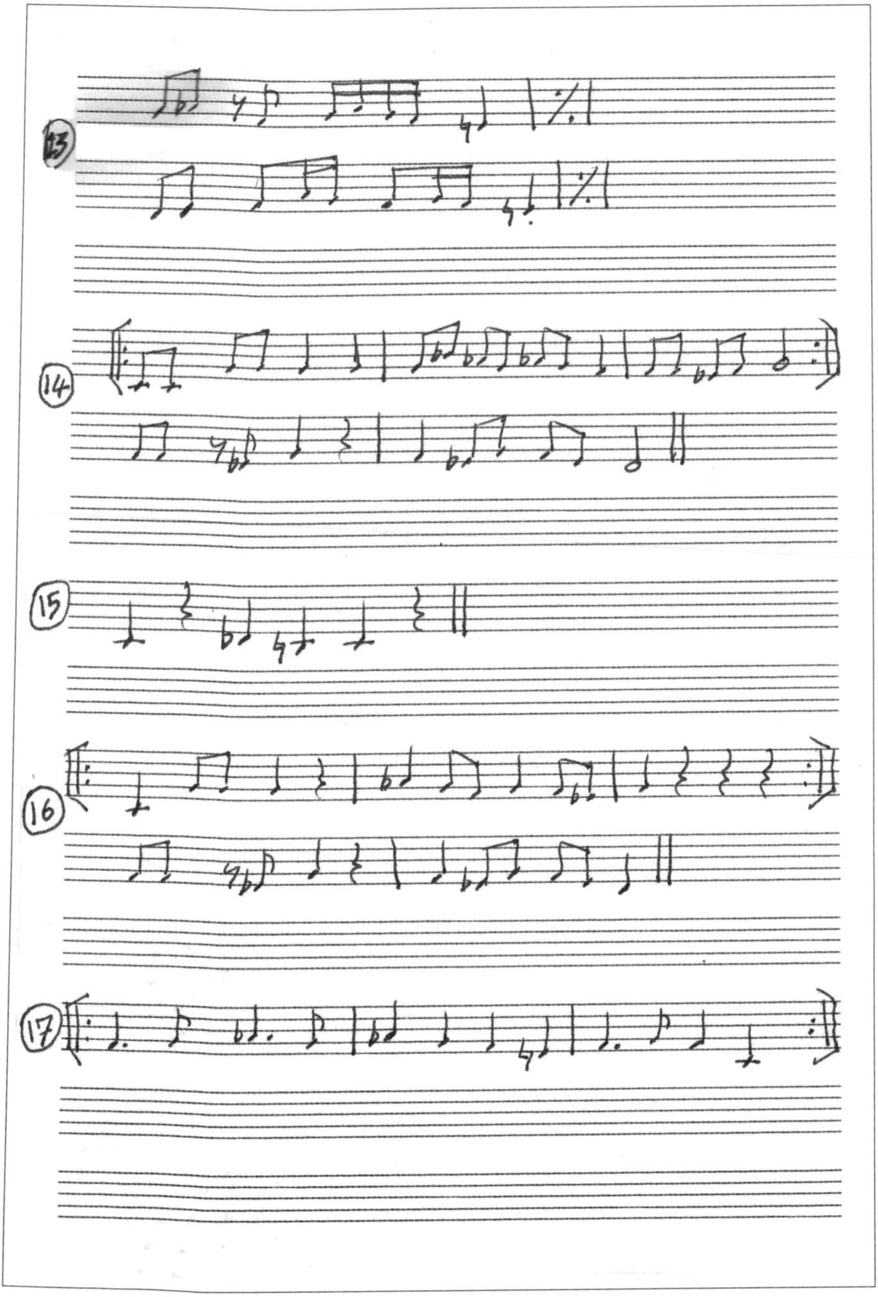
13
14
15
16
17

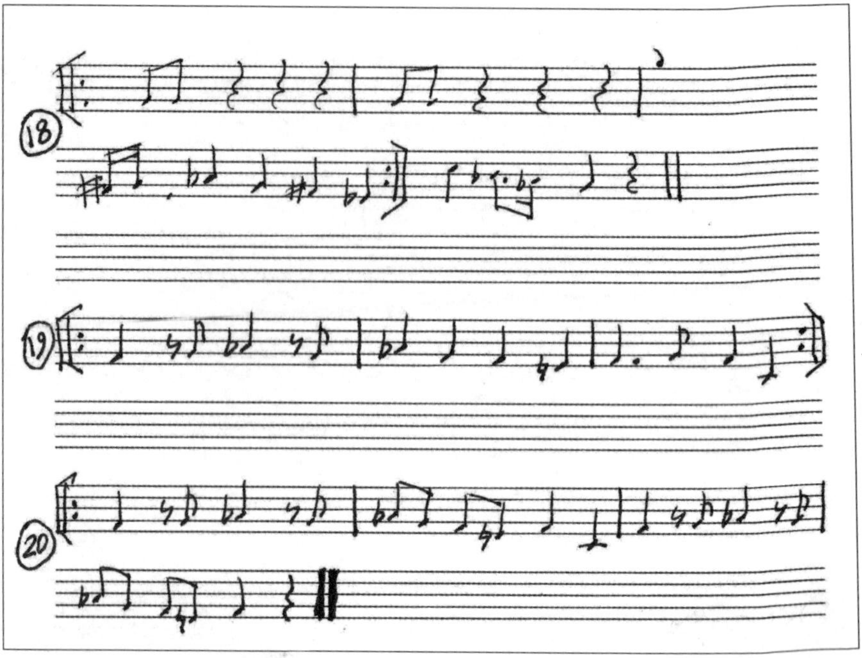
18
19
20